TEACHING AND LEARN

Team-Based Learning

Team-Based Learning

A Transformative Use of Small Groups

Edited by
Larry K. Michaelsen
Arletta Bauman Knight
L. Dee Fink

Westport, Connecticut
London

Library of Congress Cataloging-in-Publication Data

Team-based learning : a transformative use of small groups / edited by Larry K. Michaelsen,
Arletta Bauman Knight, and L. Dee Fink.
    p.   cm.
  Includes bibliographical references (p.) and index.
  ISBN 0-89789-863-X (alk. paper)
    1. Group work in education. 2. Team learning approach in education.   I. Michaelsen,
Larry K., 1943– II. Knight, Arletta Bauman.   III. Fink, L. Dee, 1940–
LB1032.T38   2002
371.39'5—dc21   2002038103

British Library Cataloguing in Publication Data is available.

Library of Congress Catalog Card Number: 2002038103
ISBN: 0-89789-863-X

First published in 2002

Praeger Publishers, 88 Post Road West, Westport, CT 06881
An imprint of Greenwood Publishing Group, Inc.
www.praeger.com

Printed in the United States of America

The paper used in this book complies with the
Permanent Paper Standard issued by the National
Information Standards Organization (Z39.48-1984).

10 9 8 7 6 5 4 3 2 1

Contents

Preface

This book is about team-based learning, an instructional strategy that is based on procedures for developing high performance learning teams that can dramatically enhance the quality of student learning—in almost any course. Where did this idea come from? Why is it important for teachers and others in higher education to learn about it and understand it more fully?

ORIGIN OF THE IDEA OF TEAM-BASED LEARNING

The idea of team-based learning originated with Larry Michaelsen in the late 1970s. As a faculty member at the University of Oklahoma, Michaelsen was confronted with a new and daunting pedagogical challenge. Because of enrollment pressures in his department and college, he was forced to triple the size of his primary course from 40 to 120 students.

He had used group activities and assignments in the smaller classes, and this method was effective in helping students learn how to apply concepts, rather than simply to learn about them. Based on this experience, he was convinced that the same kinds of group activities would work in large classes as well. As a result, he rejected the advice of his colleagues who advised turning the class into a series of lectures, in favor of an approach that involved using the vast majority of class time for group work.

By the middle of the first semester in which he tried this approach, it was obvious that this new teaching strategy was working. In fact, it was working so well that it accomplished three things that Michaelsen had not even anticipated. First, the students themselves perceived the large class setting as being far more beneficial than harmful. Second, the approach created several conditions that would enhance learning in any setting. In spite of the size of the class, for example, the approach was prompting most students to take responsibility for their own and their peers' learning. Third, Michaelsen was having fun. Because the students were getting their initial understanding of the content through their own efforts, he could concentrate his efforts on the aspect of teaching that he enjoyed most: designing assignments and activities that would enable students to discover why the subject matter that was so near and dear to him was important to them as well.

DEVELOPMENT AND REFINEMENT

After this modest but auspicious beginning, Michaelsen knew that he was on to something important, something that had major significance for other college teachers as well as for himself. As a result, he has devoted much of his professional attention since that time to increasing his own understanding of why this way of using small groups works so well. He has also concentrated on helping other teachers take advantage of this innovative teaching strategy. Over time he discovered that his ability to increase his own understanding of these processes was directly related to two sets of activities.

The first set of activities relates to the research literature on the development and management of teams in multiple settings. Although he was already familiar with this literature, he was now able to read and understand it in a new way. As a result of observing hundreds of newly formed groups go through the process of maturing into effective teams, he could more clearly see the parallels between educational teams and teams in other settings. In addition, he discovered that his use of small groups raised the dynamics within groups to a higher level of capability. His student groups were being transformed by the team-based learning process into powerful learning teams, a phenomenon not well described in the literature. As a result, he was able to collect and analyze new data on the team development process and contribute articles of his own to the scholarly literature on the development and management of effective teams (Michaelsen, Watson & Black, 1989; Watson, Kumar, & Michaelsen, 1993; Watson, Michaelsen, & Sharp, 1991).

The other activity involved making contacts with people who either used or wanted to use teams in both business and educational settings. Over the years he has worked extensively with business executives to find ways to develop and manage effective work teams in corporate settings. In the academic setting, he has worked extensively to help professors find ways of building effective learning teams. He has conducted over 200 workshops for faculty members and published articles in a wide range of journals focused on college teaching (Michaelsen, 1983a,b, 1992, 1999; Michaelsen & Black, 1994; Michaelsen, Watson, Cragin, & Fink, 1982). As a result of this involvement in both business and academia, he has both taught and been taught by thousands of people who are actively "working in the trenches" to develop effective teams. The most important consequence of this activity for Michaelsen is that he has developed an ability to see patterns of effective team development across a wide range of academic and business settings.

REASONS FOR WRITING THIS BOOK

While Michaelsen is clearly the person who created and refined the idea of team-based learning, we [Fink and Knight] have worked closely with him for many years in writing articles and conducting workshops on the subject. As director and associate director of the Instructional Development Program at Oklahoma for many years, we have often recommended this approach to teaching for faculty who are facing problems in their courses. When faculty members complain that students are not showing interest in their courses, will not do the homework, or just generally do not seem to be understanding the material, team-based learning is one of the most powerful tools we can recommend.

As awareness of, and interest in, the use of team-based learning has grown nationally and internationally, all three of us have seen a steep rise in the number of requests for more information about team-based learning: "What is it? How do you do it? Will it work in my special situation?" This increased interest made the time seem right to put together a book on the subject that would answer as many of these questions as possible. And we were anxious to join in that effort.

OUR HOPES FOR THIS BOOK

When the three of us considered what prompted us to take on the sizeable task of creating a book, we discovered strong excitement and strong frustration shaping our hopes of what this book might accomplish.

The excitement comes from our observation and conviction that team-based learning can truly change and transform the quality of the classroom experience for both the teacher and the students. We have seen teacher after teacher, on our own campus and on other campuses, shift to using team-based learning and report extraordinary results. The students enjoy the class more and they learn more; teachers often rediscover their joy for teaching again. One of our hopes for this book is that it will enable more teachers to transform their teaching in similarly positive ways.

Along with this excitement, though, we have also felt strong frustration coming from two opposite directions. One source of frustration is with individuals who have observed or experienced a poorly designed use of small groups and, as a result are ready to "throw the baby out with the bath water." Periodically we hear or read stories about students in a class in which the teacher did all the wrong things with groups. The students involved, and others who read and hear about such events, conclude correctly that this was a terrible experience, but they are wrong when they generalize from these situations and conclude that teaching with small groups is generally a bad form of teaching. Such people have not yet learned that there are principles involved in the effective use of small groups and have not taken the time to learn what these principles are; we hope this book will help readers understand these principles and learn how to use them.

Ironically, our other source of frustration is with some of our colleagues who are powerful and competent advocates of teaching with small groups. Our frustration is not that they have not made positive contributions to teaching. In fact, it is just the opposite. The problem is that they have been so successful and effective in selling their message—that is, that structured small group activities are a powerful and effective way to promote active learning in existing courses—that they and others have had difficulty differentiating *small group learning* from *team-based learning*. As a result, the message that learning *teams* can produce extraordinary outcomes, even in very difficult teaching settings, has been difficult to disseminate. Hence, our final hope is that this book will allow those who already value small group teaching to more fully understand the difference between groups and teams and to see the possibility that teams can take small group learning to a whole new level of significance.

THE STRUCTURE OF THIS BOOK

With these hopes and goals in mind, we have created four parts in the book. Part I lays out the key ideas that are important for understanding what team-based learning is, how it works, and what is necessary to make it work effectively.

Part II, "The Voices of Experience," contains chapters written by teachers who have used team-based learning effectively in a variety of situations. We intentionally sought out contributors who had taught different kinds of subject matter, taught with different sized classes and in different cultural settings, and even in the rapidly emerging world of online learning. These writers, in essence, provide the evidence in support of our claim that team-based learning is a transformative use of small groups. That is, team-based learning can be applied in a wide variety of teaching situations with extraordinary results.

The concluding chapter summarizes the reasons teachers decided to try team-based learning and how they overcame any initial concerns. More important, it is a summary of the impact this teaching strategy can have on student learning, student attitudes toward learning, and the ability of teachers ot enjoy teaching again.

The set of appendices contains a variety of charts, tables, forms, and recommendations that may be useful when using team-based learning and when trying to explain this special teaching strategy to others (e.g., students, colleagues).

INTERACTIVE WEBSITE ON TEAM-BASED LEARNING

We also invite readers to visit the interactive website that has been set up for people interested in learning more about team-based learning: www.teambasedlearning.org.

This website serves two primary functions. First, it will be a forum for continuing the conversation about team-based learning. The e-mail and listserv functions will allow people to ask questions, share successes and problems, find out who might be using team-based learning with a similar subject or in a similar situation, and so on. The second function is to archive important and helpful information. Our sense of what this should include will undoubtedly evolve over time. But initially we expect to create three sections: one on "Frequently Asked Questions" (which will continue to grow from the one included in this book), a brief description of courses in multiple disciplines in which team-based learning has been used effectively, and video clips of various activities and exercises from Larry Michaelsen's classes.

We hope you will visit the website, find ideas of value to you, and—when appropriate—contribute material about your own experiences with team-based learning for the benefit of others.

ACKNOWLEDGMENTS

We are especially indebted to the able and generous work of Carolyn Ahern in shaping and editing this manuscript. Her knowledge of proper form and eye for consistency have made this a much more readable manuscript.

REFERENCES

Michaelsen, L. K. (1983a). Developing professional competence. In *Learning in groups*. Ed. C. Bouton and R. Y. Garth. *New directions for teaching and learning*, Vol. 14. San Francisco: Jossey-Bass.

———. (1999). Myths and methods in successful small group work. *National Teaching and Learning Forum* 8(6): 1–5.

———. (1992). Team learning: A comprehensive approach for harnessing the power of small groups in higher education. In *To improve the academy: Resources for faculty, instructional, and organizational development*, Vol. 11. Ed. D. H. Wulff and J. D. Nyquist. Stillwater, OK: New Forums Press.

———. (1983b). Team learning in large classes. In *Learning in groups*. Ed. C. Bouton and R. Y. Garth. *New directions for teaching and learning*, Vol. 14. San Francisco: Jossey-Bass.

Michaelsen, L. K., & Black, R. H. (1994). Building learning teams: The key to harnessing the power of small groups in higher education. In *Collaborative learning: A sourcebook for higher education*, Vol. 2. State College, PA: National Center for Teaching, Learning and Assessment.

Michaelsen, L. K., Watson, W. E., & Black, R. H. (1989). A realistic test of individual versus group consensus decision making. *Journal of Applied Psychology* 74(5): 834–839.

Michaelsen, L. K., Watson, W. E., Cragin, J. P., & Fink, L. D. (1982). Team learning: A potential solution to the problems of large classes. *Exchange: The Organizational Behavior Teaching Journal* 7(1): 13–22.

Watson, W. E., Kumar, K., & Michaelsen, L. K. (1993). Cultural diversity's impact on group process and performance: Comparing culturally homogeneous and culturally diverse task groups. *Academy of Management Journal* 36(3): 590–602.

Watson, W. E., Michaelsen, L. K., & Sharp, W. (1991). Member competence, group interaction and group decision-making: A longitudinal study. *Journal of Applied Psychology* 76: 801–809.

The Key Ideas of Team-Based Learning

The primary purpose of part I of this book is to present all the key ideas needed by anyone who is interested in using team-based learning in their teaching. Part II will then offer examples of courses in which teachers have successfully used team-based learning, that is, the "Voices of Experience."

Dee Fink begins part I by putting the ideas of team-based learning into the larger context of teaching with small groups. During the past decade or so, many college-level teachers have been experimenting with the use of small groups in their teaching, and the literature on this subject has grown rapidly. The good news about this development is that there are many interesting and different ideas about how to teach with small groups. The bad news is that this very plethora of ideas can create confusion by teachers who are just learning about small groups and about what they should or should not do. Fink offers an organizing perspective that helps explain why some writers advocate one practice and others advocate a different way. The main point of Fink's chapter is that team-based learning is a unique and powerful way of using small groups, and that its unusual capability is a result of two factors: the power of teamwork in comparison to group work, and the fact that team-based learning is an instructional strategy, rather than just an instructional technique.

In Chapter 2, Larry Michaelsen lays out a full description of what team-based learning is and what one needs to do to use it effectively. The key to effective use of team-based learning is figuring out what must be done to help newly formed groups evolve into teams. This involves setting up the right procedures for team formation, team and individual student accountability, team assignments, and high quality feedback. Once these key principles have been established, Michaelsen then shows how to apply these principles when creating the sequence of instructional activities, that is, the team-based learning strategy, that begins on the first day of class and continues until the end of the course.

As can be seen from the preceding, there are a number of changes that need to be made if one is ready to shift from a traditional form of teaching to team-based learning. But, as Michaelsen shows, if a teacher can learn how to make these changes, the benefits are enormous. Not only does it transform traditional content and application learning, it has major benefits in those special situations that involve large classes, at-risk students, the need to improve students' interpersonal skills, and the teacher's own enthusiasm for teaching.

Of all the procedures involved in successfully using team-based learning, however, the most significant single task is creating assignments that are effective for teams. As Larry Michaelsen and Arletta Knight point out in Chapter 3, this is often not done right. And when bad assignments are given to groups, both the teacher and the class end up dissatisfied with small group learning. The key argument of this chapter is that a good assignment is one that is effective in enhancing team development as well as in furthering high-level student learning. Michaelsen and Knight identify the five key variables that must be directed to make this happen and explain why these factors play such a key role. They conclude with a checklist of criteria for determining whether a given group assignment will be effective or not.

Chapter 4, by Carolyn Birmingham and Mary McCord, summarizes an important body of research on team dynamics in general. They have examined several decades of research literature, focusing on the question of what it takes to change a group into a high-performance team. Their conclusions clarify the conditions that have to be created for team members to be ready to contribute to team-based activities in important ways and to feel free to voice their views without fear of creating unmanageable conflict. For any teacher wanting to exploit the educational potential of high-performance learning teams, this chapter sheds considerable light on what they need to do.

CHAPTER 1

Beyond Small Groups

Harnessing the Extraordinary Power of Learning Teams

L. Dee Fink

Using small groups is a good way to introduce active learning into one's teaching. There are, however, significantly different ways of using small groups. This chapter offers a critical analysis of the benefits and challenges of three different ways of using small groups: casual use, cooperative learning, and team-based learning.

During the last two decades, there has been a rapid growth in the use of small groups in college-level teaching. When I talk to professors these days, the majority say that they use small groups in one way or another in at least one of their classes. The majority of students say that they have had a small group learning experience in at least one of their classes. What has led to this rise of interest in teaching with small groups?

Several factors have prompted teachers to explore this form of teaching. In part, teachers are feeling pressure both from the younger TV generation of students who are not very tolerant of lectures and from older students who want a learning experience that consists of more than "information dumping." In addition, colleges are getting feedback from employers saying that they want college-educated employees who have important human-interaction and problem-solving skills as well as content knowledge.

All of this is encouraging teachers to search for ways to make their classes more interesting and worthwhile, and that means making their classes more active. Of those teachers who reach this level of awareness, many discover that using small groups is both an obvious way of engaging students in active learning and a way that can make a significant difference in the quality of student learning.

My general purpose in this chapter is to give the big picture of teaching with small groups and the special place of team-based learning within this picture. First, I want to note that, despite the value of small groups for promoting active learning, some students and teachers have encountered significant problems. This implies that it is important for teachers to learn how to discriminate among different ways of using small groups. Second, I want to identify what I see as three general uses of small groups within higher education: casual use, cooperative learning, and team-based learning. And finally, I want to identify the similarities and differences between the two more sophisticated uses: cooperative learning and team-based learning. This will include a review of the different recommendations put forth by the advocates of cooperative learning and team-based learning on how to use small groups, as well as on the special situations in which team-based learning is particularly valuable.

THE TRANSFORMATIVE VALUE OF TEAM-BASED LEARNING

In my view, "team-based learning" is a special approach to the use of small groups that takes both teaching and learning to a new level of educational significance. This is why the title of this book refers to it as being transformative. When used properly, team-based learning drives four kinds of transformations:

- It transforms "small groups" into "teams."
- It transforms a technique into a strategy.
- It transforms the quality of student learning.
- For many teachers, it transforms (or restores) the joy of teaching.

These are large claims. What is the basis of claiming such unusual capabilities? The answer is that team-based learning has two special features that make it distinctive. The first is the unusual capability that teams have, as compared to groups. The second is the relative power of a teaching strategy, compared to a teaching technique. More will be said about these two special features later in this chapter, but I have introduced them here because these two features give team-based learning an educational capability that is so enormous that many people dismiss its claims when they first hear about it. However, as the chapters in part II of this book illustrate dramatically, when teachers take time to learn about team-based learning and how to implement it properly, it solves several challenging teaching problems and takes student learning, in any discipline, to levels that teachers could barely imagine after years of teaching in more traditional ways.

PROBLEM:
SOME STUDENTS HAVING NEGATIVE EXPERIENCES

Although teaching with small groups obviously has great potential, some survey research (Feichtner & Davis, 1985) and my own conversations with students indicate that this potential is not always realized. While many students find small group learning to be very powerful, a significant percentage of students report negative experiences with small group learning. What is the problem?

When I encounter students who have had courses in which small groups were used in a substantial way, I ask them whether they felt the experience overall had been a positive or a negative one. Almost half the time they say it was a negative experience. When I ask why, they report a number of familiar problems. Perhaps the most common one is, "I had to do most of the work and yet all of us got the same grade" (i.e., it was unfair). Somewhat related but different is, "Several of the students in my group simply didn't care what grade they got (but I do), and they therefore didn't put much time in on the project." Also frequently heard is the lament, "We were supposed to meet outside of class, but our group never found a good time to do that. So we didn't have many meetings where most of the group was there."

What these conversations and the literature on this topic are increasingly showing is that there are good and bad ways of using small groups for educational purposes. As a result, teachers need to (1) learn about the different ways of using small groups in their teaching, and (2) learn how to assess the different recommendations in this literature on how to use groups properly.

THREE DIFFERENT WAYS OF USING SMALL GROUPS

The view that will be presented in this chapter is that despite the many different terms and descriptions of how to use small groups, these variations can be described under three general headings: casual use, cooperative learning, and team-based learning.

Different authors have used different terms when writing about small groups: learning groups (Bouton & Garth, 1983), collaborative learning (Bruffee, 1999; Hamilton, 1997), cooperative learning (Johnson, Johnson, & Smith, 1991; Millis & Cottell, 1998; Slavin, 1983), and team-based learning (Michaelsen, 1983; Michaelsen & Black, 1994; Michaelsen, Black, & Fink, 1996). Despite the varying terminology, these several authors are all referring to the same general idea: putting individual students in a class into small groups for the purpose of promoting more active and more effective learning.

The concept of small group learning is the overall umbrella that unites these various approaches, much like the concept of "water" unites the multiple forms it can take of ice, liquid, and steam. Then when one looks at the different ways teachers use small groups and the different ways described in the literature on small groups, three general patterns emerge: casual use, cooperative learning (the use of carefully structured individual small group activities), and team-based learning. One can conceive of the relationship among these approaches as shown in Figure 1.1.

Casual use is flexible and easy to use because it is a relatively unstructured activity. Cooperative learning greatly enhances the capabilities of small group learning with its emphasis on carefully structured activities.[1] Team-based learning in turn creates and uses a different course structure that enables a whole new level of educational capabilities.

Some authors (for example, Millis & Cottell, 1998) clearly have a different mental map of small group learning. In their minds, cooperative learning is the umbrella

FIGURE 1.1
Three Uses of Small Groups

concept with team-based learning being but one of several variations under that concept. In my view, this conceptualization overlooks the fact that, as will be discussed later in this chapter, many of the procedures recommended by the proponents of cooperative learning are counterproductive to transforming newly formed groups into learning teams. Hence, as shown in Figure 1.1 and the remaining comments in this chapter, I suggest that cooperative learning and team-based learning be seen as complementary but distinct approaches under the general concept of small group learning (see Table 1.1).

Casual Use

The easiest, and therefore often the initial use by a teacher, is to employ small groups in a "casual" way. A typical situation would be for the teacher to lecture for 15–20 minutes and then have students pair up with a student seated next to them, to either discuss a question or solve a problem. After giving the student pairs a few minutes to work together, the teacher then calls on a number of them to share their answers with the whole class, comments on their responses, and then proceeds to introduce some new ideas or whatever.

This level of use offers the benefit of breaking up the potential tedium of nonstop lecturing, adds variety, and gets students into an active cognitive mode. Psychologically it also makes the class less of an isolated and isolating experience by adding a degree of social interaction. The casual use of groups requires little or no advance planning and can be used in classes of any size. The problem with this level of use is that it generally does not generate a particularly powerful form of learning. It can provide a few minutes of practice in a narrowly defined exercise, but nothing much more significant than that.

Frequent Use of Structured Activities

During the 1980s and 1990s, several writers began advocating the use of more structured small-group activities under the name of collaborative or cooperative learn-

TABLE 1.1
Three General Uses of Small Groups

I. **Casual Use**

- "Turn to the student next to you and talk about this."
- Uses relatively ad hoc exercises, therefore little or no advance planning required
- No need to worry about grading, course structure, group composition, etc.

II. **Frequent Use of Structured Activities: Cooperative Learning**

- Frequent use of carefully planned and carefully structured group activities
- Inserts small group activities into preexisting course structure
- Calls for attention to: accountability issues, group formation, student roles, etc.
- Does not change the structure of the course

III. **Transformative Use of Groups: Team-Based Learning**

- Makes small group work the primary in-class activity
- Calls for procedures that support the transformation of newly formed "groups" into "high performance learning teams"
- Takes advantage of the special capabilities of high performance learning teams
- Often requires a change in the structure of the course

ing. This approach represents a significant step up from the casual use of small groups in terms of the potential for significant learning.

Although the particular recommendations vary depending on the perspective of the author, the general pattern of cooperative learning has several common features. Writers recommend using small group activities frequently. They recommend advance planning to think through a variety of issues, for instance, how to achieve individual and group accountability, how to form groups, how long to leave the groups together, whether to assign roles, and so forth. In general, though, this approach does not involve a substantial change in the overall structure of the course. Rather, it focuses on a series of group activities associated with particular lessons to be taught. If the course was basically a lecture or discussion course before, it can basically stay a lecture or discussion course afterward. The planning is focused on a series of small-group activities associated with a particular lesson. The small-group activities fit into the rest of the course; the other parts of the course are generally not changed to support the small-group activity.

Transformative Use of Small Groups

Team-based learning represents an even more intense use of small groups in that it changes the structure of the course to develop and then take advantage of the special capabilities of high-performance learning teams. Such teams have two features that offer major advantages in an educational situation. As members of a team, individual students become willing to commit to a very high level of effort in their learning, and learning teams are capable of solving problems that are beyond the capability of even their most talented members. As is well-known in the world of sports, for example, a team that plays well as a team is far better than a team that has one star but does not know how to play together well as a team. The same is true with effective learning teams. They do not need an academic superstar to do super work. Such teams help individual members of the team better understand the material, and the team becomes capable of solving very challenging and complex problems that are well beyond the capability of the best student in the class working alone (Michaelsen, Watson, & Black, 1989).

Can team-based learning be used in a wide variety of courses? Experience shows that the answer is clearly yes. To use team-based learning, a course only needs to satisfy two conditions:

1. The course contains a significant body of information and ideas (i.e., the content) that students need to understand.
2. One of the primary goals for the course is for students to learn how to apply or use this content by solving problems, answering questions, resolving issues, and so on.

Although some college courses are focused on the development of special skills (e.g., learning a foreign language, how to use particular kinds of technology), most courses easily meet these two conditions for using team-based learning.

WHAT IS DISTINCTIVE ABOUT TEAM-BASED LEARNING?

Although Michaelsen will provide a more detailed description of team-based learning in the next chapter, a brief description will be provided here. By my definition, *"team-based learning" is a particular instructional strategy that is designed to (a) support the development of high-performance learning teams, and (b) provide opportunities for these teams to engage in significant learning tasks.*

There are two key ideas in this definition. The first is that team-based learning is a particular instructional strategy, not a series of independent small-group activities. Although teachers can and have borrowed pieces of team-based learning (usually the "individual–small group" sequence for testing), team-based learning itself consists of a particular instructional strategy, that is, a particular combination and sequence of learning activities. Using such a strategy will often involve the task of restructuring the course. The second key idea is that team-based learning revolves around the development of teams, a kind of social unit that is quite distinct from groups. At this time I will comment on each of these two key ideas.

Team-Based Learning as an Instructional Strategy

The key point here is that team-based learning is an instructional strategy, not just a teaching technique. It is a set of learning activities in a particular sequence, not just an individual activity or teaching technique that can be plugged in more or less wherever. This is an important distinction to understand because a strategy is more effective than an individual activity. A strategy uses a set of activities that work together synergistically to create a high level of energy on the part of the students that can then be applied to the task of learning. When implemented properly, a good strategy can generate a very powerful level of educational energy. And team-based learning has the potential to do exactly this.[2]

Although the particular sequence of activities can be and has been modified to fit particular teaching circumstances, the following is a description of what typically happens in a 15-week semester format. The whole course is restructured by dividing it up into five to seven units focused on the major topics of the subject. This results in several units that are two to three weeks long. Within each of these topical units, the teacher then sets up a three-phase sequence: preparation, application, and assessment (Figure 1.2).

In the *preparation phase*, students do the reading assignments for the whole unit. The goal in this initial phase is not for the students to gain an in-depth mastery or full comprehension of all the readings but to get a good introduction to the information and ideas on this topic; in-depth understanding will come later. First, students are assigned to read the primary content material for this topic outside of class. Then, when they come to class, they engage in the Readiness Assurance Process, or RAP. The purpose of the RAP is to assure that students are ready for the next phase of the sequence, which is when they learn how to apply or use the content. In the RAP, students begin by taking a test on the readings individually, preferably a relatively short test (often multiple choice in form) that can be graded in class. When finished, students turn in their individual answer sheets and then immediately take the same test as a group. Both tests are graded in class and both count as part of the course grade. The third step, which is optional, is an appeals process. If any of the groups think one or more of their answers should have been counted as correct, they can submit a written appeal, making reference to material in the reading assignment that supports their answer. The teacher later decides whether to grant credit for the appeal or not. If so, only the group(s) that made the appeal get(s) the credit. The fourth and final step is for the teacher to offer corrective instruction. That is, after the students have shown what they can learn individually and in groups, the teacher can offer any additional comments that he or she feels are necessary for a correct understanding of the key concepts. The benefit of waiting until now is that the teacher knows what ideas the students were not able to understand on their own and can focus his or her comments only on those ideas that students were not able to understand on their own. And the students, having just struggled to "get a handle on this material," are more ready to listen closely to a set of brief, focused statements. By the end of the preparation phase,

FIGURE 1.2
The Sequence of Learning Activities in Team-Based Learning

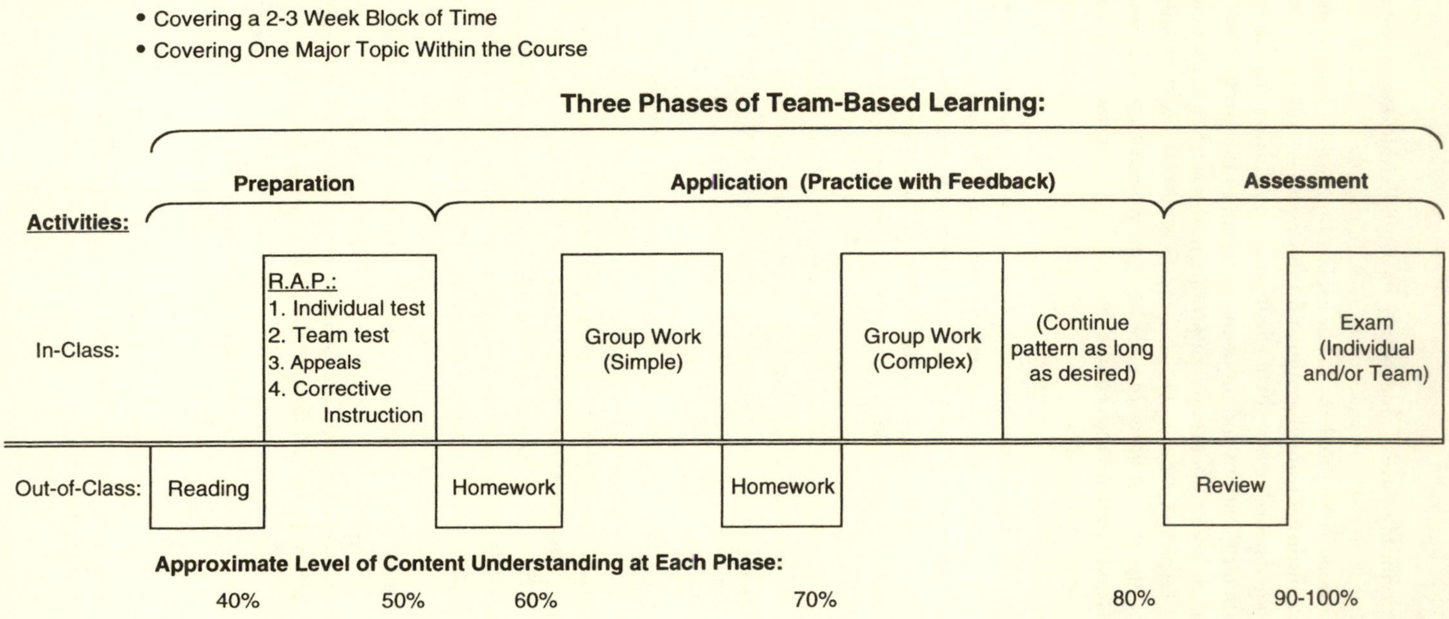

- Covering a 2-3 Week Block of Time
- Covering One Major Topic Within the Course

Three Phases of Team-Based Learning:

Activities:	**Preparation**	**Application (Practice with Feedback)**			**Assessment**

In-Class:

Reading

R.A.P.:
1. Individual test
2. Team test
3. Appeals
4. Corrective Instruction

Group Work (Simple)

Group Work (Complex)

(Continue pattern as long as desired)

Review

Exam (Individual and/or Team)

Out-of-Class:

Homework

Homework

Approximate Level of Content Understanding at Each Phase:

40%   50%   60%   70%   80%   90-100%

students typically have a moderate level of understanding of the material and are thereby ready to start the *application phase*. In this phase, they use the content to answer questions, solve problems, create explanations, make predictions, or do whatever it is that constitutes using the content for this particular subject. The next several class sessions are devoted to a series of small group application exercises in which increasingly difficult questions and problems are given to the groups. The groups each formulate their own responses to the problems, the teacher leads a comparison of the different responses by the groups, and offers feedback on the quality of their responses. Chapter 3 of this volume has specific recommendations on how to generate questions and problems that simultaneously accomplish two goals: helping the groups learn how to use the material, and helping them become more cohesive, that is, more committed to the success of the team.

Finally, after the teams have practiced applying the material for some time, they are ready for the *assessment phase*. Here the teacher, in essence, says, "You have solved these problems several times. Now do it one more time and I will grade your responses as part of the course grade." Following this, the groups are ready to go on to the next unit and repeat the cycle, but this time, they can start to integrate previous material with the new course material.

This interdependent sequence of in-class and out-of-class activities that moves through the preparation, application, and assessment phases is what constitutes the distinctive instructional strategy of team-based learning.

Special Characteristics of Teams

The second distinguishing characteristic of team-based learning is the reliance on the special characteristics of teams to accomplish a special kind of learning. People who have not had the good fortune of having had a personal experience that allowed them to be a member of something that was a team, rather than just a group, may need an explanation of what the differences between the two entities are.

Groups and teams both consist of two or more people who interact in some common activity. What distinguishes teams from groups is that teams are characterized by:

- A high level of individual commitment to the welfare of the group;
- A high level of trust among the members of the group.

The process of having a "group" of people become a "team" requires:

- Time interacting together;
- Resources (especially intellectual);
- A challenging task that becomes a common goal;
- Frequent feedback on individual and group performance.

When this happens, "teams" becomes capable of:

- Motivating a very high level of individual effort;
- Challenging each other with a high tolerance for the give and take of honest communication without taking offense;
- Working together very effectively;
- Successfully accomplishing very complex and challenging tasks.

DIFFERENT RECOMMENDATIONS ON HOW TO USE SMALL GROUPS

Figure 1.1 shows cooperative learning and team-based learning as two subcategories under the larger umbrella concept of "small group learning." Proponents of cooperative learning often see that concept (i.e., "cooperative learning") as the large umbrella concept, with team-based learning being simply one version of cooperative learning. I believe it is important to see team-based learning and cooperative learning as equivalent sub-categories under the larger concept of "small group learning." The reason is that many of the prescriptive recommendations put forth for cooperative learning do *not* apply to team-based learning and in fact are often counterproductive to the process of building high-performance learning teams. Why is this?

The fundamental difference between the two approaches lies in the relative time frame they are using and in the degree of integration they are striving for. Cooperative learning generally views small groups as a teaching technique that is applied in a series of independent learning activities, each of which is aimed at accomplishing a specific set of learning objectives. In contrast, team-based learning views small groups as the basis of a semester-long instructional strategy in which a sequence of small-group activities is designed and linked in such a way that they accomplish two purposes simultaneously: deepening student learning, and enhancing team development. These two different perspectives lead to one clear similarity, but several differences in terms of their recommendations for managing small groups.

Table 1.2 summarizes a list of common questions that faculty members frequently ask about using small groups, as well as the answers typically offered by these two perspectives. For each of these, I will try to explain the thinking behind the different answers offered by the two approaches.

Should Groups Work In-Class or Out-of-Class?

This is one area in which both perspectives agree: Groups should be given time in class to do their work. Groups need all members to be present, and this becomes difficult when students try to meet outside of class. When groups search for a time and place to meet, frequently not all of the members will be able to attend. This automatically creates a disadvantage for those students who are absent and for those groups with only some of their members present. Thus the teacher who asks groups to meet outside of class has created a problem that students cannot easily solve on their own.

TABLE 1.2
Recommendations for Using Small Groups

AREA OF AGREEMENT	Recommendations of:	
	Cooperative Learning	Team Learning
Groups: work in-class or out-of-class?	In-class	In-class
AREAS WHERE RECOMMENDATIONS DIFFER		
Duration of groups?	Half-term (or so)	Whole term
Size of groups?	4 or fewer students	5-7 students
Use assigned roles?	Yes	No; counterproductive
Grade the group work?	Maybe; maybe not	Yes; critical
Spend class time teaching and analyzing group process skills?	Critically important	Nice but not critical
Ensure *prompt* feedback on individual and group performance?	Nice but not critical	Critically important
Use peer assessment?	Maybe	Yes; critical

A second, related reason is that, when groups are asked to meet outside of class, this increases their tendency to look for ways to divide up the work and do it separately because they want to avoid the need to meet outside of class, if possible. But letting them divide up the work eliminates the group character of the assignment and changes it back to a collection of individual assignments.

How Long Should the Groups Stay Together?

Proponents of cooperative learning offer several reasons groups should be changed periodically. Changing the composition of the groups allows each student to get to know and work with more of the other students in the class. In classes with a diversity of students, working with other people who are significantly different from oneself can be an important learning achievement in itself. Changing students also moves any "freeloading" students around from group to group during the course of the semester, so that any one set of students doesn't have to carry them the whole semester. Finally, students sometimes fall into predictable patterns in their relationships with one another. Changing students breaks up these patterns and allows the groups to be more dynamic and vital.

For teachers who use team-based learning, however, periodically changing the composition of the teams is absolutely the wrong thing to do. The reason is that it takes time for a group of students to get to know each other well enough to start functioning effectively as a team. Thus, whenever you change the composition of a group, you move the group back to "square one" in terms of its becoming an effectively functioning team.

In essence, you have made it virtually impossible for most groups to ever become a team, and have significantly reduced the payoff time when they can work on challenging educational tasks effectively.

What about helping students get to know more of the other students in the class? This does have educational value and it happens with team-based learning somewhat during the whole-class discussions. But the other view is that it is more important educationally to learn how to work together as a team than it is to get acquainted with other students in the class. Students who keep changing groups never learn the difference between a newly formed group and a well-developed team, and hence never discover what a real team can do. That is a serious educational cost.

What about the problem of freeloading students? When team-based learning is used effectively, this problem seldom occurs. When groups start functioning as a team, individuals who might be inclined to be freeloaders become very uncomfortable in that role and tend to become contributing members. But even when there are individuals who persist in not contributing, the groups are large enough that they can work around the problem students. Then, at the end of the semester, each group assesses the contribution of all members through the process of peer assessment. This reduces the credit that nonproductive students receive for work done by the group. (See more on peer assessment later.) Hence, students simply do not get to freeload in a team-based learning course.

How Big Should the Groups Be?

Cooperative learning proponents tend to recommend relatively small groups, meaning four or fewer people per group, while team-based learning recommends larger groups, generally five to seven students per group. Both agree that groups of eight or more tend to be inefficient and ineffective.

The small group size is also a primary reason that cooperative learning advocates recommend assigning roles to individual students within groups. Because small groups in cooperative learning are together for a shorter period of time, they need help in becoming semi-cohesive and organized as quickly as possible. To help the groups get started quickly, teachers using cooperative learning often assign roles, and this is easier to do with smaller groups than with larger groups. There are four roles that are usually assigned—reporter, recorder, spokesperson, and folder monitor. Hence, groups of four are ideal. More than this leaves some members without an assigned role.

For teachers trying to use team-based learning, this quick fix for group formation can generate problems over time. The smaller size and the assigning of roles limit the ability of the groups to evolve into effective teams. When groups are small (meaning four or fewer), they have fewer intellectual resources and perspectives at their disposal. This is why groups should be as large as possible, until they become too large for all members to participate. This seems to happen when the groups have eight or more members. Hence, a group of five to seven people seems to be an optimum size. The problems created by assigned roles are discussed next.

Should Students Be Given Assigned Roles?

As noted earlier, cooperative learning proponents often use assigned roles. Generally, the teacher assigns these roles and then periodically changes the role for each person. The belief here is that rotating the roles enables all group members to learn different skills and to contribute equitably.

Team-based learning, on the other hand, finds assigned roles to be unnecessary at best and counterproductive at worst. A lot of time ends up being spent on determining who has what role, what that role entails, what that person therefore needs to do, and so on. And when the roles are rotated periodically, this just multiplies the time spent on role issues.

The belief in team-based learning is that, as groups learn how to function effectively as teams, they naturally and automatically begin to manage the various functions themselves. Everyone makes sure that everyone gets heard, watches how much time is left, decides who will report out, and so forth. They do this quickly and easily, in a fraction of the time taken when roles are assigned. But more importantly, *it is the students themselves who learn how to handle roles and functions*. When the teacher takes over the responsibility of assigning and distributing roles, this in fact prevents students from learning on their own what needs to be done and how to get that accomplished effectively and efficiently.

Should I Grade the Work of the Group?

Advocates of cooperative learning seem to have mixed feelings on this topic. Some, like Kagan (1995), argue strongly against grading group work on the basis that grades should reflect individual work and nothing else. Others, like Millis and Cottell (1998), at times argue both ways. In one part of their book, they write that "Individual accountability precludes this practice [of group grades]" (12). Yet in other parts of their book, they offer advice on how to grade group work. Eventually they clarify their opposition by stating that they are against "undifferentiated group grades," meaning they believe that all members of a group should not automatically receive the same grade for work performed by the group. That seems to be a more valid stance.

The reason for this ambivalence seems to be a concern that grading group work will result in unfairly raising or lowering the grades of some individuals within the group. The fear is that hardworking students in a poor group may end up with a lower course grade because of poor group work, and poor students may be carried along by hardworking members.

The team-based learning perspective is that it is critically important for graded group work to constitute a significant percentage of the course grade, say 30–40 percent. Groups need an incentive for becoming an effective team and they need feedback on how well they are performing as a team. Graded group work meets both these needs. If a major part of the course grade depends on high-quality team performance, the individual and the team have the necessary incentive to work hard, and to do well.

In addition, the feedback on team performance, both graded and ungraded, gives teams the information they need to monitor and improve their performance as a team. Hence, grading group work is critically important.

What about the unfairness issue? That is an important issue. Giving the same grade to all members in the group would result in grades that are unduly high or unduly low for many students in a class. But this potential problem is ameliorated by a number of different processes in team-based learning.

First, when individual students come underprepared, the other members know it quickly and typically make their concern known to that individual, directly or subtly. This creates significant pressure from the team for each individual to be more prepared in the future. Hence there are fewer under-contributing members overall.

Second, the teams are also in a good position to recognize multiple and different kinds of contributions from individual members. Some contribute a wealth of creative ideas for the team to consider; others are stronger in analyzing and assessing those ideas; and yet other students are very helpful in managing the group work. Hence the team members develop a clear understanding of the varied ways in which individual members contribute to the work of the group.

Finally, in those rare cases in which some individuals persist in not contributing, the other members will know that and will indicate that on their peer assessment at the end of the course. This ensures that those who do not contribute will not receive the same credit as everyone else for the quality of the group work.

Should I Spend Class Time Teaching and Analyzing Group Process Skills?

In general, advocates of cooperative learning strongly recommend that instructors spend class time: (1) teaching students how to analyze group processes, and (2) periodically having groups examine the question of how well they are working together as a group (e.g., Johnson, Johnson, & Smith, 1991:22–24). The idea is to help the groups identify any problems they are having so corrective action can be taken. For advocates of team-based learning, teaching about group processes is not seen as bad other than the fact that it is usually not necessary. They strongly believe that good assignments (for recommendations on this, see Chapter 3 of this book) and prompt feedback do much more to help teams to improve their functioning than does teaching them about group interaction and having them discuss how they think they did at the conclusion of each assignment. Hence it simply isn't necessary to spend a significant amount of class time teaching about group-process issues.

How Important Is It to Provide Prompt Feedback on Individual and Group Work?

There is little or no discussion of this issue in the general literature on cooperative learning. For team-based learning proponents, however, prompt feedback is essential to both learning and team development. In their view, even if students are taught to use some sort of group process framework, they are reluctant to engage in the difficult task of seriously evaluating how their group is functioning. When there is a delay, even a day or two, between when the groups do their work and when the assessment comes back, the typical reaction is to see "what they got" and move on. By contrast, when the teams receive immediate feedback on individual and team performance, they instinctively and inevitably engage in an analysis of what went wrong when they still have a clear enough recollection of their experience to make the necessary corrections. Teachers only need to support and encourage this process by providing immediate feedback. When they do this, most teams will quickly and effectively improve the quality of their learning and performance. Thus, in most cases, providing immediate feedback is all that is required for teams to quickly and effectively improve the quality of their learning and performance.

Should I Have the Group Members Assess Each Other?

The practice of having students assess how well each member of the group has contributed to the work of the group, is known as "peer assessment." Proponents of cooperative learning seem to have mixed feelings about this practice. If a teacher decides to grade the group work, then peer assessment is appropriate. But even then, the process is recommended only if students are given proper training and the teacher monitors the process sufficiently (see, for example, Millis & Cottell, 1998:193–94).

In team-based learning, peer assessment is considered to be an essential component of the grading process. Team-based learning proponents would agree with most cooperative learning proponents, that undifferentiated group grades are potentially problematic. If the team is effective and everyone contributes in important ways to the group (which is often the case), then everyone in the group deserves the same credit for whatever grade the group receives for its work. However, in those teams in which there is variation in the quantity or quality of individual contribution, then this needs to be reflected in the way the course grade is calculated. This is best accomplished by peer assessment. The students, not the teacher, have the best knowledge of the quantity and quality of each member's contribution to the work of the group.

In general, the process of peer assessment works as follows. The group does its work and receives a grade for that work. Near the end of the semester the group engages in peer assessment in which each member assesses the work of the other members of the group in terms of how much each person contributed to the learning and the success of the group. This assessment is then used, either (1) as a component to be added to the group grade, or (2) as a component that is used as a percentage multiplier of all graded group work. When there is variation in individual contribution, this procedure results in variation in individual credit received for group work: individuals who contribute more receive more credit than individuals who contribute less. Doing this resolves the fairness issue in grading group work. (For more information on peer assessment, see Appendix B.)

POTENTIAL IMPACT ON STUDENT LEARNING

What are the possible educational benefits that teachers might expect to see if they move from using cooperative learning to using team-based learning? Since both ways of teaching are variations of teaching with small groups, this question will be addressed by looking at the four kinds of learning that are likely to be encouraged by any substantial use of small groups:

- Understanding the course content;
- Applying the course content to problem solving, decision making, etc.;
- Developing the skills for working effectively on a team;
- Valuing the team approach to solving complex intellectual tasks.

Understanding the Course Content

All courses have a certain amount of content learning (factual information, conceptual ideas, etc.) that students need to understand and remember. Team-based learning and cooperative learning are both capable of maintaining a high level of content learning while also promoting other kinds of learning. However, the two approaches rely on different activities to accomplish this.

Cooperative learning activities are generally aimed at learning how to apply the course content rather than helping students acquire their initial understanding of the content itself. Hence cooperative learning relies on the usual procedures for accomplishing the initial learning of the content: in-class lectures, out-of-class readings, homework exercises, and so on. Advocates of cooperative learning sometimes note the need for teachers to create motivating homework assignments and for students to do the homework responsibly. But the small-group activities themselves are generally aimed at application learning, not the initial content learning.

Team-based learning, on the other hand, uses small group activities to directly support the students' initial understanding of the content as well as their subsequent efforts to learn the content by applying it. The structure of the team-based learning sequence (Figure 1.2) gives students several passes at increasing their understanding of the content. The first pass occurs when the students study the material on their own before class, a task for which they are held individually accountable on the first test. Then, during the four steps of the Readiness Assurance Process, students increase their understanding by trying to answer questions individually and through group discussion, reviewing the assigned readings to make appeals, and receiving additional focused input from the professor. Following this, students get repeated opportunities to enhance their understanding of the content by working on assignments in which they apply their knowledge to a variety of problems, questions, and so forth.

As a result of students' going through these three phases of the team-based learning process, teachers generally report that students maintain a very high level of content learning (see the level of understanding of the content in Figure 1.2). (The authors of several of the chapters in part II of this book comment on the high level of content learning when they use team-based learning.)

Ability to Apply the Course Content

Application learning is where one can expect to see a major difference when using team-based learning. Cooperative learning and team-based learning both offer significant opportunities for students to learn how to apply course material. However, for a number of different reasons that are described below, team-based learning has the potential for both a quantitative and qualitative increase in application learning.

The quantitative increase happens because students spend a higher percentage of class time in application activities. Most cooperative learning exercises are application exercises, but the time spent on these exercises seldom exceeds 25–40 percent of total class time. With team-based learning, that percentage increases to 75–80 percent. The Readiness Assessment Procedure is so effective and efficient in providing students with a basic mastery of the course content that students are left with substantially more time to spend on application exercises.

The qualitative increase results from students being able to take on more complex and more challenging problems. Several factors make this possible. First, having larger groups means each group has more intellectual resources at its disposal for addressing the application problems. Second, by spending more time together, the groups become more capable of working together effectively; that is, they can operate as a high-performance team rather than simply as a group. Third, the fact that the group work is graded provides a direct incentive for the teams to invest substantial time and effort into high-quality group work.

Developing Team Skills

Society at large, as well as most professional organizations, is increasingly recognizing the value of people who know how to work effectively in teams on intellectual tasks, and they are calling on colleges and universities to incorporate this kind of learning into the higher education curriculum. Any small group activity is potentially capable of developing students' ability to work in teams. But cooperative learning and team-based learning use very different strategies for accomplishing this.

Cooperative learning in general relies on (1) using assigned roles within groups, (2) having the teacher monitor the groups to see how they are handling the content and how well the groups are working, and (3) spending time after the small-group exercise to "process" (i.e., review and analyze) the small-group activity.

Team-based learning, by contrast, relies on the teams themselves to monitor individual and group performance and to improve performance as necessary. To do that, the teams only need prompt discriminating feedback on individual and team performance. This feedback is provided immediately in the Readiness Assessment

Procedures and in the team application exercises. This feedback makes each team aware of both the absolute and relative quality of its performance, and thereby allows them to assess how well they are working together as a team. If they are not functioning well as a team, the problems are not difficult for them to diagnose:

- Is everyone coming prepared?
- Is everyone speaking up when he or she needs to?
- Is everyone listening carefully to everyone else?

Is there reason to believe that college students, working in teams, are capable of improving their team work skills without input from the instructor? Although we do not have data comparing cooperative learning and team-based learning, there are data clearly documenting that when groups are given the right conditions, they dramatically improve their ability to use their members' intellectual resources and work together as a team to solve complex problems (Watson, Michaelsen, & Sharp, 1991). What are the right conditions? They need time to work together, freedom to learn how to manage their own affairs, and ongoing and timely feedback on the quality of their work.

Why is team-based learning especially effective in helping individual students learn how to improve their team skills? In team-based learning, groups (1) have more time together, because they are left together for the whole semester; (2) are allowed to manage their own interactions; and (3) are given lots of prompt feedback that tells them how well they are doing and gives them incentives to do well.

Valuing the Team Approach to Intellectual Tasks

In addition to wanting people who know how to work in teams, society needs, and is calling for, people who understand the value of this approach in dealing with the challenging intellectual tasks of our time. Team-based learning seems especially well equipped to help students see the value of the team approach to complex problems. Students repeatedly see the data from the Readiness Assurance Process and this data essentially always shows that the teams outperform even the highest individual scores over time (see Exhibit D–A8.3, p. 267; Michaelsen, Watson, & Black, 1989).

Then, in the application phase of team-based learning, teachers need to provide complex, challenging tasks for the teams to work on and to give them clear feedback on the relative quality of their performance. When this happens, it is crystal clear to everyone that an effective team approach produces results superior to what could be accomplished by even a very bright individual, working alone.

THE VALUE OF TEAM-BASED LEARNING IN PARTICULARLY CHALLENGING TEACHING SITUATIONS

Various teachers have found that team-based learning can be especially helpful in dealing with a number of situations that can be and often are particularly challenging for teachers. Four situations in which this is true are when teachers are faced with: large classes, classes with a high level of student diversity, courses with extended meeting times, and courses that emphasize thinking skills.

Large Classes

When teachers are faced with the responsibility of teaching large classes of 100 or more students and seek advice on how best to do this, they frequently get technical suggestions: get more organized, try to make your lectures lively, use more audiovisual materials, and so on. But technical changes like these do not have the ability to make a significant impact on the two biggest problems with large classes from a learning perspective: student anonymity and passivity.

I would urge teachers with large classes to consider using team-based learning as a strategic response. By changing the structure of the course (that is, changing the primary type and sequence of learning activities), the teacher can make a large class operate like a small class and thereby directly impact these two key problems. Students no longer feel anonymous because they participate regularly in a group where everyone knows them and they know everyone else. Student passivity is obviously no longer a problem because essentially every class session consists of active learning. In the application phase of team-based learning, which constitutes the majority of class sessions, students are working on problems and getting feedback on how successful they are. Students in a team-based learning course may complain about being overworked, but they never complain about being passive or bored.

There are some adjustments that need to be made when using team-based learning in classes of 100 students or more. Michaelsen identifies these in his chapter "Team-Based Learning in Large Classes" in this volume. Overall, though, these are relatively easy to make.

Back in the mid-1980s, Michaelsen and I made a mistake that allowed us to realize just how effective team-based learning is in making a large class to operate like a small class. Michaelsen was using the IDEA course evaluation system to obtain student evaluations in a large team-based learning class with over 100 students in it. In the IDEA system, the overall evaluation is made on a percentile scale of 1 (low) to 100 (high), with 50 being average. But it compares students' responses in a given course with other courses of similar size. So we had to note the size of the class on the initial information sheet. Somehow the class size got recorded as having "11" students instead of "111" students. We were surprised when the results came back. His course was rated in the 90–95th percentile whereas in the past they had always been well above the 95th percentile. When we finally figured out that the reason for the drop was that his course was being compared to other courses with 15 or fewer students, we realized the significance of our discovery. Most teachers of large classes would feel exceedingly successful if student ratings came even close to the average ratings in a small class. But Michaelsen's class, with more than one hundred students in it, had been rated in the 90–95th percentile, two standard deviations above the average when compared to small classes. Seeing these results made us realize how enormously successful team-based learning had been in a large class setting.

Classes with a High Level of Student Diversity

Teachers frequently have classes in which students are diverse in terms of key factors such as prior preparation, age, related background experiences, ethnicity, attitudes toward the subject, and so forth.

Team-based learning creates conditions in which people who are very different from one another learn that they need to work together and that they can work together. They find ways to make their differences an asset rather than a liability.

But again, the conditions necessary to make this happen are the same conditions that make groups evolve into teams: time together, freedom to find ways to work out their differences, feedback on their individual and group performance, and incentives. When teachers can create these conditions, students who are very different from one another have a reason to want to work together effectively.

Courses with Extended Meeting Times

I frequently get frantic calls for help from teachers who are facing the prospect of teaching weekend courses in which intersession courses, or condensed courses in which students meet for half-days or several whole days at a time. "What should I do? I can't lecture for three hours at a time!"

I frequently suggest that they consider using team-based learning. This allows the teacher to move some or most of students' initial exposure to the content to out-of-class reading time. That leaves the teacher and students free to use some or most of the class sessions for learning how to apply the content. Once they have created a team-based learning structure for the course, teachers generally have little difficulty figuring out how to use the extended class meeting time to engage students in learning how to apply the course material. This prospect is seen as attractive, not problematic.

Courses That Emphasize Thinking Skills

Team-based learning can be especially helpful to anyone who wants to emphasize the development of students' thinking skills in their courses. In contrast to memorization, thinking is an intellectual activity in which the interaction between people—if properly structured—can be particularly valuable. Whether the skill is critical thinking (judging the value of something), practical thinking (problem solving and decision making), or creative thinking (imagining and creating new ideas or objects), learning how to incorporate the ideas and perspectives of several people and learning how to work through differences can greatly enhance each student's own ability to think effectively. The extended application phase of team-based learning supports this kind of learning very well. Students have multiple opportunities to exchange ideas with others, practice thinking, and get feedback on the quality of their thinking.

TEAM-BASED LEARNING AND PROBLEM-BASED LEARNING

Before finishing this chapter, we should take time to examine the relationship between team-based learning and problem-based learning (PBL). These two approaches to teaching are quite similar in three important respects. First, they are both clearly teaching strategies and not just teaching techniques. Each involves a specific course structure. Second, they both involve a great deal of in-class small-group work, and third, both give the groups challenging, decision-based assignments (Duch, Groh, & Allen, 2001; Wilkerson & Gijselaers, 1996; PBL websites at the University of Delaware, Samford University, and San Diego State University).

There are, however, two important differences. One relates to the focus of the decision-based problems that form the basis of the group assignments. The problems in team-based learning generally aim at teaching students how to apply information and ideas that have been previously studied; PBL problems are designed to teach students to *learn how to learn* new material. That is, PBL aims at having students complete assignments based on complex, unstructured problems that can only be solved by acquiring and using knowledge not yet studied. In practice, though, the distinction between the problems given in team-based learning and in PBL is not that great. Many PBL teachers in fact do have students study some content information first and then give the groups a problem to solve that requires using this previously studied content plus more content that has not yet been learned (University of Delaware, 1995–96).

The second difference between team-based learning and PBL is that although PBL has its own specific ideas about the kinds of tasks given to learning groups, it does not have distinct ideas on how to use small groups. Rather, it seems to borrow ideas from the general literature and practice on this topic. Most PBL teachers seem to use small groups in a way that is more akin to cooperative learning than to team-based learning. As a result, instead of employing strategies that help newly formed groups evolve quickly into high-performance learning teams, they tend to rely on tutors to keep the groups functioning effectively and focused on completing their assigned tasks. As a result, there is sometimes a high cost in the form of the faculty or staff tutors needed to coach each group of students, especially in the model used by most medical schools.

Thus, it would seem that most PBL teachers could benefit from the prescriptions of team-based learning in two important ways. One is that by using the procedures that promote high-performance learning teams, they could eliminate the costly need to provide tutors. The other is that they could increase the effectiveness and capabilities of the learning teams. For example, in a team-based learning version of PBL, instructors might (1) use the RAP over assigned readings to ensure that students master a set of foundational concepts and to enhance the promotion of team development; (2) have students practice using this content, in teams, with one or more application problems; and then (3) assign additional problems that require the teams to identify, learn—and learn how to apply—relevant new content on their own. The incorporation of team-based learning procedures in this way would allow PBL teachers to keep what is distinctive and exciting about PBL without the heavy cost of tutors.

CONCLUDING COMMENTS

This chapter has presented team-based learning as an advanced form of teaching with small groups. Even as carefully structured group activities represent a major improvement beyond the casual use of small groups, team-based learning offers major educational benefits that go beyond the capability of the periodic use of individual small-group activities.

By creating an instructional strategy and a course structure that involve small groups in the initial acquisition of course content, in learning how to apply that content, and in the assessment of student learning, the procedures of team-based learning offer teachers an extremely powerful tool for creating several kinds of higher-level learning. The key to using this tool successfully lies in understanding a few key principles of team dynamics and then learning how to apply those principles with specific subject matter and in a variety of teaching situations. The remaining chapters of this book address these principles and describe how they can be applied in multiple situations.

People who have used team-based learning effectively, such as the authors of the chapters in Part II of this volume, testify to the transformational character of this approach to teaching:

- It transforms small groups into teams.
- It transforms a technique into a strategy.
- It transforms the quality of student learning.
- And, for many, it transforms the joy of teaching!

NOTES

1. For the purposes of this chapter, I am putting ideas about "collaborative learning" and "cooperative learning" under the same heading because they both advocate the use of carefully structured small group activities that can be inserted into a variety of existing course structures.

2. The significance of an instructional strategy is developed more extensively in Chapter 4 of another book of mine, *Creating Significant Learning Experiences in College Classrooms*, which will be published by Jossey-Bass in 2003.

REFERENCES

Bouton, C., & Garth, R. Y., eds. (1983). *Learning in groups. New directions for teaching and learning,* Vol. 14. San Francisco: Jossey-Bass.

Bruffee, K. A. (1999). *Collaborative learning: Higher education, interdependence, and the authority of knowledge.* 2d ed. Baltimore: Johns Hopkins University Press.

Duch, B. J., Groh, S. E., & Allen, D. E., eds. (2001). *The power of problem-based learning.* Sterling, VA: Stylus.

Feichtner, S. B., & Davis, E. A. (1985). Why some groups fail: A survey of students' experiences with learning groups. *The Organizational Behavior Teaching Review 9*(4): 58–71.

Hamilton, S. J. (1997). *Collaborative learning: Teaching and learning in the arts, sciences, and professional schools.* 2d ed. Indianapolis, IN: IUPUI Center for Teaching and Learning.

Johnson, D. W., Johnson, R. T., & Smith, K. A. (1991). *Cooperative learning: Increasing college faculty instructional productivity.* ASHE–ERIC Higher Education Report, No. 4. Washington, DC: George Washington University.

Kagan, S. (1995). Group grades miss the mark. *Educational Leadership 52*(8): 68–71.

Michaelsen, L. K. (1983). Team learning in large classes. In *Learning in groups. New directions for teaching and learning series,* Vol. 14. Ed. C. Bouton & R. Y. Garth. San Francisco: Jossey-Bass.

Michaelsen, L. K., & Black, R. H. (1994). *Building learning teams: The key to harnessing the power of small groups in higher education.* In *Collaborative learning: A sourcebook for higher education,* Vol. 2. Ed. S. Kadel & J. Keehner. State College, PA: National Center for Teaching, Learning and Assessment.

Michaelsen, L. K., Black, R. H., & Fink, L. D. (1996). What every faculty developer needs to know about learning groups. In *To Improve the academy: Resources for faculty, instructional and organizational development,* Vol. 15. Ed. L. Richlin. Stillwater, OK: New Forums Press.

Michaelsen, L. K., Watson, W. E., & Black, R. H. (1989). A realistic test of individual versus group consensus decision making. *Journal of Applied Psychology 74*(5): 834–839.

Millis, B. J., & Cottell, P. G. (1998). *Cooperative learning for ligher education faculty.* Phoenix: Oryx Press.

PBL Websites. University of Delaware: www.udel.edu/pbl; Samford University: www.samford.edu/pbl/pbl_main.html; San Diego State University: edweb.sdsu.edu/clrit/PBL_WebQuest.html.

Slavin, R. E. (1983). *Cooperative learning.* New York: Longman.

University of Delaware. (1995–96). Problem-based learning in undergraduate education. Newsletter No. 47. Center for Teaching Effectiveness, University of Delaware, Newark, DE.

Watson, W. E., Michaelsen, L. K., & Sharp, W. (1991). Member competence, group interaction and group decision-making: A longitudinal study. *Journal of Applied Psychology, 76:* 801–809.

Wilkerson, L., & Gijselaers, W. H., eds. (1996). *Bringing problem-based learning to higher education. New Directions for Teaching and Learning Series,* Vol. 68. San Francisco: Jossey-Bass.

CHAPTER 2

Getting Started with Team-Based Learning

Larry K. Michaelsen

This chapter has been written for teachers who are ready to consider using team-based learning in their courses but who want a clearer picture of why this approach has such great potential and what it takes to make it work effectively. After explaining what it is that gives learning teams their unusual and special capability for promoting significant learning, I will identify the four key principles that govern the effective use of learning teams (part 1) and then describe what happens from start to finish in a team-based learning course (part 2). At the end of the chapter, I also have a few comments about why I believe team-based learning is such an attractive option for teachers in a variety of teaching situations.

The purpose of this chapter is to provide readers with a broad understanding of the characteristics of team-based learning along with the capability to implement it as an instructional strategy. It must be emphasized, however, that the tremendous power of team-based learning is derived from a single factor: the high level of cohesiveness that can be developed within student learning groups. In other words, the effectiveness of team-based learning as an instructional strategy is based on the fact that it *nurtures the development of high levels of group cohesiveness* that, in turn, results in a wide variety of other positive outcomes. When one fully understands the importance of group cohesiveness as the foundation for building learning teams, the relative significance of the procedures and activities described herein become readily apparent.

Based on evidence from both personal experience and empirical research (see Chapter 4), it clearly takes a transformation process to evolve a small group into a powerful, cohesive learning team. The paragraphs that follow will outline a set of principles and practices that are critical to this transformation process. The first part of this chapter presents four key principles for implementing team-based learning, and outlines why they must be followed. The next part provides a discussion of the steps involved in actually implementing team-based learning, and the first part of the chapter describes the benefits of team-based learning, especially its adaptability across a variety of teaching and learning situations.

THE FOUR ESSENTIAL PRINCIPLES
OF TEAM-BASED LEARNING

Teachers who shift from traditional forms of teaching to a team-based learning approach, will find that this shift leads to significant changes in: (1) the focus of their instructional objectives, (2) the nature of the "events" through which learning occurs, and (3) the role of both instructor and student.

Traditionally, the primary learning objective of most classes is to familiarize students with course concepts. By contrast, the primary learning objective in team-based learning is to ensure that students have the opportunity to practice *using course concepts*. As a result, the vast majority of class time is used for teamwork on application-focused team assignments. This in turn requires that the instructor's primary role shift from one who is dispensing information to one who designs and manages the overall instructional process. Furthermore, instead of being a passive recipient of information, students are required to accept responsibility for the initial exposure to the course content so that they will be prepared for the in-class team work.

Changes of this magnitude do not just happen automatically. They are, however, the reliable and natural outcome when the four essential principles of team-based learning have been implemented. The essential principles are:

1. groups must be properly formed and managed;
2. students must be made accountable for their individual and group work;
3. group assignments must promote both learning and team development;
4. students must have frequent and timely performance feedback.

When these principles are in place, mere groups of students evolve into cohesive learning teams. A description of each of these principles is provided in the following paragraphs.

Principle 1: Groups Must Be Properly Formed and Managed

Forming effective groups involves managing two important variables. One is that the groups must be formed in a way that avoids establishing groups whose membership characteristics are likely to interfere with the development of group cohesiveness. The other is ensuring that the groups have approximately the same talent pool to draw from in completing their assignments. Otherwise, the teacher will encounter a great deal of difficulty in designing assignments that are manageable but challenging enough to promote learning. In addition, the groups should be large and diverse enough to ensure that they have adequate resources to complete their assigned tasks and should remain intact for the duration of the course. (See Chapter 4 for a review of empirical literature related to these issues).

Minimizing Barriers to Group Cohesiveness

Probably the greatest inhibitors to the development of group cohesiveness are either a previously established relationship between a subset of members in the group (e.g., boyfriend/girlfriend, fraternity brothers, etc.), or the potential for a cohesive subgroup based on background factors such as nationality, culture or native language. In newly formed groups, these factors are likely to become the basis for a cohesive subgroup from which other members are likely to feel excluded for the entirety of a course. As a result, allowing students to form their own groups practically ensures the existence of potentially disruptive subgroups (Fiechtner & Davis, 1985; Michaelsen & Black, 1994). Thus, teachers should use a group formation process that mixes students up in a way that forces the groups to build themselves into teams "from the ground up."

Distributing Member Resources

For groups to function as effectively as possible, they should also be as diverse as possible. That is, every group should have access to those students in the class who have the potential for making a significant contribution to the success of their group. Diversity issues focus on factors such as student assets and liabilities as well as student characteristics such as gender, ethnicity, and so on. For groups to be more evenly matched, relevant student assets, liabilities, and characteristics should be distributed equitably across the groups. Member assets may include full-time work experience, previous relevant course work, access to perspectives from other cultures, or other characteristics. Member liabilities may be in the form of negative attitudes toward the course, limited fluency in English, no previous relevant course work, and so forth. When relevant member assets, liabilities, and characteristics are evenly distributed, learning teams will work more effectively. However, it takes input from the teacher to determine which student characteristics may serve as either assets or liabilities for this particular class. In other words, students do not intuitively have enough information or the inclination to wisely form groups; therefore the task must always be the responsibility of the teacher. (See the section entitled "Forming the Groups" on p. 40.)

Learning Teams Should Be Fairly Large and Diverse

Because team-based learning assignments involve highly challenging intellectual tasks, teams must be fairly large and diverse. That is, teams should be comprised of five to seven members and as heterogeneous as possible. If teams are smaller and/or homogeneous, some are likely to face the problem of not having a sufficiently rich talent pool of individual resources needed to be successful.

Groups Should Be Permanent

Students should stay in the same group for the entirety of the semester. Although even a single well-designed group assignment usually produces a variety of positive outcomes, it is only when students work together over time that they become cohesive enough to evolve into self-managed and truly effective learning teams. Team development occurs through a series of interactions that enable individual members to test the extent to which they can trust their peers to take them seriously and treat them fairly. In newly formed groups, members typically begin the testing process by engaging in small talk and by carefully avoiding disagreements, even though doing so (i.e., avoiding disagreements) inevitably limits their ability to work productively. As a result, newly formed groups tend to rely heavily on their most competent member and have a limited ability to tap the resources of the rest of the group. If properly nurtured, most groups will, in time, develop more productive interaction patterns. Realistically, however, even under favorable conditions, most groups require working together in excess of 20–25 hours before they can fully assess and benefit from the resources of all members of the group (Watson, Michaelsen & Sharp, 1991). In addition, membership diversity initially inhibits both group processes and performance, but becomes a clear asset when members have worked together over an extended period of time (Watson, Kumar, & Michaelsen, 1993).

As groups develop into teams, communication becomes more open and, as long as members have information relevant to the issues at hand, is far more conducive to learning. In part, this occurs because trust and understanding build to the point that members are willing and able to engage in intense give-and-take interactions without having to worry about being offensive or misunderstood. In addition (and in contrast to temporary groups), team members are willing to risk challenging each other because they see their own success as being integrally tied to the success of their team. Thus, over time, members' initial concerns about creating a bad impression by being "wrong" are outweighed by their motivation to ensure that their team is successful. When this occurs, studies have shown that 98 percent of teams will outperform their own best member on learning-related tasks (Michaelsen, Watson, & Black, 1989).

Groups Must Be Formed by the Teacher

Given the requirements for minimizing barriers to group cohesiveness and evenly distributing resources across teams, the teacher must directly control the group formation process. Even stating a desired group size and then inviting students to form their own groups flirts with disaster. Because of the heavy influence of where students are likely to be sitting when the invitation is given, it is highly unlikely that the resulting groups will have members that will have membership characteristics that will enable them to develop into cohesive teams.

Principle 2: Students Must Be Made Accountable

Establishing accountability requires creating two conditions. One is ensuring that the quality of students' individual and group work can be monitored. The other is ensuring that the quality of their work will have significant consequences (good and bad).

In traditional classes, because there is no real need for students to be accountable to anyone other than the instructor, it is possible to establish a reasonable degree of accountability by simply assigning grades to students' work. By contrast, developing groups into cohesive learning teams requires assessing and rewarding a number of different kinds of student behavior. Students must be accountable for individually preparing for group work, devoting time and effort to completing group assignments, and interacting with each other in productive ways. Fortunately, however, using learning groups also offers opportunities for meaningfully involving students in establishing accountability for these important behaviors.

Accountability for Individual Pre-Class Preparation

The first step in developing cohesive learning teams is making members accountable for pre-class individual preparation. If individual students fail to complete pre-class assignments, they will be unable to contribute to the efforts of their team. Lack of preparedness hinders the development of group cohesiveness, and better students resent having to carry their less willing or less able peers. As a result, effectively using learning groups requires making students accountable for individually preparing for class.

In team-based learning, the basic mechanism that ensures individual accountability for pre-class preparation is the *Readiness Assurance Process* (see Table 2.1, and Michaelsen & Black, 1994) that occurs at the beginning of each major unit of instruction. The first step in the process is an individual Readiness Assessment Test (RAT—typically 18–20 multiple-choice questions) covering a set of pre-assigned readings. Next, students turn in their answers and are given an additional answer sheet so that groups can retake the same test and turn in their consensus answers for immediate scoring. This process promotes students' accountability to both the instructor and to each other. First, students are responsible to the instructor because the individual scores count as part of the course grade (discussed later in detail). Second, during the group test, each member is invariably asked to voice and defend their choice on every question. As a result, students are clearly and explicitly accountable to their peers for not only completing their assigned readings, but also for being able to explain the concepts to each other.

Accountability for Contributing to Their Team

Confirming that members are prepared for group work is an essential first step in ensuring that students contribute to their group in ways that promote learning. The next step is ensuring that members contribute time and effort to group work. To accurately assess members' contributions to the success of their teams, it is imperative that instructors involve the students themselves in the assessment process. An excellent tool for this kind of evaluation is peer assessment. That is, members are given the opportunity to evaluate one another's contributions to the activities of the team. Contributions to the team include activities such as individual preparation for team work, reliable class attendance, attendance at team meetings that may have occurred outside of class, positive contributions to team discussions, valuing and encouraging input from fellow team members, and so forth. Peer assessment is essential because team members are typically the only ones who have enough information to accurately assess one another's contributions. (See the next part in this chapter and Appendix B for additional information on peer evaluations.)

Accountability for High-Quality Team Performance

The third significant factor in ensuring accountability is developing an effective system to assess the performance of the teams. There are two keys to assessing teams effectively. One is using assignments that require teams to create a "product" that can be readily compared across teams and with "expert" opinions (including those of the instructor—see the following). The other is using procedures to make sure that teams receive frequent feedback on their work.

Accountability and Rewards

Students are, after all, rational human beings who tend to behave in ways they believe will result in positive consequences. Thus, it is essential that we use an assessment system that encourages the kind of behavior that will promote learning in, and from, group interaction. As a result, an effective assessment and reward system requires three elements. One is regular and timely assessment of the extent to which students are prepared for and contribute to their groups. Another is assessing the quality of the work done by groups. Finally, irrespective of the extent to which students are involved in the assessment process, a significant proportion of students' grades should be based on the behaviors that are needed to promote high-quality group interaction. Thus, creating cohesive and effective learning teams requires using a grading system in which individual members' contributions to the success of their teams, and team performance, are assessed and rewarded (see pp. 88–90 and Appendix A).

Principle 3: Team Assignments Must Promote
Both Learning and Team Development

The development of appropriate group assignments is a critical aspect of successfully implementing team-based learning. In fact, most of the reported "problems" with learning groups (free-riders, member conflict, etc.) are the direct result of inappropriate group assignments. When bad assignments are used, poor results are both predictable and very nearly completely preventable. In most cases, the reason that group assignments produce problems is that they are not really group assignments at all. Instead, individuals working alone rather than members working together as a group do the actual work. Further, since discussion time is so limited, these kinds of assignments both inhibit learning and prevent, rather than promote, team development.

The most fundamental aspect of designing effective team assignments is ensuring that they truly require group interaction. In most cases, team assignments will generate a high level of interaction if they require teams to use course concepts to make decisions that involve a complex set of issues, and enable teams to report their decisions in a simple form. When assignments emphasize making decisions, intragroup discussion is the natural and rational way to complete the task. However, assignments that involve producing complex output such as a lengthy document are likely to limit discussion because the rational way to complete the task is to divide up the work and have members individually complete their part of the total task. Therefore, tasks that can be divided among team members should always be avoided. (A thorough discussion of effective team assignments follows in Chapter 3).

Principle 4: Students Must Receive Frequent and Immediate Feedback

Providing immediate feedback is key to successful team-based learning for two very different reasons. One that is well documented in the education literature is that feedback is essential to content learning and retention (e.g., Bruning, Schraw, & Ronning, 1994). The other, that is seldom mentioned in the education literature but well documented in the small groups research literature (see chapter 4, pp. 90–91), is that feedback is important because of its impact on group development. Further, the positive impact of feedback on both learning and team development is greater when it is immediate, frequent, and discriminatory (i.e., enables learners to clearly distinguish between good and bad choices, effective and ineffective strategies, etc.).

Timely Feedback from the Readiness Assessment Tests

The Readiness Assessment Tests (RATs, as mentioned previously and discussed in detail later in this chapter) are an excellent example of the importance of feedback for both learning and team development. Because they are given at the beginning of each major instructional unit, feedback from the RATs facilitates the shift from concept coverage to concept applications by allowing the instructor to minimize the time devoted to ensuring that students have the conceptual skills required for completing the application focused assignments. In addition, feedback from the RATs facilitates the team development process in two important ways. One is that because the group scores are made public, group members are highly motivated to pull together to protect their public image. The other way in which the RATs build group cohesiveness is that the immediate feedback on both the individual and group scores enables the groups to learn how to work together more effectively. Because the feedback is immediate, students are both aware of situations when the group failed to capitalize on the knowledge of one or more of their members, and are highly motivated to do something about it (Watson et al., 1991). As a result, they very quickly learn the importance of including everyone in the decision making process. Thus, over time, naturally extroverted or more assertive members do more listening and less talking, quieter students become much more active in team discussions, and cohesiveness increases because members develop a genuine appreciation of each other's contribution to their group's success.

Timely Feedback on Application-Focused Team Assignments

Providing immediate feedback on application-focused team assignments is just as important for both learning and team development, but typically presents a much greater challenge than providing immediate feedback on the RATs. Unlike the RATs, which are designed to ensure that students understand basic concepts, most application-focused team assignments are aimed at developing students' higher-level learning skills and, as a result, can be much more difficult to evaluate. One key to providing immediate feedback on application-focused team assignments is requiring the right kind of output from the teams (i.e., assignments that require students to make complex decisions, but represent their work in a simple form). The other is using procedures that enable teams to assess and provide feedback on each other's work.

For most teachers, designing application-focused assignments that enable timely feedback requires modifying both their assignments and the way they use them. Fortunately, the task of modifying assignments so that they facilitate timely feedback (and team accountability) is fairly straightforward once you understand the key elements in the process. The kinds of changes that typically need to be made can be illustrated by the experience of a colleague who teaches in a medical school.

As a professor in a medical school, this teacher used a series of case files to develop medical students' diagnostic skills. For many years, she assigned groups to write a series of one-page memos identifying a preliminary diagnosis for the patient portrayed in each case. She was, however, always disappointed in the learning outcomes. Her disappointment was a result of the fact that students only worked with a fraction of the cases because groups delegated the work to individual members. In addition, given the large size of the class, correcting the assignment took so long that students were more interested in their grade than the substance of the papers.

Because of her disappointment with the learning outcomes, the teacher modified the assignment and was much more pleased with the results. Her modifications include the following changes. Although she still has students read the same cases, she has changed the team assignments so that the emphasis is on *deciding* rather than writing. She also changed classroom management procedures to enable groups to become involved in the assessment and feedback process. For example, first, she pre-assigns the same set of cases. Then, in class, she adds a vital piece of new information to the assigned case and gives teams a specified length of time to either select a most likely diagnosis from a limited set of alternatives, or commit to a position that they do not have enough information to make a definite diagnosis. When the time for deciding has elapsed, the teacher has teams hand in a one-page form on which they report their choice and the key items of evidence that support their conclusion (for grading purposes). Then she gives a signal and the teams simultaneously hold up a legal-sized sheet of paper to reveal their choices to the class as a whole. The outcome of the assignment in this form is a series of lively discussions. The discussions first occur within the teams. Then there is always a vigorous interchange between groups as students challenge the rationale for each other's choices. Further, the give-and-take discussion in both phases fosters concept understanding and team cohesiveness.

The Four Essential Principles: Summary Comments

Although learning groups have positive effects on students' engagement and learning in most courses, their educational value is dependent on two conditions. One is the extent to which students are motivated to prepare for group work. Peer teaching simply cannot occur unless the "teachers" have something to teach (i.e., no amount of discussion can overcome absolute ignorance). The other is the extent to which students are willing to engage in give-and-take discussions (i.e., students' individual knowledge is of no value unless they are willing to voice what they know). Although constructive disagreements are essential to significant learning, the level of trust required for members to be willing to challenge each other's views requires a level of cohesiveness and trust that only develops through a series of positive group interactions.

By adhering to the Four Essential Principles of Team-Based Learning, teachers ensure that the vast majority of groups will develop a level of cohesiveness and trust required to transform groups into effective learning teams. Appropriately forming the teams puts them on equal footing and greatly reduces the possibility of mistrust from preexisting relationships between a subset of team members. Holding students accountable for preparation for and attending class motivates team members to behave in ways that build cohesiveness and foster trust. Using assignments that promote both learning and team development provides incentives to motivate members to challenge each other's ideas for the good of the team. Using RATs and other assignments that provide ongoing and timely feedback on both individual and team performance enables teams to develop confidence in their ability to capture the intellectual resources of their members. Also, over time, students' confidence in their teams grows to the point that they are willing and able to tackle difficult assignments with little or no external help.

IMPLEMENTING TEAM-BASED LEARNING

One of the greatest benefits of team-based learning is that teachers are forever freed from the burden of covering all of the course content; instead, it is the students who do this work. With team-based learning, students spend time studying the material individually before class and then interacting in class with their teammates during the Readiness Assurance Process. This sequence of events ensures that the students gain a strong initial coverage of the content of the course. As a result, they are then prepared to use the majority of class time on assignments aimed at enhancing their ability to apply the knowledge. As a result, effectively using team-based learning typically requires redesigning a course from beginning to end and the redesign process should begin well before the start of the school term.

The redesign process involves making decisions about and designing, activities at four different points in time: before class begins, the first day of class, each major unit of instruction, and near the end of the course.

Before Class Begins

The pre-class work in implementing team-based learning involves making decisions related to issues in the following three categories: (1) partitioning the course content into macro-units, (2) identifying the instructional goals and objectives, and (3) designing a grading system.

Partitioning the Course Content

The first step in the implementation of team-based learning is to partition the course content into four to seven macro-units based on the major topics of the course. These major units of instruction form the basis for defining objectives and for designing both the RATs and the application-focused assignments. Typically, these units consist of two to four chapters from the course text and perhaps additional readings that can be tied together with an overall conceptual theme.

Macro-units of instruction in team-based learning typically involve three different types of in-class activities, each of which is preceded by pre-class preparation by the students. The first type of in-class activity, the Readiness Assurance Process, enables the instructor to ensure that students are familiar with key unit concepts by assessing and extending the level of understanding students achieved after completing the pre-class reading assignment. Next come one or more activities designed to provide students with opportunities to practice (and receive feedback) on actually applying the key unit concepts. Finally, students are typically required to demonstrate their mastery of unit concepts through completing an individual or group application-focused assignment or exam. In other words, students work independently outside of class studying and preparing for each event (i.e., test, assignment, project, etc.) that occurs in class. This sequence of events is illustrated in Figure 2.1. The diagram (fondly referred to as the castle-top diagram) graphically portrays the pattern of activities that occur, over time, during a typical instructional unit. One can readily see the flow of events from out-of-class preparation to in-class tests and assignments.

FIGURE 2.1
Team-Based Learning Instructional Activity Sequence

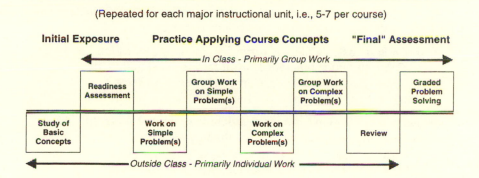

(Repeated for each major instructional unit, i.e., 5-7 per course)

Identifying the Instructional Goals and Objectives

The second step in redesigning a course for team-based learning is identifying content-related learning objectives for the entirety of the course, each major instructional unit, and often for sub-units as well. If instructors are able to design with their desired end in mind—that is, by determining what they want students to *do* with the ideas and concepts as a result of studying this unit of instruction—they are far more likely to end up, educationally, where they want to be.

With team-based learning, it is important to identify two different types of content-related instructional objectives. The first type of instructional objective, and, by far the most important, involves identifying what students will do with their newly acquired knowledge (see Table 2.1; Michaelsen & Black, 1994). The second type of instructional objective focuses on identifying the course concepts and terminology that students must know in order to achieve the "doing" objectives.

The "doing" objectives are important for two very different reasons. First, because there is not enough time for the teacher to cover all of the material, focusing on how we want students to use their knowledge is an extremely powerful and reliable aid in deciding which elements of the course content are really important. Second, although most students are willing to put in the effort needed to understand basic concepts, they are likely to rebel at the expectation that they should be primarily responsible for their initial exposure to course content unless they know why the concepts are important. If the only payoff from the students' pre-class study and reading is covering more meaningless minutia (at least in their minds), they are likely to complain about "having to pay tuition to be in a class where the teacher doesn't teach." On the other hand, if studying the basics on their own enables them to work on challenging and relevant application-focused assignments (e.g., see Michaelsen & Black, 1994), most students both appreciate and support what the teacher is trying to do. As a result, the instructor must have a clear answer to the question, "What do I want

TABLE 2.1
Readiness Assurance Process

---

1) <u>Assigned Readings</u>. In most instances, the students are initially exposed to concepts through assigned readings.

2) <u>Individual Test</u>. Additional exposure during the individual test helps reinforce students' memory of what they learned during their individual study (for a discussion of the positive effects of testing on retention see Nungester & Duchastel, 1982).

3) <u>Team Test</u>. During team tests, students orally elaborate the reasons for their answer choices. As a result, they are exposed to peer input that aids in either strengthening or modifying their schemata related to key course concepts. In addition, they gain from acting in a teaching role (for a discussion of the cognitive benefits of teaching see Bargh & Schul, 1980; Slavin & Karweit, 1981).

4) <u>Appeals</u>. During this step students are given the opportunity to restore credit for questions missed on the team test by making a successful written appeal. Because students have the opportunity to increase their score, they are highly motivated to engage in a focused re-study of troublesome concepts.

5) <u>Oral Instructor Feedback</u>. Steps 1-4 ensure that the instructor is aware of students' level of concept understanding. In step 5, the instructor provides feedback and corrective instruction that is specifically aimed at resolving any misunderstandings that remain after students have done the focused review in preparing the appeals.

students to be able to do when they have finished the course?" Otherwise, I would strongly recommend against using team-based learning. However, if instructors are able to articulate higher-level objectives, they are well on their way to being a successful user of learning teams.

Designing a Grading System

The third step in redesigning the course is to ensure that the grading system is designed to reward the right things. An effective grading system for team-based learning must address the concerns of both students and the instructor. For both, the primary concern is related to past situations in which too many groups have had free-riders. Students worry that they will be forced to choose between getting a low grade or getting a higher grade—but at the expense of carrying their less able or less-motivated peers. Instructors worry that they will have to choose between grading rigorously and grading fairly.

Fortunately, both sets of concerns tend to be alleviated by a grading system in which a significant proportion of the grade is based on: (1) individual performance, (2) team performance, and (3) each member's contributions to the success of their teams. Having a significant part of the grade based on each of the first two principles is key to ensuring that students will be rewarded for their individual effort and that teams will have the resources they need to complete team assignments. In other words, having part of the grade based on team performance provides an incentive for students to invest the time and effort needed to complete (and learn from) the team assignments. Students must first perceive that each of the factors (i.e., individual performance, team performance, and members' contributions to the success of their teams) is important to their course grade. After that, the only concern left is that the relative weight of the factors is acceptable to both the instructor and the students.

The First Hours of Class: Getting Started on the Right Foot

Activities that occur during the first few hours of class are critical to the success of team-based learning. During that time, the teacher must see that four objectives are accomplished. The first objective is to lay the groundwork for team-based learning in general. That is, team-based learning must be explained to the students to ensure their understanding of why the teacher is using team-based learning, and how the class will be conducted. The second objective is to actually form the groups. The third and fourth objectives include alleviating students' concerns about the grading system and setting up mechanisms to encourage the development of positive group norms.

Laying the Groundwork for Team-Based Learning

Because team-based learning is so fundamentally different from traditional courses, it is important that students understand both how the class will be conducted and the rationale for this approach to learning. Educating the students about team-based learning requires (at a minimum) providing students with information about the grading system and the sequence of assignments. This information should be printed in the course syllabus and presented orally by the teacher.

In order to foster students' understanding of team-based learning, I typically use two activities that work quite well. The first, which I always use on the first day, involves the use of an overhead transparency (or a PowerPoint presentation). This presentation describes how learning objectives for this course will be accomplished through the use of team-based learning, as compared to a course that is taught with a more traditional approach. (see Appendix D–A1.1 and D–A1.2). The second activity that, with class periods of less than an hour, might occur on the second day, involves using part of the first class as a demonstration of a Readiness Assessment Test with the course syllabus as the "content" material to be covered. That is, as soon as I have formed the groups, I have students read the course syllabus (on the spot) and then take an individual test over the contents of the syllabus. That test is followed by a group test. The tests are a simulation of the Readiness Assessment Tests the students will be taking during the semester.

Forming the Groups

As discussed, two factors that must be taken into consideration when forming the groups are the assets and liabilities of the students, and the potential for the emergence of sub-groups. As a result, the starting point in the group-formation process is to gather information about the specific student assets and student liabilities that could potentially impact student performance in this class. Assets and liabilities for a particular course might include such things as work experience, previous relevant course work, access to perspectives from other cultures, and so on.

The second factor that can impact student performance in a group is the emergence of sub-groups, for example, boy- or girlfriends, sorority or fraternity members, ethnic groups, and so forth. Regardless of the process used to form the groups, both of these categories of individual member characteristics need to be evenly distributed across the groups.

After student characteristics have been identified, actually assigning students to groups can be done in a variety of ways. The first decision that must be made, however, is the size of the groups. As discussed earlier, the groups should be composed of five to seven members. This ensures that the vast majority of groups will have ample resources (i.e., input from individual students). Once group size is determined, it is time to begin the process of distributing individual member characteristics across the groups.

One common practice is to collect the relevant student information on a set of cards. Then, before the second class, the teacher uses the information on the cards to sort students into specific groups. This method has the advantage of giving the teacher time to work out the group assignments. Its disadvantage, however, is that students tend to wonder how much the instructor might have somehow given one or more of the groups an unfair advantage.

Although using student information to form groups outside of class works very well, I recommend actually forming the groups in class in the presence of the students. This procedure virtually eliminates student concerns about any ulterior motives the instructor may have had in forming the groups.

To form groups in class, the teacher begins the process by simply asking questions about the factors that are important to group success. For a class in management, typical questions could include, "How many of you have four or more years of full-time work experience?" "How many have access to a laptop computer you can bring to class?" "In which country did you attend high school? and other queries. Students respond to each of the questions either orally or with a show of hands. Then students possessing a series of specific assets are asked to form a single line around the perimeter of the classroom with the rarest or most important category at the front of the line. After students are lined up, they simply count off down the line by the total number of groups in the class. All "ones" become Group 1, all "twos" become Group 2, and so on. With this simple method, individual student characteristics have been easily distributed across the teams (see video clip at www.teambasedlearning.org).

Alleviating Student Concerns about Grades

The next step in getting started on the right foot with team-based learning is to address student concerns about the grading system. For the most part, students' uneasiness about grades in a group-oriented course are based on past experience in which they have been forced to choose between carrying the group or getting a bad grade. Fortunately, their anxiety largely goes away when they understand two of the essential features of team-based learning. One is that two elements of the grading system—"counting" individual scores on the RATs and basing part of the grade on a peer evaluation—create a high level of individual accountability for pre-class preparation and class attendance. The other is that there is little danger that one or two less-motivated members can put the group at risk because the team assignments will be done in class and will require thinking, discussing, and deciding.

Based on years of experience, the most effective way to alleviate student concerns about grades is to directly involve them in the development of the grading system. Students become involved by participating in an exercise called "Setting Grade Weights" (Michaelsen, Cragin, & Watson, 1981; see Appendix C). Within limits set by the instructor, representatives of the newly formed teams negotiate with one another to reach a mutually acceptable set of weights for each of the grade components: individual performance, team performance, and members' contributions to the success of their teams. After an agreement has been reached regarding the grade weight for each component, the standard applies for all groups for the remainder of the semester.

Involving students in the process of setting grade weights is highly effective because it is an immediate demonstration of just one of the ways that instructor and student roles in this class will be different from most other classes. It also helps to ensure that students truly understand a grading system that counts group performance and peer evaluation as essential components. As group members work together to reach an agreement about grade weights, they are beginning the team-building process.

Each Major Unit of Instruction

Units of instruction in team-based learning (approximately 6–10 class hours) follow the activity sequence shown in Figure 2.2. Each of the in-class activities should be designed to accomplish two ends. One is to build students' understanding of course content. The other is to increase group cohesiveness to the point that the majority of the groups successfully develop into self-managed learning teams.

FIGURE 2.2
Team-Based Learning Instructional Activity Sequence

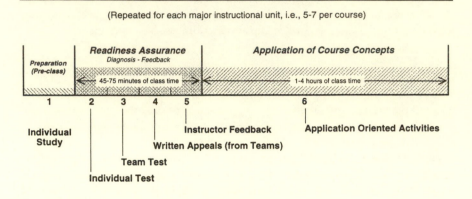

Ensuring Content Coverage with the Readiness Assurance Process

In team-based learning, the basic mechanism to ensure that students are exposed to course content is the Readiness Assurance Process. This process occurs five to seven times per course and constitutes the first set of in-class activities of each major instructional unit. It also provides the foundation for individual and team accountability as one of the building blocks of team-based learning as mentioned earlier. The Readiness Assurance Process has five major components: (1) assigned readings, (2) individual tests, (3) group tests, (4) an appeals process, and (5) instructor feedback (Figure 2.2). Each of the individual components is discussed in the following paragraphs.

Assigned readings. Prior to the beginning of each major instructional unit, students are given a reading assignment that is to be completed outside of class. The readings should contain information on the concepts, issues, and ideas that students should understand by the conclusion of the instructional unit. The readings constitute the first component of the Readiness Assurance Process. Students are to complete the readings and come to the next class period prepared to take a test covering the material they have just read.

Individual tests. The first in-class activity in each instructional unit is the Readiness Assessment Test (RAT) over the set of assigned readings. The RATs typically consist of short true–false or multiple-choice questions that provide the opportunity for peer teaching and enable the instructor to assess whether or not students have a sound understanding of the key concepts from the readings. As a result, the RAT questions should focus on foundational concepts (and avoid picky details), but be difficult enough to create discussion within the teams (see Appendix A for information on how to create effective RATs).

Team tests. When students have finished the individual RAT, they turn in their answers and immediately proceed to the third phase of the Readiness Assurance

Process. During the third phase, students retake the same test, but this time as a group. And to complete the group test, members must reach agreement on each test question. As an integral part of the Readiness Assurance Process, the discussion required to choose a group answer both serves as an excellent review of the readings and provides the opportunity for peer teaching.

In addition, the feedback members receive from each other—immediate scoring of the team RATs—provides students with a means of discovering misunderstandings either on a question-by-question basis using IF-AT answer sheets (Epstein, 2000) or as soon as the team test is completed (see Appendix A for a discussion of alternative methods for quickly scoring the RATs). As soon as the team tests are completed and scored, students pick up their individual answer sheets (the individual tests are scored *during* the group tests) so that they have concrete and immediate feedback on both individual and team scores. Thus, by comparing individual and team answer sheets, they know how effective they have been in using the intellectual resources of group members. At this point, the teacher (or a group member) also posts their group scores on the board; however, individual scores remain anonymous. Public posting of the team scores allows students to monitor their performance by making comparisons between their scores and those of their peers.

Appeals. At this point in the Readiness Assurance Process, students proceed to the fourth phase. This phase gives students the opportunity to refer to their assigned reading material to appeal any questions that were missed on the group test. That is, students are allowed to do a focused re-study of the assigned readings to challenge the teacher about their responses on specific items on the group test or about confusion created by either the quality of the questions or inadequacies of the pre-class readings. Discussion among group members is usually very animated while the students work together to "build a case" to support their appeals. The students must produce compelling evidence to convince the teacher to award credit for the answers they missed on the group test. Again, as an integral part of the Readiness Assurance Process, this exercise provides yet another review of the readings. This time, however, the review is specifically focused on the material that needs additional clarification, that is, the material related to the questions that the teams answered incorrectly.

Instructor feedback. The fifth and final part of the Readiness Assurance Process involves oral feedback from the instructor. This feedback comes immediately after the appeals process and allows the instructor to clear up any confusion students may have about any of the concepts presented in the readings. As a result, input from the instructor is typically limited to a brief, focused review of only the most challenging aspects of the pre-class reading assignment.

The Readiness Assurance Process in summary. The Readiness Assurance Process allows instructors to virtually eliminate class time that is often wasted in covering material that students can learn on their own. Time is saved because the instructor's input occurs after students have: (1) individually studied the material, (2) taken an individual test focused on key concepts from the reading assignment, (3) retaken the same test as a member of a learning team, and (4) completed a focused re-study of the most difficult concepts. As a result, the instructor is aware of any specific concepts that need additional attention so that he or she can correct students' misunderstandings and still have ample time to allow students to tackle the application-oriented assignments to develop students' higher-level learning skills.

It is also important to emphasize the significance of the Readiness Assurance Process for developing and using learning teams. In fact, the Readiness Assurance Process is the backbone of team-based learning because of its effect on team development. The RATs are the single most powerful team development tool I have ever seen because they promote team development in four specific areas. First, starting early in the course (usually in the first few class hours) the students are exposed to immediate and unambiguous feedback on both individual and team performance. As a result, each member is explicitly accountable for his or her pre-class preparation. Second, because team members work face-to-face, the impact of the interaction is immediate and personal. Third, students have a strong vested interest in the outcome of the group and are motivated to engage in a high level of interaction. The strong interest results from the fact that the students receive both intrinsic and extrinsic rewards for successful team performance. Finally, cohesiveness continues to build during the final stage of the process, that is, when the instructor is presenting information. Groups become more cohesive because, unlike lectures, the content of the instructor's comments is determined by the results of the RATs and is specifically aimed at providing value-added feedback to the teams.

Even though the impact of the Readiness Assurance Process on student learning is limited primarily to ensuring that they have a solid exposure to the content, it is still an extremely valuable teaching and learning activity because it creates a feedback-rich learning environment. By encouraging pre-class preparation and intensive give-and-take interaction, this process also increases students' ability to solve difficult problems. Pre-class preparation and lively discussion build the intellectual competence of team members and enhance students' ability and willingness to provide high-quality feedback to one another. This, in turn, is an invaluable tool for instructors because it dramatically reduces the teacher's burden of providing feedback to individual students. As a result, the Readiness Assurance Process provides a practical way of ensuring that, even in large classes, students are exposed to a high volume of immediate feedback that, in some ways, is actually better than having a one-on-one relationship between student and instructor (e.g., Vygotsky, 1978).

Promoting Higher-Level Learning with Application Exercises

The next stage in the team-based learning instructional activity sequence for each unit of instruction is one or more assignments that provide students with the opportunity to deepen their understanding by using the concepts to solve some sort of a problem. As previously outlined, good application-focused group assignments foster give-and-take discussions because they focus on decision making (not writing) and enable students to share their conclusions in a form that enables prompt cross-team comparisons and feedback.

TABLE 2.2
Examples of Decision-Based Assignments

From a list of 2-5 plausible, but differentially defensible, outcomes that are related to the concepts of the course and have students choose the one that would be most affected by (plug in an example from the list below):

❑ **A specific temperature increase [in a course in chemistry or botany].**

❑ **A Democratic victory in the next election [in a course in sociology or political science].**

❑ **A specific increase in the primary lending rate [in a course in economics or finance].**

Several examples of potential application-focused assignments meeting these criteria are shown in Table 2.2. In each case, the assignment requires teams to use course concepts to make a complex decision that can be represented in a simple form. As a result, because each of these assignments could be implemented so that teams could receive prompt and detailed peer feedback on the quality of their work, they would also enhance both learning and team development. Learning would increase because students would be forced to reexamine (and possibly modify) their assumptions and interpretations of the facts and the teams would become more cohesive as they pulled together in an attempt to defend their position.

Encouraging Positive Team Norms by Tracking Attendance and Performance

Learning teams will only be successful to the extent that individual members adopt the two most critical group norms: pre-class preparation and class attendance. Fortunately, if students have ongoing feedback emphasizing the fact that pre-class preparation and class attendance are critical to their team's success, these norms will pretty much develop on their own. One very simple, yet effective, way to provide such feedback to the students is through the use of team folders. The folders should contain an ongoing record of members' attendance, along with the individual and team scores on the RATs and other assignments (see Appendix D, Exhibit D–B1.1). The act of recording the RAT scores and attendance data in the team folders is particularly helpful because it ensures that every team member knows how every other team member is doing. Members also know how their group is faring compared to the rest of the groups. This comparison of scores reinforces acknowledgment of the dependence of the group on each individual member's input. This recognition of the significance of each member's contribution to the team strongly encourages the development of positive team norms.

Near the End of the Term

Although team-based learning provides students with multiple opportunities for learning along the way, instructors can solidify and extend student understanding of both course content and group process issues by using specific kinds of activities near the end of the term. These are activities that cause students to reflect on their experience during the past semester. Their reflecting is focused on several different areas. In most cases, these end-of-the-semester activities are aimed at reminding students of what they have learned about the following:

1. Course concepts;
2. Concept applications;
3. Value of teams in tackling intellectual challenges;
4. Kinds of interaction that promote effective team work;
5. Themselves.

Learning about Course Content

One of the greatest benefits of using team-based learning is also a potential danger. Since so little class time is aimed at providing students with their initial exposure to course concepts, many tend to forget how much they have learned and, based on the reduced volume of lecture notes alone, some may actually feel that they have been cheated. An effective way to prevent this potential problem is to devote a class period to a concept review. In its simplest form this involves: (1) giving students an extensive list of course concepts (usually on a single sheet), (2) asking them to individually identify any concepts they do not recognize, (3) compare their conclusions in the teams, and (4) review any concepts that teams identify as needing additional attention.

Understanding Content Applications

The best way to remind students that they are able to actually apply course concepts is to have them use course concepts in solving a series of meaningful problems. In some cases, the application-focused assignments associated with individual instructional units may not be complex enough to enable students to see them as more than hypothetical situations. By the end of most courses, however, instructors can largely solve this problem by assigning teams to solve problems that are both increasingly unstructured and require using concepts from multiple content areas. For example, a common activity for a specific unit of instruction for students in a statistics course would be to decide whether or not some treatment had produced a significant result in a given situation. Later, the instructor might enrich the students' understanding by using a case in which different groups were using statistics to argue for different policies and asking them to decide which group had the soundest argument for their position. In my own courses, I often use novels and full-length feature films to provide a complex setting in which students can practice integrating a wide range of management and organizational behavior concepts.

Learning about the Value of Teams

Although concerns about the better students being held back by less motivated or less able peers are commonplace with other group-based instructional approaches, team-based learning enables instructors to provide compelling empirical evidence of the value of teams for tackling difficult intellectual challenges. For example, in taking the individual and team RATs, students generally have the feeling that the teams are outperforming their own best member, but they are seldom aware of either the magnitude or the pervasiveness of the effect. Near the end of each term, I create a transparency that shows five cumulative scores from the RATs for each team—the low, average, and high member score, the team score, and the difference between the highest member score and the team score (see Appendix D, Exhibit D–A7.3). Most students are literally stunned when they see the pattern of scores for the entire class. In the past fourteen years, over 99 percent of the teams have outperformed their own best member by an average of nearly 11 percent. In fact, in the majority of classes, the lowest team score in the class is higher than the best individual score in the entire class (e.g., see Michaelsen, Watson, & Black, 1989).

Recognizing Effective Team Interaction

Over time, teams get better and better at ferreting out and using members' intellectual resources in making decisions (e.g., Watson et al., 1991). However, unless instructors use an activity that prompts members to explicitly think about group process issues, they are likely to miss an important teaching opportunity. This is because most students, although pleased about the results, generally fail to recognize the changes in members' behavior that have made the improvements possible.

I have used two different approaches for increasing students' awareness of the relationship between group processes and group effectiveness. The aim of both approaches is to have students reflect on how and why members' interaction patterns have changed as their teams became more cohesive. One approach is an individual assignment that requires students to:

1. review their previous observations about the group;
2. formulate a list of "changes or events that made a difference";
3. share their lists with team members;
4. create a written analysis that addresses barriers to team effectiveness and keys to overcoming them.

The other, and more effective approach, involves the same assignment, but having students prepare along the way by keeping an ongoing log of observations about how their team has functioned (see Hernandez, 2002).

Learning about Themselves

One of the most important contributions of team-based learning is that it creates conditions that can enable students to learn a great deal about the way they interact with others. In large measure, this occurs because of the extensive and intensive inter-action within the teams. Over time, two important things happen. One is that members really get to know each other's strengths and weaknesses and, as a result, have clear insights of what kind of feedback is needed. The other is that, in the vast major-ity of teams, members develop such strong interpersonal relationships that they feel morally obligated to provide honest feedback to each other.

Although students learn a great deal about themselves along the way, the instructor can have a significant positive impact on many students' understanding of themselves by using a well-designed peer evaluation process. In its simplest form, this involves formally collecting data from team members on how much and in what way they have contributed to each other's learning and making the information (but not who provided it) available to individual students.

Some prefer collecting and "feeding back" peer evaluation data two or more times during the term (usually in conjunction with major team assignments). Others (my-self included) favor involving teams in developing peer evaluation criteria part way through the term but only collecting the peer evaluation data at the very end of the term. The biggest advantage of collecting and feeding back peer evaluation data along the way is that it gives students the opportunity to make changes. The disadvantage is that having students formally evaluate each other can measurably disrupt the team development process. (See Appendix B for a discussion of these issues and copies of instruments that can be used to collect peer evaluation data).

BENEFITS OF TEAM-BASED LEARNING

Using groups, even in a casual way, produces benefits that cannot be achieved with students in a passive role (see Bargh & Schul, 1980; Fiechtner & Davis, 1985; Slavin & Karweit, 1981). While even the casual use of groups is beneficial, it must be stressed that team-based learning allows the achievement of important outcomes that simply cannot be obtained with temporary groups or occasional group activities (e.g., see Michaelsen, Jones, & Watson, 1993; Watson et al., 1991). Some of these include: (1) developing students' higher-level cognitive skills in large classes, (2) providing social support for at-risk students, (3) promoting the development of interpersonal and team skills, and (4) building and maintaining faculty members' enthusiasm for their teaching role.

USING LEARNING TEAMS IN LARGE CLASSES

A key advantage of learning teams is that they can be used to offset many of the disadvantages of large classes (see Chapter 11, and Michaelsen, Watson, Cragin, &

Fink, 1982). In fact, developing and using learning teams may be the only means for building students' higher-level cognitive skills in large classes (see Kurfiss, 1988). Team-based learning is also effective in motivating attendance, handling discipline problems, and engaging members who would benefit from group work but, given the opportunity, would rather work alone (e.g., see Light, 1990). Although temporary groups can provide a valuable aid in small classes where the instructor's physical presence is sufficient to ensure that no one "escapes" (either physically or mentally) and that students are actually working on assigned tasks, they simply cannot exert enough influence on their peers to motivate attendance, handle discipline problems, engage members, and so on.

Increased Social Support for Various Types of At-Risk Students

Students in team-based learning classes have a social support base that is beneficial in multiple ways, unlike temporary groups whose social support typically ends when the class period is over. For example, group-based instructional approaches have been shown to reduce stereotypes of racial and ethnic minorities and physically handicapped students (Johnson, Johnson, & Maruyama, 1983) and increase self-esteem (Johnson & Johnson, 1983). In most classes, the social interaction, which is a natural part of team-based learning, provides benefits to students who often do not feel at ease in a traditional classroom. For example, international students often find lasting friendships and grow in their understanding of a new culture; older students discover that their accumulated life awareness is an appreciated and valuable asset; students who are at risk of dropping out form working relationships that continue to be of help in future assignments and other classes; and students who are having difficulty maneuvering their way through the campus bureaucracy have a ready source for answers to their questions and concerns.

Development of Interpersonal Skills

Students also benefit from interacting in a situation in which group work really counts. Unlike temporary groups, in which tough interpersonal issues can be avoided simply by waiting until the groups are re-formed, students in team-based learning classes cannot easily escape the problems they encounter in their groups. As a result, many learn lessons about themselves that allow them to be more effective and productive when they finish school and enter the work force. For example, students who are intellectually capable, but socially unskilled, learn through being exposed to more positive role models and through input from peers who have enough at stake that they are willing to give them helpful (but not always positive) feedback. In addition, because students have to learn to work together, they develop the understanding and skills they need to work productively as task-group members. Finally, part of effective group work is believing that the benefits of working in groups outweighs the costs.

Unlike groups used in a supplementary way, the vast majority of team-based learning groups provide solid evidence of the terrific potential of effective learning teams for accomplishing difficult intellectual tasks.

Building and Maintaining an Enthusiasm for Teaching

Probably the greatest benefit of team-based learning is that it has a tremendous positive impact on the instructor. Being responsible for creating enthusiasm and excitement about basic, but essential, material is a burden that few are able to carry for long without burning out. As a result, even the most dedicated and talented instructors are likely to try to find ways of reducing their teaching load. With team-based learning, however, the groups handle most of the aspects of teaching that, for most, are simply drudgery. For example, the instructor almost never has to go over basic concepts or answer simple questions. The RATs handle that task with ease and many of the remaining questions, even in basic courses, are challenging enough to be interesting. In addition, instructors rarely have to worry about attendance problems. Students come to class because they want to.

Another reason that team-based learning builds enthusiasm for teaching is that most of the necessary changes are structural in nature. Instead of trying to make one's presentations more interesting and exciting, the major emphasis with team-based learning is on designing courses to give students opportunities and incentives to accept more responsibility for ensuring that learning occurs. Thus, the focus of the instructor shifts from "How should I teach?" to "How can students best learn?" and the challenge for instructors has to do with designing courses and group activities with that new and different perspective in mind.

Finally, team-based learning also produces instructor enthusiasm because it taps into the energy that is released as the student groups develop into learning teams. Although there are typically some initial struggles, most groups' capabilities steadily improve to the point that students behave more like colleagues than "empty vessels." This is the natural outcome of empowering groups by structuring them so that they have needed resources, are exposed to appropriate performance evaluation systems, and have the opportunity to engage in meaningful and challenging assignments. As a result, the vast majority of students willingly share responsibility to ensure that learning occurs. When this happens, teaching with team-based learning is simply more fun.

REFERENCES

Bargh, J. A., & Schul, Y. (1980). On the cognitive benefits of teaching. *Journal of Educational Psychology 74*(5): 593–604.

Bruning, R. H., Schraw, G. J., & Ronning, R. R. (1994). *Cognitive psychology and instruction.* 2d ed. Englewood Cliffs, NJ: Prentice-Hall.

Epstein, M. L. (2000). A testing/teaching multiple-choice answer form. Workshop presented at the Fourteenth Annual Conference, Teaching of Psychology: Ideas and Innovations, Ellenville, NY. http://enigma.rider.edu/~epstein/ifat/>

Fiechtner, S. B., & Davis, E. A. (1985). Why some groups fail: A survey of students' experiences with learning groups. *The Organizational Behavior Teaching Review* 9(4): 58–71.

Hernandez, S. A. (2002). Team-based learning in a marketing principles course: Cooperative structures that facilitate active learning and higher-level thinking. *Journal of Marketing Education* 24(1): 45–75.

Johnson, D. W., & Johnson, R. T. (1983). The socialization and achievement crisis: Are cooperative learning experiences the solution? In *Applied Social Psychology Annual,* Vol. 4. Ed. L. Bickman. Beverly Hills: Sage.

Johnson, D. W., Johnson, R. T., & Maruyama, G. (1983). Interdependence and interpersonal attraction among heterogeneous and homogeneous individuals: A theoretical formulation and a meta-analysis of research. *Review of Educational Research* 53(1): 5–54.

Light, R. J. (1990). *The harvard assessment seminars: Explorations with students and faculty about teaching, learning, and student life.* Cambridge MA: Harvard University.

Michaelsen, L. K., & Black, R. H. (1994). Building learning teams: The key to harnessing the power of small groups in higher education. In *Collaborative learning: A sourcebook for higher education,* Vol. 2. Ed. S. Kadel & J. Keehner. State College, PA: National Center for Teaching, Learning, and Assessment.

Michaelsen, L. K., Cragin, J. P., & Watson, W. E. (1981). Grading and anxiety: A strategy for coping. *Exchange: The Organizational Behavior Teaching Journal* 6(1): 8–14.

Michaelsen, L. K., Jones, C. F., & Watson, W. E. (1993). Beyond groups and cooperation: Building high performance learning teams. In *To improve the academy: Resources for faculty, instructional, and organizational development.* Ed. D. L. Wright & J. P. Lunde. Stillwater, OK: New Forums Press.

Michaelsen, L. K., Watson, W. E., & Black, R. H. (1989). A realistic test of individual versus group consensus decision making. *Journal of Applied Psychology* 74(5): 834–839.

Michaelsen, L. K., Watson, W. E., Cragin, J. P., & Fink, L. D. (1982). Team learning: A potential solution to the problems of large classes. *Exchange: The Organizational Behavior Teaching Journal.* 7(1): 13–22.

Nungester, R. J., & Duchastel, P. C. (1982). Testing versus review: Effects on retention. *Journal of Applied Psychology* 74(1): 18–22.

Slavin, R. E., & Karweit, N. L. (1981). Cognitive and affective outcomes of an intensive student team-based learning experience. *Journal of Experimental Education* 50(1): 29–35.

Vygotsky, L. S. (1978). *Mind in society: The development of higher psychological processes.* Boston: Harvard University Press.

Watson, W. E., Kumar, K., & Michaelsen, L. K. (1993). Cultural diversity's impact on group process and performance: Comparing culturally homogeneous and culturally diverse task groups. *The Academy of Management Journal* 36(3): 590–602.

Watson, W. E., Michaelsen, L. K., & Sharp, W. (1991). Member competence, group interaction and group decision-making: A longitudinal study. *Journal of Applied Psychology* 76: 801–809.

CHAPTER 3

Creating Effective Assignments
A Key Component of Team-Based Learning

Larry K. Michaelsen and Arletta Bauman Knight

The single biggest challenge for teachers wanting to use team-based learning is that of creating effective group assignments. The challenge is to find an important question or problem and then learn how to create an assignment around that problem that will simultaneously foster group cohesiveness and promote higher-order learning. In this chapter Michaelsen and Knight analyze the processes that detract from group cohesiveness (in the form of social loafing) and then identify the variables and procedures that must be managed to create an effective assignment. They conclude by providing a checklist of key characteristics that will allow teachers to assess the effectiveness of their group assignments.

As more and more teachers use small groups in their courses, some find that the results are as exhilarating as they had hoped. Others, however, are seriously disappointed. It has been our experience that instructors are almost always unhappy the related to problems that are a natural consequence of using poorly designed group assignments.

Probably the most common problem affecting the use of small groups involves individuals who dominate the discussions to the point that quieter members' ideas are either unexpressed or largely ignored. A second common problem arises when individuals within the group believe they are forced to do the work for their less able or less willing counterparts. And the third problem occurs when groups are reporting the results of their work to the total class. Even when there has been a high level of engagement in the small groups, subsequent whole-class discussions sometimes "fall flat."

Based on our experience, these "problems" are actually symptoms that are the natural consequences of the real problem: poorly conceived group assignments. In fact, we strongly believe that almost all failed efforts to successfully use learning groups can be traced back to inappropriate group assignments.

Because the nurturing of group cohesiveness is critical to the success of team-based learning and to student learning, we begin by outlining the forces that lead to the uneven and low levels of member participation that inherently limit the learning that occurs in noncohesive groups. We then identify five key variables that must be managed to create a level of group cohesiveness that is conducive for broad-based member participation and learning and why some commonly used assignments inhibit both members participation and learning. Next, we discuss how member interaction affects how we process information and the related implications for the design and selection of effective group assignments. Finally, we present a list of principles that are essential for designing effective group assignments along with a checklist for evaluating the effectiveness of group assignments in a wide variety of instructional settings and subject areas.

CAUSES AND CONSEQUENCES OF UNEVEN MEMBER PARTICIPATION

In noncohesive groups, a high percentage of group members simply prefer to sit back and let someone else work on their behalf. This phenomenon, which has come to be known as social loafing (Latane, Williams, & Harkins, 1979) is a serious problem because it significantly constrains the interaction necessary for a productive learning environment. Further, if left unchecked, the conditions that produce social loafing will also prevent the development of the social fabric that is necessary for effectively functioning learning groups. For example, when quieter members decline to contribute to the group, more assertive members inevitably take charge. By doing so, assertive members not only reduce the need for additional input from their fellow group members, but also create a kind of caste system in which quieter members often feel that their ideas will not be welcomed.

Forces that Promote Social Loafing (Uneven Member Participation)

We have identified six forces which, unless recognized and dealt with by the instructor, will produce a level of social loafing that can seriously affect the development of group cohesion (see Table 3.1). Three of these forces have to do with the characteristics of group members. For example, some group members are resistant to participation because they are just naturally shy. Second, members with more assertive personalities actually prefer to dominate a discussion, and third, some group members may feel they lack content knowledge required for the task at hand. As a result, these

TABLE 3.1
Forces that Promote Social Loafing

(Uneven Contributions in Group Discussions)

❏ Some individuals naturally resist participation (shyness).

❏ Some individuals prefer to dominate discussions.

❏ Members may believe they lack the content knowledge required for making a meaningful contribution.

❏ Members may not be committed to the success of the group.*

❏ Members may be concerned about appearing to be disagreeable or overly agressive.*

❏ The task may be inappropriate for groups because it:

   ◆ can be completed by one or two members working alone.

   ◆ does not require members to reach an agreement.

  * These are especially important problems with new groups.

individuals are reluctant to speak because they are concerned about being viewed as incompetent.

Of the remaining forces that can produce social loafing, two are especially problematic in temporary and newly formed groups. For example, members of these kinds of groups are typically so concerned about creating a positive impression that they will nearly always gloss over differences of opinion in order to avoid being perceived as being disagreeable or overly assertive. The fact that some members start out by being more concerned with politeness than rightness is especially troublesome because it inhibits the kind of give-and-take discussion that produces both learning and group development. (See summary of research on the impact of group maturity in chapter 4, pp. 81–85.) Along with concerns about politeness, an additional problem arises when there are group members who see themselves as having little to lose if the group fails to perform effectively—so they do not make the effort to contribute.

The last force that must be examined is probably the most problematic cause of social loafing in learning groups and, as a result, is one of the greatest barriers to the development of group cohesion. This problem is the use of assignments that can be completed by independent, individual work. When members of a group have no need to work together to complete a task, they will miss the opportunity to bond as a group. For example, when the rational way to complete a task is to parcel out the work to individual members, that is exactly what will happen. And it has been our experience that dividing up the work commonly occurs in two situations: when the assignment is too easy, and when the task requires a great deal of writing. In the first situation, the groups quickly realize that group interaction is not needed; therefore, one member will simply act on behalf of the group to complete the assignment. When the assignment involves writing, which is inherently an individual activity, the only real group aspect of completing the assignment is deciding how to divide up the overall task. The real work is completed by individual members working alone. (See summary of research on group tasks in chapter 4, pp. 86–88.)

Negative Impact of Uneven Member Participation

Whatever the cause, uneven member participation defeats two of the key purposes for using learning groups. One effect is that students learn very little about the content. The other is that, because the groups are seldom very effective, students are often left with a negative impression regarding the value of group work.

Both problems are particularly serious when the uneven participation results from assignments that require a great deal of written work and students resort to a divide-and-conquer approach. Because the work-allocation decisions are the first step in completing the assignment, content learning is limited. That is, students are likely to volunteer to work on the aspect of the project that will require the least amount of effort. In other words, they gravitate away from the aspects of the assignment that will expose them to new concepts and ideas.

The divide-and-conquer approach also inhibits the development of students' team interaction skills in three significant but very different ways. First, because the work is being done by individuals working on their own, there is little opportunity for members to practice the listening and persuasion skills that will be so important to their success in future jobs. Second, it robs them of the opportunity to experience one of the primary benefits of group work that of honing their thinking during the give-and-take discussions. As a result, instead of viewing peers as resources for tackling intellectually challenging tasks, students are predisposed to think of team members simply as bodies among whom work can be divided. Third, when individual students think they have done more than their fair share of the work, the divide-and-conquer approach can leave them with a bitter taste about group work. Although the complaints of individuals who believe they did an inordinate amount of the work may be valid, other students (often minorities) sometimes see the same situation in a very different light. For example, these students believe that the complainer(s) did the most work because they dominated the group, thereby denying them the opportunity to contribute. As a result, these students (the ones being criticized) are usually very angry if they receive low peer evaluations (even though they did not do equal work) because they feel the situation was unfair.

CREATING BROAD-BASED MEMBER PARTICIPATION
WITH EFFECTIVE ASSIGNMENTS

The single most effective strategy for eliminating uneven member participation, or social loafing, is to make sure that group assignments foster the development of cohesive learning teams. As groups become more cohesive, so does the level of trust and understanding among group members. With well-designed assignments, most groups become cohesive to the extent that even naturally quiet members become willing to engage in intense give-and-take interactions without worrying about being offensive or misunderstood (Michaelsen, Black, & Fink, 1996; Michaelsen, Watson, & Black, 1989; Watson, Kumar, & Michaelsen, 1993; Watson, Michaelsen, & Sharp, 1991). In addition, a primary characteristic of a truly cohesive team is that members see their own well-being as integrally tied to the success of their group. As a result, members of cohesive groups are often highly motivated to invest personal energy doing group work (Michaelsen, Jones & Watson, 1993; Shaw, 1981).

Assignments that Promote Group Cohesiveness

We have identified five key variables that determine whether or not a particular assignment will effectively build group cohesiveness:

1. Does it promote a high level of individual accountability for team members?
2. Does it bring members into close physical proximity?
3. Does it motivate a great deal of discussion among team members?
4. Does it ensure that members receive immediate, unambiguous, and meaningful feedback (preferably involving direct comparisons with the performance outputs from other teams)?
5. Does it provide explicit rewards for team performance?

Variable # 1: Ensuring Individual Accountability

Ensuring that assignments promote individual accountability is especially critical for the initial group assignments. That is, initial assignments set the stage for the rest of the course. In new groups, the innate forces against broad-based participation are so powerful that they must be offset early on (see Figure 3.1). If a group is even modestly successful with input from only one or two members in an initial assignment, it is very easy for that group to develop a norm for future activities that says some members will contribute a lot and others will contribute very little (Feldman, 1984).

On the other hand, using an initial group task that explicitly requires pre-work and input from all group members produces a set of dynamics that largely prevents social loafing from occurring in the first place. In part, this results from the fact that using tasks that hold members accountable for pre-work tends to have a positive effect on members at both ends of the assertiveness continuum. For example, quieter members tend to speak up and more assertive members tend to tone down. Quieter members tend to contribute more because they are likely to actually have something of substance to say. And they intuitively realize that they are likely to be seen in a negative light if they do not contribute.

FIGURE 3.1
Impact of Assignment Characteristics of Team Development
and Social Loafing

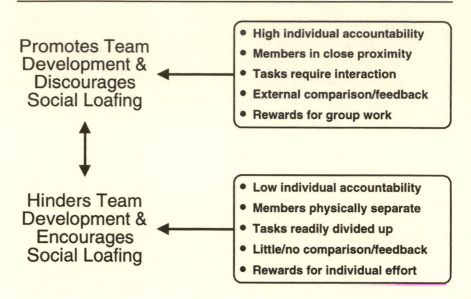

By contrast, these same dynamics have the opposite effect on members at the other end of the assertiveness spectrum. Members whose natural tendencies often cause them to dominate discussions tend to tone down for just the opposite reasons. When every member is required to contribute, the more assertive members have greater confidence that others may have something of value to say. As a result, they intuitively realize that they are likely to be seen in a negative light if they do not give the quieter members the opportunity to speak. Finally, with tasks that really do require broad-based input, groups are more likely to succeed and be rewarded when they get input from all members. Thus, their initial success reinforces a norm in which everyone is expected to provide input to the group on a regular basis (Feldman, 1984).

The Readiness Assurance Process (RAP), described in detail in Chapter 2, illustrates both how and why assignments that promote individual accountability have such a powerful impact on both learning and team-building (Michaelsen & Black, 1994; Michaelsen, Black & Fink, 1996). Since members have individually answered each of the questions on the Readiness Assessment Test (RAT)—and part of their grade depends on how well they do—when it comes time for the group RAT,[1] the group naturally proceeds in a way that sets a desirable pattern for future discussions. A typical scenario is one member (usually a more vocal one) initiating the process by polling his or her peers to determine how they answered each question. Then, unless everyone selected the same answer, the natural next step is to explore the members' reasons for their choices. Almost without exception, the ensuing discussion enables members to learn from each other and also to discover important principles for doing well on subsequent assignments. For example, they learn that it is wise to ask each person to provide reasons for their answers every time differences occur within the group. As a result, each individual learns that it is wise to be well prepared. In addition, quieter members tend to be rewarded for talking and assertive members tend to be rewarded for listening.

Variable # 2: Promoting Close Physical Proximity

The degree to which a group becomes cohesive is directly related to the extent to which members do things together. Unless members interact, groups simply will not become cohesive. Being in close physical proximity virtually ensures that group members will at least begin the team development process by acquiring a set of common experiences. As a result, we strongly recommend using in-class group work and avoiding assignments that allow students to complete the assigned task outside of class, working individually.

Our experience strongly suggests that requiring groups to do their work outside of class creates an overwhelmingly powerful barrier to the development of group cohesiveness. In most cases, the "cost" of meeting outside of class is so great that students will meet only long enough to divide up the work so that they can independently complete the components of the assignment. As a result, they produce a group product in name only, and whatever cohesiveness was developed during the initial meeting is usually offset by the worry about whether or not other members will actually do their part.

Variable # 3: Promoting Discussion Among Team Members

A high level of interaction and discussion within a group greatly enhances group cohesiveness. Although a number of different types of tasks can produce such interaction, a highly reliable rule-of-thumb is that assignments increase group cohesiveness (and, over time, eliminate social loafing) when they require members to *make a concrete decision that is based on the analysis of a complex issue*. A common example of this kind of assignment is asking students to apply a rule or solve a truly challenging problem. These types of tasks typically require students to use a broad range of intellectual skills that include recognizing and defining concepts, making discriminations, and applying principles or procedural rules (Gagné, 1970). Further, everyone typically has both opportunity and incentive to actively participate in completing the task because of the genuine need for broad-based member input. The net result is that problem-based tasks almost universally immerse students in information-rich, give-and-take discussions through which their content learning increases. Further, if the assignment is thoughtfully crafted, students are also likely to reinforce two important lessons about group interaction: (1) other members' input is a valuable resource, and (2) we can accomplish things by working together that none of us could have accomplished on our own.

Variable # 4: Providing Teams with Meaningful Feedback

Another very powerful force for the development of group cohesiveness is providing team members with immediate, unambiguous, and meaningful feedback. The feedback is particularly powerful when it involves being compared with other teams who have been faced with solving the same problem. The knowledge that any other team has the potential to outperform "your" team is extremely motivating to students. In fact, Shaw (1981) writes that the presence of an outside influence that is perceived to be threatening to individual member goals or the well-being of the group has a significant impact on the outcome of the group. In this situation, the potentially threatening outside influence becomes the other teams in the class. In the scheme of things, this type of influence is quite valuable because differences among individual group members become less important as they pull together to protect themselves and their public image from the outside force, that is, challenges from the other teams. As a result, providing performance data that allow comparisons between groups is a very powerful tool for increasing group cohesiveness.

Some assignments are clearly better than others at providing such comparisons. In general, the more that assignments provide unambiguous performance feedback, the better they are at promoting team development. Further, the more immediate the feedback, the greater its value to both learning and group cohesiveness.

By contrast, assignments are likely to limit the development of group cohesiveness (and encourage social loafing) if they force groups to do the majority of their work in the absence of feedback. When groups have no way of knowing how they are doing (e.g., when groups are asked to produce some sort of a complex "product" such as a group paper), members are likely to experience a great deal of stress when trying to work with one another. In addition, differences in members' work styles can also produce a great deal of tension in the group. For example, members who have a strong preference for a systematic and orderly approach grow increasingly anxious as deadlines approach and often find themselves in conflict with peers who put off their work until the last minute because they feel they work best under pressure.

Variable # 5: Rewarding Group Success

It would be wonderful if students completed group assignments simply for the love of learning. However, most students feel so many pressures on their time that they are prone to be distracted from working on even the most interesting of assignments. Thus, if we fail to create conditions in which doing good work as a group pays off in some meaningful way, we are, in effect, asking our students to behave irrationally. As a result, teachers have to take on the responsibility for creating a situation in which it actually makes sense for students to work hard to complete an assignment.

The most obvious way to create incentives for members to devote time and energy to group work is to include *group performance* in our grading system. If group work "counts," then cohesiveness increases because group members have a clear and concrete reason to work together. On the other hand, if students are graded only on their individual work, group cohesiveness will be blocked by the fact that they will correctly see themselves as competing with other members of their own group.

Rewarding group performance also helps meet the basic human need for social validation. Typically, everyone wants to feel they can offer something of value to others. Thus, by creating a situation in which the output from the group will be assessed, rewarded, and challenged by peers from other groups, we are creating an environment that promotes both group cohesiveness and learning.

Assignments that Reduce Group Cohesiveness

To fully understand the characteristics of a well-designed team assignment, it can be enlightening to take a look at the kinds of assignments that typically result in low levels of energy and learning and, in fact, can even lead to open warfare within the groups. It is our experience that the worst assignment when trying to build group cohesiveness is to ask students to write a term paper as a group. Group papers seldom provide any support for building group cohesiveness and almost universally result in social loafing, or at least what is perceived by other students as social loafing. Writing is inherently an individual activity; therefore, the rational way to accomplish the overall task is to divide up the work so that each member independently completes part of the assignment (usually the part that he or she already knows the most about). As a result, there is seldom any significant discussion after the initial division of labor, and feedback is generally unavailable until after the project is handed in. At that time, it is too late to create either individual accountability or meaningful comparisons with other groups

Further, under these conditions, having part of the student's grade based on group work is a much more negative experience than it is a positive one. Members are well aware that the failure of any member of the group to do well on his or her share of the writing can force the rest of the group members to accept a low grade or engage in a last-minute attempt to salvage a disaster. In fact, high-achieving students often express the feeling that getting an acceptable grade on a group term paper feels like having crossed a freeway during rush hour without being run over. That is an experience that none of us wishes to impose on our students.

INCREASING HIGHER-LEVEL LEARNING WITH EFFECTIVE ASSIGNMENTS

The characteristics of group assignments profoundly affect learning and retention because of two different factors. One is that they affect members' exposure to new information because of their impact on group interaction as mentioned previously. The other to be discussed has to do with the fact that changes in character and substance of peer interactions have a powerful impact on the cognitive processes through which learning occurs.

How We Learn

On the surface, when we make reference to what we know, we appear to be referring to the sum total of the information to which we have been exposed. Taking information in, however, is only part of the learning process (Bruning, Schraw, & Ronning, 1994). Information that is taken in and stored in short-term memory decays very rapidly. Thus, from a practical standpoint, what we "know" is more a function of our ability to retrieve and use information than it is the sum total of the information that we have taken in.

Impact of What We Know

Our ability to learn is profoundly affected by both information to which we have previously been exposed and the way this information is stored in our long-term memory. Most important, our capability to learn depends on the extent to which the related components of our memory are clustered into well-organized structures (i.e., sometimes referred to as schemata—see Anderson, 1993; Bruning, Schraw, & Ronning, 1994; Mandler, 1984). These information structures are important because they provide "hooks" that help establish links between new information that is related to what we already know and the individual components of our existing structures. In addition, these structures provide a backdrop that helps us recognize what we do not know (i.e., information that does not fit).

Information Structures and Learning

What we "know," then, is largely a function of the number, complexity, and interconnectedness of the information structures in our long-term memory and, for practical purposes, the information that we are able to retrieve and use. In other words, significant learning has taken place when we increase the amount of information we are able to retrieve and use. This ability to retrieve information usually occurs when new information motivates us to: (1) add information to existing structures, (2) establish new structures, or (3) establish new links within or between existing structures.

Elaborative Rehearsal

If a learning activity exposes us to new information that neatly connects to a "hook" in one of our information structures, then it is simply attached to the appropriate link. If new information appears to conflict with existing grouping, the learning process takes a very different, but even more beneficial, course. Initially, we will search through our long-term memory to review the linkages upon which the apparent conflict is based. If this review confirms the existence of a conflict, we will be in a state of discomfort until we find a harmonious accommodation. If none is found and the information's credibility is sustained, we are motivated to eliminate the conflict by modifying or adding to existing structures. This memory retrieval and examination process, called "elaborative rehearsal" (Craik & Lockhart, 1986), facilitates learning because each stage has a positive impact on our long-term memory. Consequently, the greater the extent to which an assignment exposes students to credible information that conflicts with their existing information structures, the greater its impact on their long-term memory.

Increasing Higher-Level Learning

The importance of providing opportunities for elaborative rehearsal is dramatically illustrated by a series of studies involving learning groups (summarized by Slavin, 1995). In all of the studies, students were divided into four-member groups as part of a "jigsaw" activity. Each member was assigned to become a subject-matter expert with respect to one of four areas and then given the opportunity to teach the material to the other members of his or her jigsaw team. In most instances, students in jigsaw groups scored higher on an overall summative test than students from a control group who had been taught with a more traditional method. The positive benefits of the jigsaw activity, however, were primarily due to students' mastery of the material they had taught to their peers. Hearing someone else explain a set of concepts (i.e., listening to a lecture) had a minimal positive effect on learning as compared to the impact of having to synthesize the information, organize a presentation, and present the information to a group of peers.

In two other studies, Lazarowitz (1991) and Lazarowitz and Karsenty (1990) added an additional learning task for the jigsaw groups. After the jigsaw peer instruction, each of the groups was given a discovery-oriented problem to solve that required students to actively use information presented by each of the four subject-matter experts. The most significant finding from these studies was that requiring students to engage in higher-level thinking increased students' ability to recall and use the information that was originally presented by the other subject-matter experts

Based on the overall results of the jigsaw studies, it appears that just listening to another peer in a learning group, even when combined with the opportunity to ask clarifying questions, produces only modest gains in long-term memory. On the other hand, learning activities that require higher-level thinking skills, such as those involved in teaching others or using concepts to solve a discovery-oriented problem, produce substantial long-term gains in students' ability to recall and use course concepts.

Other types of learning activities that focus on using higher-level thinking skills have also been shown to produce similar gains when compared to simple cognitive tasks such as listening to lectures or going over one's notes. These include taking tests (Nungester & Duchastel, 1982), writing "minute papers" (Wilson, 1986), and being exposed to opposing views on a subject and then having to resolve the conflict in the process of making a decision (Smith, Johnson, & Johnson, 1981).

In combination, the findings from these studies convincingly argue that the long-term educational impact of group work will be much greater if group assignments go beyond simply exposing learners to new information to requiring active engagement in higher-level cognitive skills. As a result, the key to designing assignments that promote both greater depth of understanding and retention is to use assignments that require higher-level thinking and problem solving.

PRINCIPLES FOR DESIGNING EFFECTIVE TEAM ASSIGNMENTS

In combination, the preceding sections of this chapter have pointed out the need for assignments and procedures that promote high levels of individual accountability and group discussion (both within and between groups). When students are accountable for preparing for group work, they are motivated to work with the ideas and concepts enough to enter the discussions with a personal schemata within which the set of related ideas have been organized. The discussion—both within and between teams—increases learning and retention by exposing them to new information that is often inconsistent with their current schemata.

The Three Ss

The question for the teacher then is how does one create assignments that both create accountability and foster discussion? We have found that three procedures, fondly referred to as the "3 Ss," are very effective in creating assignments with the necessary characteristics. These are: (1) all of the students in the class should be working on the *same problem* or assignment, (2) students should be required to make a *specific choice*, and (3) groups should *simultaneously report* their choices (Figure 3.2). Further, these procedures apply to all three stages of effective group assignments—individual work prior to group discussions, discussions within groups, and total class discussions.

Procedure #1: Same Problem

One of the essential characteristics of an effective group assignment is the necessity for discussion both within and between groups. It is through such discussions that students receive immediate feedback regarding the quality of their own thinking.

In order to facilitate such an exchange, groups must have a common frame of reference. That commonality is derived from working on the same problem, that is, the same assignment or learning activity. Having a common task allows for comparison,

FIGURE 3.2
Essential Principles for Designing and Implementing Effective Group Assignments

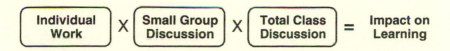

To obtain the maximum impact on learning, assignments at each stage should be characterized by "3 Ss":

- **Same problem**–Individuals/groups should work on the same problem, case, or question.

- **Specific choice**–Individuals/groups should be required to use course concepts to make a specific choice.

- **Simultaneously report**–If possible, individuals/groups should report their choices simultaneously.

first between group members, and then between groups, and provides students with important feedback on their own thinking and their performance as a learning team.

Procedure #2: Specific Choice

As previously discussed, cognitive research shows that learning is greatly enhanced when students are required to engage in higher-level thinking. To challenge students to process information at higher levels of cognitive complexity, we must provide them with assignments that create those challenges.

After many years of experience, we have discovered that the best activity to accomplish this goal is to word the assignment in such a way that students are required to make a specific choice. While the terminology may sound vague at this point, in the following paragraphs, we will provide both several examples of "make-a-specific-choice" assignments and a rationale for why they work so well in promoting both student learning and team development.

Procedure #3: Simultaneous Reports

When teachers have the groups work on a problem, they then have the choice of having the groups share the result of their thinking with the rest of the class in one of two ways, sequentially or simultaneously. The big problem with having groups report sequentially is that later groups are tempted to change their mind by simply endorsing what seems to be emerging as the most popular. Unfortunately, the natural tendency to avoid "rocking the boat" often eliminates the disagreements that provide the basis for potentially valuable give-and-take discussions. Having the groups report simultaneously solves this problem, since all of the groups are required to report the results of their thinking and decision making before they know what the pattern is among the other groups. Hence they have to commit to and be ready to defend their answer, regardless of whether the other groups agree or disagree with them.

The opposite scenario, however, is usually quite grim. For example, if the teacher gives each group a different problem to work on and has the groups give an oral report sequentially, the result is almost invariably a long, drawn-out, and very low-energy event. On the other hand, if the teacher has students work on the same problem and has the groups report simultaneously, the natural result is a very high energy, give-and-take total class discussion.

Impact of Make-a-Specific-Choice Assignments

The degree to which assignments stimulate higher-level cognitive skills (elaborative rehearsal) is largely a function of what we ask students to produce. For example, suppose an English composition instructor wanted to ensure that his or her students were able to recognize the effective use of active versus passive voice in written communication. Three alternative versions of the English composition assignment are shown in Table 3.2 (see also Michaelsen, Black, & Fink, 1996). In these examples, the order of the tasks reflects the degree to which each of them would require the use of higher-level cognitive skills. For example, alternative #1 simply asks students to make a list. It is unlikely that this kind of assignment would stimulate higher-level thinking because students could make a list by simply going to a reference source that cites examples of typical mistakes, copying the list and, turning it in. With this obvious bit of information in hand, one would readily concede that assignment #1 is not particularly challenging. Assignment #2, having to "make-a-choice," is a considerably better assignment. This assignment requires students to critically examine the sentences in the sample passage and then use the criteria that define active versus passive voice to identify examples of the same.

Although assignment #2 does require more thinking, assignment #3, "make-a-specific-choice," provides the students with even more practice in using higher-level cognitive skills. Assignment #3 is better, in part, because students will not be able to complete task #3 unless they can also complete tasks #1 and #2. As is typical with make-a-specific-choice assignments, picking a single best example of the correct use of passive voice will require students to develop and use a number of higher-level cognitive skills. At a minimum, these higher-level skills include making multiple comparisons and discriminations, analyzing content information, and verifying rule application (see Gagné, 1970).

Granting that make-a-specific-choice assignments are beneficial for individual students working alone, these assignments also produce great gains in learning groups. In part, learning increases because make-a-specific-choice assignments provide an additional reason for students to take their work seriously. For example, group interac-

TABLE 3.2
Wording Assignments to Promote Higher-Level Cognitive Skills and Team Development

___

"Make-a-list"

1. "List the 'mistakes' that writers frequently make that detract from their efforts to write in active 'voice'."

"Make-a-choice"

2. "Read the following passage and identify a sentence that is a clear example of: a) active, and b) passive 'voice.'"

"Make-a-specific-choice"

3. "Read the following passage and identify the sentence in which passive 'voice' is used most appropriately."

___

tion provides two additional opportunities to stimulate active learning: the discussion within groups and the discussion between groups. When used in a group context, make-a-specific-choice assignments increase learning in each step of the process as students prepare individually, as they interact within their group, and as they become engaged in the discussion between groups (Figure 3.3).

Impact on Individual Preparation for Group Work

Using a series of assignments that requires students to make a specific choice enhances individual preparation for group work in three quite different ways. One is that learners have to use higher-level thinking skills to actually make a choice. As a result, most will enter the group discussion having made a serious attempt to think through the issues. Second, unless the group is in complete agreement, members gain additional self-insight when they are preparing to explain the reasons behind their selections to their peers. Third, students' motivation to prepare for subsequent group work is typically enhanced because they realize that make-a-specific-choice assignments practically eliminate the opportunity to hide and let someone else carry the group.

Impact on Discussions Within Groups

The difference between make-a-list and make-a-specific-choice assignments is even more evident in intra-team discussions. For example, listing choices that are possibilities tends to be a low-energy team task. One reason for the low energy is that a search for what should be on a list focuses on quantity rather than quality. Another

FIGURE 3.3
Impact of Assignment Wording on Learning and Team Development

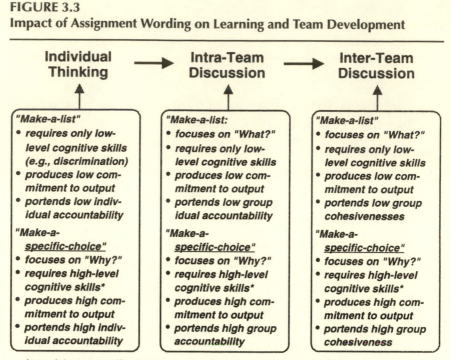

| Individual Thinking | → | Intra-Team Discussion | → | Inter-Team Discussion |

"Make-a-list"
- requires only low-level cognitive skills (e.g., discrimination)
- produces low commitment to output
- portends low individual accountability

"Make-a-specific-choice"
- focuses on "Why?"
- requires high-level cognitive skills*
- produces high commitment to output
- portends high individual accountability

"Make-a-list:
- focuses on "What?"
- requires only low-level cognitive skills
- produces low commitment to output
- portends low group idual accountability

"Make-a-specific-choice"
- focuses on "Why?"
- requires high-level cognitive skills*
- produces high commitment to output
- portends high group accountability

"Make-a-list"
- focuses on "What?"
- requires only low-level cognitive skills
- produces low commitment to output
- portends low group cohesivenesses

"Make-a-specific-choice"
- focuses on "Why?"
- requires high-level cognitive skills*
- produces high commitment to output
- portends high group cohesiveness

* At a minimum, specific choices require: Multiple comparisons and discriminations, exchange and analysis of content information, and verification of rule applications.

reason is that once several items go on the list, it is easy for quieter or less self-assured participants to get "off the hook" by saying that their ideas are already listed. The last reason is that making a list seldom leads to a feeling of pride in the group output because the majority of the items are likely to be in common with other groups.

By contrast, when groups are asked to select a single best choice based on specific criteria and are aware that other groups have been given the same assignment, members are likely to engage in an intense give-and-take discussion regarding why any given choice is better than another. No one wants to be the only group to have made a particular choice and not be able to present a clear and cogent rationale for their position. As a result, most groups will engage in make-a-specific-choice tasks with a great deal of energy. They are also likely to be able and very willing to defend their choices.

Impact on Discussions Between Groups

Group assignments phrased in make-a-specific-choice terms produce their greatest gains in class discussions between groups. Two of the benefits arise from the simplicity of the output. We have discovered that assignments that compel groups to make a specific choice invariably promote group accountability because any differences between groups are absolutely clear. For example, an assignment that asks groups to select the single best example of an appropriate use of passive voice will produce a much more productive between-group discussion than an assignment that asks groups to merely identify examples of appropriate use of active and passive voice. Comparing "best examples" (i.e., specific choices) is likely to produce a more intense and informative discussion than just listing examples because groups have a vested interest in defending their position to the other groups. In addition, the discussion will focus on the reasons one choice is superior to another.

By contrast, group assignments that result in either lists or nonspecific choices often result in two problems: low-energy class discussion and poor group analyses going unchallenged. The lack of energy results from the fact that groups tend to be far more interested in their own work than that of other groups. Poor analysis often goes unchallenged because: (1) having students either make a list or a nonspecific choice is likely to produce so much data that the task of finding something to challenge can be quite difficult, and (2) the absence of clear comparisons allows groups to overlook inconsistencies in both their own and other groups' analyses.

Impact of Simultaneous Reporting

Although make-a-specific-choice assignments produce substantial benefits at each of the three stages shown in Figures 3.2 and 3.3, their value is often much greater when the choices are reported simultaneously. This is particularly evident in making the transition from group to total class discussions. Even if students are required to make the same specific decision, having them report sequentially is far less effective than having them report simultaneously. An excellent example of the disparity between the two methods is described below:

After using the RAP, a colleague who teaches marketing uses a make-a-specific-choice group assignment to ensure that students can "coherently weigh the factors involved in evaluating alternative sites for locating different types of businesses" (Michaelsen, Black, & Fink, 1996). He asks his students to: "*Select what you think would be the ideal site for a new dry cleaning business in the city of_____ (a specific city about which students can gain access to relevant data), identify the single most compelling reason for your decision, and be prepared to explain the rationale for your selection*" (Michaelsen et al., 1996:233). Although the assignment clearly requires students to use course concepts to make a specific choice, its impact is greatly enhanced by how he has his groups report their choices.

Effect of Sequential Reporting

For several years, this professor gave RATs, allowed students to use class time to work on the project, and had each of five groups make a ten-minute presentation in which students revealed their choices and the reasons for making them. After the final presentation, he then opened up the floor for questions and class discussion. With very few exceptions, however, he was disappointed by his students' low energy and shallow analysis of the issues. In part, the problem was that the repetitive nature of the presentations tended to put everyone to sleep, including the teacher. However, the problems did not end there. Differences in the groups' choices—the key to stimulating intergroup discussions—were obscured by several factors. First, the sheer volume of data in five, ten-minute presentations made it difficult for students to keep track of all the information. Second, the relevant facts were presented over a fifty-minute time span. As a result, the key points tended to get lost in a maze of less relevant commentary. Third, since the groups were likely to use different approaches for representing their analyses, establishing links between key ideas was likely to seem like comparing apples and oranges.

Effect of Simultaneous Reporting with Pushpins

After modifying the assignment by replacing sequential reporting with simultaneous reporting, the marketing professor has had tremendous success. Instead of the repetitious sequential reports from each group, he now has them come to class having selected the location for the dry cleaning business and prepared to defend their choice. Then, at the beginning of the class, he:

1. Gives each group a pushpin with their group number on it, a felt-tipped marker and a legal-sized sheet of paper.
2. Allows a specified time period (5–10 minutes) for groups to identify and record the single most compelling reason for their decision on the legal-sized paper.
3. Requires each group to simultaneously stick their pushpin in a city map (attached to a classroom board) indicating their selected location for the dry cleaning establishment and tape their "most compelling reason" in a place that is visible to the entire class.
4. Allows groups to take 5–10 minutes to examine the other groups' choices and formulate questions to ask the other groups regarding the location decisions that were made.
5. Uses the remainder of the class for class discussion.

Even if the location choices are exactly the same, the two different reporting options produce dramatically different outcomes. The pushpin version of the assignment invariably produces a high-energy exchange between groups that focuses on why one reason is more compelling than another. In contrast to students being overwhelmed with data from fifty minutes of reports, the pushpin approach ensures that students are exposed to a simultaneous, common, permanent, and highly visual representation of only the essential data, which are the proposed locations and each group's rationale for their choice. Further, the students have a designated time to carefully process and digest the information in an integrated way.

In summary, properly designed make-a-specific-choice group assignments, with simultaneous reporting, virtually ensure a high level of energy in the classroom because of their profound and positive impact on cohesiveness. Reaching consensus on a difficult choice requires a great deal of thought and effort. Students, therefore, intuitively realize that differences between teams represent an important source of feedback. Thus, because differences between team choices are so clear, they represent a significant external threat.

By contrast, make-a-list assignments seldom promote group cohesiveness because the output is poorly suited for intergroup comparisons. The contrast becomes most apparent when groups share the results of their discussions. Even though groups generally do a pretty good job of making lists, the energy level in the class almost always takes a nose dive when the groups report to the class. In fact, simply getting students to pay attention to each other as representatives go over each item in their list can be a serious problem. Differences that groups might otherwise take pride in and be motivated to defend are both obscured and diminished in significance by the sheer volume of data.

How Good Are Your Assignments?

Probably the single best indicator of the effectiveness of group assignments is the presence of *task-focused energy* when groups share the results of their work with the other groups in the class. In fact, the energy level continues to rise when groups share the results of their discussions with the other groups in the class; it will also promote both group cohesiveness and learning. When the energy level is high during discussions between teams you can be confident that team members have individually prepared in advance for the team work, taken their team work seriously, and increased their ability to tackle even more difficult learning tasks. Good assignments create a high energy level in the classroom. And the energy level rises because students are interested in and willing to spontaneously challenge each other's thinking as well as defend their own.

We have observed time and again that the "3 Ss" (*Same* assignment, *Specific* choice, and *Simultaneous* reporting) have a powerful impact on both group cohesiveness and energy in the classroom. Table 3.3 provides a checklist that you can use to preassess the extent to which your assignments incorporate these three procedures.

Making Good Group Assignments into Great Ones

Every group assignment affects students' learning in two very different ways: directly (by actively engaging them with the issues and concepts) and indirectly (by actively engaging them with each other). As a result, teachers have two options for improving the learning value of their assignments. One is to modify the substance of the assignment to increase students' interaction with the material (e.g., using cases or

TABLE 3.3
A Checklist for Effective Group Activities

PRIOR TO Group Discussions

❏ **Are group members working on the same assignment and required to make a specific choice, individually and in writing?** (Note: This individual accountability is especially important in newly formed groups.)

During Discussions WITHIN Groups

❏ **Are groups required to share members' individual choices and agree (i.e., reach a group consensus) on a specific choice?**

❏ **Will the discussion focus on "Why?"** (and/or "How?")

❏ **Will the groups' choice(s) be represented in a form that enables immediate and direct comparisons with other groups?***

During Discussions BETWEEN Groups

❏ **Are group decisions reported simultaneously?***

❏ **Do group "reports" focus attention on absolutely key issues?***

❏ **Are groups given the opportunity to digest and reflect on the entire set of "reports"* before total class discussion begins?**

❏ **Will the discussion focus on "Why?"** (and/or "How?")

> **The more "Yes" answers, the better. If the answer to all eight questions is "Yes", the assignment will effectively promote both learning and group development.**

*The form in which individual and group choices are represented largely determines the dynamics of the discussions that follow. Both individual reports to groups and group reports to the class should be as absolutely succinct as possible. One-word reports are the very best (e.g., yes/no, best/worst, up/down/no change, etc.) because they invariably stimulate a discussion of why one choice is better than another.

problems that students see as relevant). The other is to increase students' interaction with their peers—either within a group or between groups—by changing the assignment so that it does a better job of increasing group cohesiveness.

Surprisingly, the indirect approach for increasing the effectiveness of group assignments, that is, having students interact with one another in ways that increase group cohesiveness, is often the most effective. For example, an agronomy professor who was using team-based learning used an "increase-cohesiveness" approach to improve a group assignment aimed at developing his students' ability to recognize the weed varieties that commonly infest turf grass lawns in the local region. Initially, he used an assignment that required groups to "identify and appropriately tag an example of each weed variety growing in plot #1 [which he had laid out] on the lawn behind this building." The assignment worked reasonably well, but he decided to modify the activity to increase its value for building team cohesiveness. The revised assignment now uses five plots (one for each group in the class) and requires an additional twenty minutes to complete.

During the first ten minutes of the assignment, the group members work individually within their team's plot to first find and then temporarily tag an example of each weed variety. During the next twenty minutes, each of the groups: (1) agrees on (and permanently tags) a sample of each weed variety in their plot (and receive ten points for each correctly tagged weed variety), and (2) prepares for a "weed finders challenge" (WFC).

During the WFC, groups have five minutes to examine each of the plots of other teams and challenge incorrectly tagged weeds. If their challenge is valid, they receive ten bonus points, but if their challenge is incorrect, they lose ten points to the group whom they challenged.

With the new version of the assignment, groups typically use approximately the first half of their time to make sure they have correctly tagged a sample of each weed variety in their own plot. Then they turn their attention to preparing for the WFC by training members to scout for potential challenges (because they do not have time to go to each of the other plots as a group), and shifting their tags to *atypical* examples of the weed varieties in an attempt to elicit bogus challenges from other groups.

Although the changes in the original assignment are relatively modest in nature, the new assignment produces positive changes in all five of the factors that affect group cohesiveness (Figure 3.1). The assignment now promotes individual accountability on both ends: individual tagging prior to group work and individuals serving as scouts during the WFC. It requires members to work in close proximity with each other (and away from other teams). The assignment produces high levels of intragroup interaction by necessitating reaching consensus on your own samples and preparing members to scout other plots. It provides rewards for group work: the opportunity to earn points for correctly tagging weeds and extra points by successfully challenging other groups. The assignment provides external comparison and feedback by giving groups the opportunity to challenge each other. As a result, the revised assignment is much more effective in building group cohesiveness.

Even though the problem on which the assignment is based is exactly the same (recognizing and tagging weeds), modifying the assignment so that it increases group cohesiveness has had a profound and positive impact on its value for learning for a variety of reasons. First, the realization that they will have to work on their own causes individual group members to be more serious about their advance preparation and peer teaching and learning. Members start out with a reasonably high level of understanding that is further enhanced during the group discussions in preparation for the weed finders' challenge. Second, the WFC generates learning that is particularly long-lasting because it involves actually finding and identifying weeds, even

under less than optimal conditions. As a result, many of the students who participated in the weed finders' challenge have reported that they are unable to have a picnic any more without thinking about what kinds of weeds are going to be covered by
their picnic blanket!

Conclusion

The primary theme of this chapter is to emphasize our belief that good group assignments are absolutely critical for the effective use of team-based learning as a teaching strategy. In addition, we have offered four specific conclusions about the
characteristics of good group assignments.

First, the vast majority of dysfunctional student behaviors (e.g., social loafing, one
or two members dominating the discussion, etc.) and complaints (e.g., having to
carry the dead wood, the instructor isn't teaching, etc.) are the result of bad assignments, not bad groups. Second, good group assignments can be very effective in promoting students' mastery of basic conceptual material and enhancing higher-level
thinking and problem-solving skills. Third, the single best way to gauge the effectiveness of group assignments is to observe the level of energy that is present during the
total class discussion stage of the assignment. And finally, the surest approach for creating effective group assignments is to maximize the extent to which the learning
tasks promote the development of cohesive learning groups. When each of these characteristics is incorporated, student learning can soar.

NOTE

1. To clarify terminology, the "Readiness Assurance Process" refers to the whole set of activities used at the beginning of a unit that makes sure students are *ready* to start learning how
to use the content. These activities include: individual study before class, the individual test on
the readings, the group test, feedback on test performance, appeals, and so forth. The "Readiness Assessment Test" refers specifically to the test used in the Readiness Assurance Process.

REFERENCES

Anderson, J. R. (1993). Problem solving and learning. *American Psychologist 48:* 35–44.

Bruning, R. H., Schraw, G. J., & Ronning, R. R. (1994). *Cognitive psychology and instruction.*
2d ed. Englewood Cliffs, NJ: Prentice-Hall.

Craik, F. L. M., & Lockhart, R. S. (1986). CHARM is not enough: Comments on Eich's
model of cued recall. *Psychological Review 93:* 360–364.

Feldman, D. (1984). The development and enforcement of group norms. *Academy of Management Review 9:* 47–53.

Gagné, R. M. (1970). *The conditions for learning.* 2d ed. New York: Holt, Rinehart &
Winston.

Latane, B., Williams, K., & Harkins, S. (1979). Many hands make light the work: The causes and consequences of social loafing. *Journal of Personality and Social Psychology 37*: 822–832.

Lazarowitz, R. (1991). Learning biology cooperatively: An Israeli junior high school study. *Cooperative Learning 11*(3): 19–21.

Lazarowitz, R., & Karsenty, G. (1990). Cooperative learning and students' self-esteem in tenth grade biology classrooms. In *Cooperative learning theory and research.* Ed. S. Sharon, 143–149. New York: Praeger.

Mandler, J. M. (1984). *Stories, scripts, and scenes: Aspects of schema theory.* Hillsdale, NJ: Lawrence Erlbaum.

Michaelsen, L. K., & Black, R. H. (1994). Building learning teams: The key to harnessing the power of small groups in higher education. In *Collaborative learning: A sourcebook for higher education,* Vol. 2. State College, PA: National Center for Teaching, Learning and Assessment.

Michaelsen, L. K., Black, R. H., & Fink, L. D. (1996). What every faculty developer needs to know about learning groups. In *To improve the academy: Resources for faculty, instructional and organizational development.* Ed. L. Richlin. Stillwater, OK: New Forums Press.

Michaelsen, L. K., Jones, C. F., & Watson, W. E. (1993). Beyond groups and cooperation: Building high performance learning teams. In *To improve the academy: Resources for faculty, instructional and organizational development,* Ed. D. L. Wright & J. P. Lunde. Stillwater, OK: New Forums Press.

Michaelsen, L. K., Watson, W. E., & Black, R. H. (1989). A realistic test of individual versus group consensus decision making. *Journal of Applied Psychology 74*(5): 834–839.

Nungester, R. J., & Duchastel, P. C. (1982). Testing versus review: Effects on retention. *Journal of Applied Psychology 74*(1): 18–22.

Shaw, M. E. (1981). *Group dynamics: The psychology of small group behavior.* 3d ed. New York: McGraw-Hill.

Slavin, R. E. (1995). *Cooperative learning.* 2d ed. Boston, MA: Allyn & Bacon.

Smith, K., Johnson, D. W., & Johnson R. T. (1981). Can conflict be constructive? Controversy versus concurrence seeking in learning groups. *Journal of Educational Psychology 73*(5): 651–663.

Watson, W. E., Kumar, K., & Michaelsen, L. K. (1993). Cultural diversity's impact on group process and performance: Comparing culturally homogeneous and culturally diverse task groups. *The Academy of Management Journal 36*(3): 590–602.

Watson, W. E., Michaelsen, L. K. & Sharp, W. (1991). Member competence, group interaction and group decision-making: A longitudinal study. *Journal of Applied Psychology 76*: 801–809.

Wilson, Wayne R. (1982). *The use of permanent learning groups in teaching introductory accounting.* Unpublished doctoral dissertation, University of Oklahoma.

Wilson, R. C. (1986). Improving faculty teaching: Effective use of student evaluations and consultants. *Journal of Higher Education 57*(2): 196–211.

CHAPTER 4

Group Process Research

Implications for Using Learning Groups

Carolyn Birmingham and Mary McCord

If we want to transform newly formed groups into high-performance learning teams, what do we need to do? This chapter summarizes some of the key findings from the reseach literature on group dynamics that indicate what groups need to become high-performance teams.

The primary objective of this chapter is to review the extant empirical literature that focuses on the development of high-performance teams. The focus of the review is identifying prescriptions for creating and managing high-performance teams, that is, teams whose primary function is to enhance members' educational development. The review is organized around the key findings that emerged from an extensive study of intact work groups (from a wide variety of work settings) that was conducted by Hackman (1990). Based on his research, no group can become a high-performance team unless its members: (1) bring adequate knowledge and skill to bear on the task, (2) employ task performance strategies that are appropriate to the work and to the setting in which the work is being done, and (3) are motivated to exert sufficient effort to accomplish the task at an acceptable level of performance.

The following paragraphs address each of these key factors. The first section examines the literature that deals with bringing adequate knowledge and skill to the work of the group, and addresses questions regarding group composition and formation in relation to the complexity of the tasks to be performed. The next section discusses conditions that affect the development of group processes that encourage active member participation. This discussion focuses on research related to the impact of the group or team maturation process and the nature of the tasks that groups are expected to perform. The final section examines the research related to the characteristics of performance and reward and feedback systems that are effective in promoting active member participation and team development.

ENSURING ADEQUATE MEMBER KNOWLEDGE AND SKILLS

In business settings, success in dealing with complex problems is primarily measured by the "products" created by employee groups. Therefore, organizations strive to recruit team members who already have needed skills, either by assembling teams from existing employees or by hiring new ones. Educational settings, however, differ from the typical workplace in the formation of groups in two important ways. One is that the most important measure of success is what group members learn, not what they produce. In fact, learning is typically enhanced by assignments that require students to struggle with challenging intellectual tasks. The other difference is that in learning groups, the primary purpose of group interaction is increasing members' skills. As a result, members seldom start out with the skills they need to accomplish their assigned tasks. Thus, in educational settings, the primary focus of the group formation process is creating groups whose members are, in combination, capable of acquiring the information and skills needed to complete the tasks through which the learning occurs.

In both workplace and classroom settings, giving groups complex intellectual tasks can be a two-edged sword. On one hand, solving complex problems requires broad-based member input and open give-and-take discussion. Thus, complex problems provide the opportunity for group members both to contribute to the success of their group and to learn from each other as a natural part of doing their work. On the other hand, to have the resources necessary for solving complex problems, groups must contain members who either have or are capable of acquiring a wide range of intellectual, process-management, and interpersonal skills. As a result, one key to using groups effectively, either for solving complex problems or for creating a rich learning environment, is forming the groups so that members either have or are capable of acquiring the resources required for their assigned work.

In general, the actual group formation process, in either business or educational settings, typically involves assessing the capabilities of a limited pool of potential members and distributing them among the number of groups that are to be formed. Thus, the process of forming groups requires varying the group size and the diversity of group members to match task requirement needs (Gersick, 1988; Gersick & Hackman, 1990; Hackman, 1990). Also included in this equation are the processes by which groups are formed and the length of time groups should remain together.

Group Size

Extant literature reporting on the optimal size for teams identifies two factors that have a significant impact on decisions about the ideal size of a group or team. One is that the lower limit for the ideal group size is determined by the difficulty of the tasks to be performed (Hackman, 1990). With simple tasks, a team would not be needed at all. However, the more complex the task, the larger the ideal size group. However, the other factor is that the relatively short duration of academic terms tends to set an upper boundary to the ideal size group. This is because the larger the group, the greater the time and effort required to develop a level of group cohesiveness required for effective group work.

To no surprise, studies which date back to the 1950s, on the appropriate size of problem-solving groups (Bales, 1950), generally involve making a judgment about a trade-off between resources and member involvement (Kowitz & Knutson, 1980; Scheidel & Crowell, 1979). On one hand, larger groups generally have more resources and, as a result, are capable of dealing with more complex problems. On the other hand, as groups become larger, fewer members actually participate in group discussions (Bales, 1950). As a result, members of larger groups tend to be less satisfied with, and less committed to, the success of their groups.

In terms of actual numbers, most researchers have concluded that for significant intellectual work, the minimum size for an effective group is five members. At the other end of the spectrum regarding size, most studies have concluded that groups larger than seven members tend to encounter significant problems with group processes (Kowitz & Knutson, 1980; Scheidel & Crowell, 1979). Given the importance of having groups or teams work on complex tasks, this research suggests that groups of five to seven would appear to be optimal.

Group Diversity

Although the ideal diversity of the team is also a function of the tasks to be performed (Hackman, 1990), empirical research on team effectiveness clearly poses a dilemma for people forming groups. On one hand, diversity typically enhances a group's information gathering and processing capacity by increasing the likelihood of having a broader set of member viewpoints. As a result, few would argue against the potential value of forming problem-solving groups so that members are likely to have a diversity of opinions (Watson, Kumar, & Michaelsen, 1993).

One must also be alerted, however, to the potential for negative impact when group members are diverse. In fact, a great deal of research tends to highlight at least the initial negative impact of member diversity (e.g., Chatman & Flynn, 2001; Watson et al., 1993; Williams & O'Reilly, 1998). In part, the initial negative impact of member diversity results from a combination of two factors. One is that diverse groups are less likely to be cohesive than homogeneous groups (Shaw, 1981). The other is that group cohesiveness generally enhances group effectiveness (Evans & Dion, 1991; Gruenfeld & Hollingshead, 1993; McGrath, 1984; Shaw, 1981). In part, the initial negative impact of having highly diverse groups is that they take longer to develop to the point where they can use member resources effectively (Watson et al., 1993). However, although diverse groups typically have more initial difficulties, after forty hours of working together they are typically more effective than homogeneous groups (Watson et al., 1993). Thus, given the importance of using assignments and tasks based on difficult problems, the empirical research on group effectiveness clearly supports using heterogeneous learning groups, assuming that the groups work together long enough to become cohesive.

Forming Groups

Regardless of the setting, anyone faced with managing multiple teams has a limited set of potential team members. Therefore, he or she has to employ some mechanism to assign individuals to groups so that two important things can occur. One is ensuring that each of the groups has members with the necessary skills and abilities to complete their assigned tasks. The other is ensuring that the process used to assign individuals to groups is perceived by the students as a process that is fair. If students are comfortable with the process, they are much more likely to be motivated to succeed to "prove" their worth. On the other hand, if the group assignment procedures are perceived as being biased in some significant way, members are likely to feel that the unfair selection process offers a ready-made excuse for failure.

Alternative Strategies

The three group-formation methods discussed in the literature are self-selection, random assignment (Griffin, 1985), and assignment by individual student ability (Evans, 1988). In general, self-selection tends to be the most problematic group-formation strategy. For instance, the data show that self-selected groups are generally homogeneous (Bies & Shapiro, 1988) and, as a result, have less potential for solving complex problems. That is, using student-formed groups creates the potential for groups with uneven and/or inadequate resources. Surprisingly, students often perceive that self-selection gives some groups an unfair advantage (Bies & Shapiro, 1988).

Forming groups by random assignment is a somewhat better method. And it has the advantage of being perceived as fair by the students (Griffin, 1985). On the other hand, with random assignment there is a risk that, as in self-selected groups, some of the groups may end up with inadequate resources (Evans, 1988).

Taken together, the empirical literature supports two practices for forming groups. One is that the teacher should form the groups. The other is that he or she should use a group-formation process through which the available resources (and liabilities) are evenly distributed among the groups so that they are generally at the same ability level. If learning groups are generally equal in ability, the instructor can use a common set of assignments without having to worry that some assignments are too difficult for some groups but too easy for others. The prescription for forming groups is that the instructor should stratify the selection pool so that assets and liabilities will be evenly spread across groups, and use some form of a random assignment procedure in actually assigning members to groups to ensure that the process is perceived as being fair.

Next Steps

Although correctly forming groups is likely to increase the extent to which members have (or are likely to be able to acquire) needed skills, getting the groups formed is only the first step in creating high-performance teams. Newly formed groups, for a variety of reasons, are simply not able to work together effectively. Thus, once the groups are formed, the next problem is to create conditions that are likely to stimulate the active give-and-take discussion that is required to complete tasks that are complex enough to provide opportunities for significant learning.

DEVELOPING PROCESSES THAT PROMOTE ACTIVE MEMBER PARTICIPATION

Helping groups become effective involves a number of important ingredients. Two of the most important steps are ensuring that members meet together over time to enable them to mature as a group, and members are required to complete tasks that are complex enough to provide opportunities for significant interaction and learning. This section discusses each of these critical steps.

The Impact of Group Maturity on Group Member Participation

The literature on small-group effectiveness identifies a number of group interaction characteristics (see Table 4.1) that are clearly different in newly formed as compared to longer-term groups. These characteristics undoubtedly have implications for the kind of give-and-take discussion that is essential to group and team effectiveness, regardless of the setting. They include individual members'

1. level of trust in, and attraction to, their group;
2. motivation to achieve group goals;
3. willingness to help each other;
4. awareness of each other's skills and abilities;
5. ability to share information effectively;
6. willingness to disagree;
7. preferred method for resolving conflict;
8. overall ability to complete difficult intellectual tasks.

Group Trust and Attraction

In part, attraction to a group depends on the level of trust that members have in each other. Further, since one of the most important conditions for developing trust is seeing other team members reliably complete tasks over time (Gulati, 1995; McAllister, 1995; Ross & LaCroix, 1996), members of newly formed groups are

TABLE 4.1
Summary of Empirical Research Interaction Characteristics of New versus Mature Groups

Interaction Characteristics	Group Maturity		Conclusions Based on Research by:
	New Groups*	Long-Term Groups	
• Trust in & Attraction to Group	Low to Moderate	Potentially High	McAllister (1995); Johnson, Johnson, & Scott (1978); Ross & LaCroix (1996); Hambrick, Davison, Snell, & Snow (1998); Gulati (1995); Jarvenpaa, Knoll & Leidner (1998)
• Motivation to Achieve Group Goals	Little identification with group or goals	High identification with group and goals	Brandon & Pratt (1999); Saunders (2000); Jarvenpaa, Knoll & Leidner (1998); Evans & Dion (1991); McGrath (1984); Langfred (1998)
• Willingness to Help Other Members	Self-interest paramount	Members support and help each other	Johnson, Johnson, Johnson, & Anderson (1976); Lazarowitz, Sjaram & Steinberg (1980)
• Awareness of Members' Skills and Abilities	LOW–Based on stereotypes of members' personal attributes	HIGH–Based on observations of members' behavior	Harrison, Price, & Bell (1998); Zalkind and Costello (1962)
• Effective Sharing of Task-Related Information	Focus on social; high dependence on group's best member	Focus on task; all members' input available to & used by group	Gersick (1988); Johnson, Johnson, Johnson, & Anderson (1976); Johnson, Johnson, & Scott (1978); Watson, Michaelsen, & Sharp (1991)
• Willingness to Disagree (potential for open give-and-take discussion)	LOW–Most discussion focuses on areas of agreement	HIGH–Members willing to voice and attempt to resolve differences	Ellis & Fisher (1975); Arrow & McGrath (1993); Moreland & Levine (1988); McGrath & Gruenfeld (1993); O'Connor, Gruenfeld, & McGrath (1993); Leana (1985); McGrath, Arrow, Gruenfeld, Hollingshead, & O'Connor (1993); Simmons & Peterson (2000)
• Method of Resolving Conflict	Mostly use face-saving strategies (e.g., voting, compromise)	Open discussion aimed at reaching group consensus	Gruenfeld, Mannix, Williams, & Neale (1996); Birmingham & Michaelsen (1999)
• Ability to Complete Difficult Intellectual Tasks	Inherently low due to low member commitment and avoidance of open discussion	Potentially high due to increased member commitment and more open discussion	Hackman (1990); Arrow & McGrath (1993); Jehn & Mannix (2001); Watson, Michaelsen, & Sharp (1991); Gruenfeld & Hollingshead (1993); Watson, Kumar, & Michaelsen (1993)

* Includes existing groups with new member(s) added

unlikely either to trust each other or to be highly attracted to their group (Hambrick, Davison, Snell, & Snow, 1998). Over time, however, as members have the opportunity to demonstrate that they will reliably contribute time and effort to ensure that the group task is completed, sociability, attraction, and cohesiveness all increase (Jarvenpaa, Knoll, & Leidner, 1998; Johnson, Johnson, & Scott, 1978; Knoll & Jarvenpaa, 1995).

Motivation to Achieve Group Goals

Group goals are a key element of the development of member trust and group cohesiveness in several different ways. In particular, groups with high levels of diversity need common goals to establish a basis for thinking of themselves as a team (Brandon & Pratt, 1999; Saunders, 2000). Working cooperatively to accomplish team tasks and goals provides members with the opportunity for ongoing interpersonal and informational exchanges between group members (Jarvenpaa et al., 1998). Further, over time, goals even provide a basis for team interaction. For example, groups with high levels of trust discuss group goals more than do groups with low levels of trust (Jarvenpaa et al., 1998).

Given the centrality of group goals in the group development process, it is not surprising that highly cohesive groups are generally more effective in achieving group goals than less cohesive groups (Evans & Dion, 1991). The ability of highly cohesive groups to achieve their goals is, however, a potential cause for caution. Generally, cohesion influences a group in the same direction as the existing group norms (McGrath, 1984). If a group is highly cohesive and has norms that are task-performance oriented, then members are motivated to outperform other groups (Langfred, 1998). If not, however, group norms often focus on unintended or undesired goals (e.g., protecting members from unreasonable demands from managers or teachers) and can motivate members to restrict their productivity (e.g., Seashore, 1954; McGrath, 1984).

Willingness to Help Each Other

Another positive aspect of increased group cohesiveness is that members of cohesive groups tend to feel a higher degree of responsibility for each others' well-being. As a result, they are more likely to provide interpersonal support (Likert, 1961) and help each other (Lazarowitz et al., 1980).

Awareness of Each Other's Skills and Abilities

In most instances, members of new groups know very little about each others' skills and abilities. In fact, members' initial perceptions of each others' skills and abilities are likely to be based on the stereotypes of what Harrison et al. (1998) called personal diversity, that is, observable physical characteristics such as race, gender, and so on (see also Zalkind & Costello, 1962). As a result, groups will be largely unable to utilize members' knowledge and skills very effectively until they have enough contact to be able to learn about each other as individuals. Over time, watching other team members at work allows members to assess each other's skills and abilities more accurately (Harrison et al., 1998).

Effective Sharing of Task-Related Information

A number of studies have found that information sharing in newly formed groups is not likely to support high task performance on intellectual tasks (see Table 4.1). For example, Gersick (1988) found that most new-group interaction focuses on social issues such as members getting to know each other. Consequently, the exchange of task-related information is likely to be both low in quantity and mostly focused on the facts and ideas that members already have in common (Johnson et al., 1976; Johnson et al., 1978). Given this limited ability to share task-related information, it is not surprising that the effectiveness of newly formed groups in dealing with intellectual tasks seldom exceeds the ability of their best individual member (Watson et al., 1991).

Over time, however, group members grow more comfortable working with each other, and group interaction shifts from interpersonal to task issues (Gersick, 1988). A number of studies have also shown that cohesive teams exhibit a higher rate of information exchange and develop expertise in eliciting and using information that, in the beginning, was known to only a single group member (Johnson et al., 1976, 1978). Similarly, Watson, et al. (1991) found that groups that had worked together for over twenty-five to thirty hours were both more effective than, and less dependent on, their best member. They reasoned that the most logical explanation for their findings was that working together had increased the quieter members' willingness to speak up and enabled the more assertive members to learn the importance of listening to what others had to say before reaching a group decision.

Willingness to Disagree

The effective performance of nonroutine tasks requires constructive conflict (task or functional conflict; see Amason, 1996; Amason & Schweiger, 1994; Jehn, 1994, 1995, 1997, 2000; Jehn, Chadwick, & Thatcher, 1997; Jehn & Mannix, 2001; Priem & Price, 1991). However, a number of studies have found that members of newly formed groups are likely to withhold the information that would make constructive conflict possible. For example, several empirical studies (see Table 4.1) found that members both of new groups (Ellis & Fisher, 1975; McGrath, Arrow, Gruenfeld, Hollingshead, & O'Connor, 1993) and of established groups that have added members (Arrow & McGrath, 1993; Moreland & Levine, 1988) intentionally suppress information that members believe may produce conflict. In addition, members of new groups respond differently from members of longer-term groups when they do become aware of differences of opinion. For example, unless group members trust each other (which is unlikely in newly formed groups), any conflict is likely to be seen as a personal attack, that is, a relationship conflict (Simmons & Peterson, 2000). On the other hand, Leana (1985) found that established groups were much more likely to challenge each other's ideas, even if the challenger held a minority opinion.

Methods of Resolving Conflict

In addition to the fact that conflicts are less likely to arise in newly formed groups (for the reasons already outlined), the methods used to resolve the conflict that does occur are very different in new groups, as compared to mature or cohesive groups. For example, even though voting is less effective than discussion as a means of handling disagreements in decision-making groups (Innami, 1994); Gruenfeld, Mannix, Williams, and Neale (1996) found that newly formed groups were likely to use voting as a means of resolving conflict. Similarly, Birmingham and Michaelsen (1999) documented that new groups generally resolved conflicts by adopting a solution that was clearly a compromise, but later on as they became more cohesive, these same groups nearly always engaged in give-and-take discussion until they were able to reach a group consensus.

Overall Ability to Complete Difficult Intellectual Tasks

Many of the dysfunctional processes that are characteristic of newly formed groups result from the fact that they are faced with the dilemma of having to complete a task at the same time they are learning to work with each other (e.g., Argote & McGrath, 1993; Gruenfeld & Hollingshead, 1993; Levine & Moreland, 1990; McGrath, 1991). Ironically, the same dysfunctional processes may actually be helpful in the long run. For example, although clearly suboptimal from the standpoint of either task effectiveness or learning, behaviors such as searching for areas of agreement, withholding information that might create conflict, and voting or compromising to minimize discussion when conflicts arise, all tend to reduce members' uneasiness about working with each other. The key is that they are all practical ways of building a level of trust that is likely to enable effective group problem solving later on.

Developing newly formed groups to the point that give-and-take discussion (the kind that promotes learning) occurs on a regular basis, is much more of a process than an event and guides much of managerial practice in nonclassroom settings. For example, even though sports teams are made up of highly skilled athletes, the standard practice of professional sports coaches is to prepare for the games that "count" by holding a training camp and playing a series of preseason games. These training camps and preseason games provide the building blocks for future productivity by enabling team members to interact enough to have the opportunity to learn from and about each other. Taken together, the evidence from both management practice and the studies cited in Table 4.1 suggests two essential conditions for the development of high-performance teams in any setting (including higher education). One is maintaining a membership that is stable long enough for members to have the opportunity to learn to work together. The other is that the groups must engage in activities that require members to interact with one another.

Tasks that Promote Ongoing Interaction
Among Group Members

Overall, the literature on small-group effectiveness suggests that ideal intellectual tasks for groups have three characteristics. One characteristic is related to the manner in which member input is combined. Another has to do with the difficulty of the tasks to be performed. The final characteristic relates to whether or not the significance of the task is likely to motivate individual members to prepare for and participate in group or team discussions.

Task Requirements for Combining Members' Inputs

Shaw (1981) identifies two different types of group tasks with respect to their requirements for combining members' input. One type, which we refer to as *joint* tasks (see "disjunctive tasks" in Shaw, 1981:174–176), requires members to jointly create a product (e.g., frame a house). The other task type, which we refer to as *independent* tasks (see "conjunctive tasks" in Shaw, 1981: 174–176), involves members independently contributing components to an overall product (e.g., a group of Boy Scouts completing a five-mile hike in the shortest possible time).

With joint tasks, group performance effectiveness is a function of the combined input and competence of group members. As a result, performance on joint tasks (e.g., a group discussion that leads to the creation of images or ideas, Frank & Anderson, 1971) is typically better in larger or more diverse groups (Bray, Kerr, & Atkin, 1978; Ziller, 1957). With independent tasks, however, a group's performance is largely determined by its least competent member. For example, although peer pressure may motivate the slowest scout to go faster than he would go on his own, he will inevitably increase the time required for the entire group to reach their destination. Thus, with independent tasks, a larger or more diverse group will likely lower the expected group performance (Frank & Anderson, 1971).

The differences between joint and independent groups appear to be particularly important when the work is intellectual in nature. Joint intellectual tasks, for instance making a complex decision, are likely to generate high levels of give-and-take discussion (and produce significant learning) because members intuitively realize that their performance is likely to be enhanced by a greater volume or diversity of member input. For example, Michaelsen, Watson and Black (1989) compared individual and group test scores and found that over 98 percent of the groups scored higher than their own highest scoring member. By contrast, independent intellectual tasks (e.g., members each creating their assigned segment of a group term paper) seldom produce any significant amount of substantive discussion because much of their time and effort is spent on members individually working on only their own component of the overall group task. Further, the larger the group, the greater the risk that a member will detract from the overall group performance by either doing poor quality work or failing to complete his or her part on time (Davis, Kerr, Atkin, Holt, & Meek, 1975).

Making a group decision is clearly a joint task (Shaw, 1981). As a result, basing grades on decision-based assignments motivates students to engage in give-and-take discussion because they realize that group or team performance is likely to be higher with greater member input. Further, the resulting give-and-take discussion both increases learning and promotes team development.

By contrast, the dynamics created by group term papers and presentations are likely to inhibit a high level of give-and-take discussion. In part, this is due to the fact that the only aspect of completing a group paper or presentation that is clearly a joint task occurs when the group is in the process of deciding which students should be responsible for the pieces of the overall product. The remaining aspects of the work (i.e., doing research on various elements of the project as well as preparing sections of a group paper or individual parts of a presentation) are, by their very nature, independent tasks (Shaw, 1981).

Further, the greater the emphasis on the form of the paper or presentation (greater length, specific evaluation criteria, etc.), the more students will tend to treat the assignment as an independent task by minimizing their discussion on substantive issues for two reasons. First, groups feel pressure to work on the part of the assignment that they think will really "count" (the actual paper and/or presentation). Second, and because emphasizing the form of the presentation tends to pressure students into dividing up the work before their groups have developed to the point that members are willing to openly disagree (e.g., Arrow & McGrath, 1993; Ellis & Fisher, 1975; McGrath & Gruenfeld, 1993; Moreland & Levine, 1988; O'Connor et al. 1993). As a result, the task allocation decisions are typically made by one or two dominant individuals who end up being resented by quieter members who do not like their part of the assignment but were unwilling to risk being seen as being either selfish (if they wanted to do more) or lazy (if they felt as if they were given more than their fair share of the work).

Level of Task Difficulty

Even joint intellectual tasks must be at an appropriate level of difficulty. If tasks are too simple, there is no need for group interaction (thus no opportunity for learning [Bray et al., 1978]), because one competent member acting on his or her own can (and likely will) complete the task on behalf of the group. On the other hand, tasks that are too difficult are just as likely to be counterproductive. Extremely difficult intellectual tasks elicit some initial discussion, but, especially in new groups, produce so much tension and interpersonal conflict that they disrupt the group development process (e.g., Eisenstat & Cohen, 1990). By contrast, using appropriately difficult tasks is one of the most effective methods for generating broad-based member participation (Harkins & Petty, 1982).

Task Significance

The other characteristic of effective group tasks, supported by empirical research on small-group effectiveness, is related to the observation that tasks that are significant (i.e., have the potential of measurably affecting people's lives) are, in and of themselves, highly motivating (Hackman & Oldham, 1976, 1980). For example, a number of management scholars (e.g., Greenburg & Baron, 2000; Lawler, 1988) point to the motivational advantages of organizing work for teams around serving a specific group of customers or producing "whole" products to make the work itself more interesting. In addition, studies have shown that intrinsically interesting tasks (Harkins & Petty, 1982) and personally relevant tasks (Brickner, Harkins, & Ostrom, 1986) are likely to elicit high levels of member interest and commitment.

While appropriate tasks and assignments are critical to the development of high-performance teams, equally important are the methods used to evaluate the performance of the teams. Therefore, the third section of this chapter is devoted to a discussion of methods for evaluating and rewarding both individual and team performance. The discussion addresses the last of the three hurdles Hackman (1990) reported that any group must surmount. That is, the group must exert sufficient effort to accomplish the task at an acceptable level of performance.

EFFECTIVE REWARD AND PERFORMANCE
FEEDBACK SYSTEMS

Groups and teams cannot be highly effective in completing intellectual tasks unless their members are motivated to engage actively in team assignments in productive ways. Specifically, completing intellectual group tasks requires that members: (1) *prepare* themselves intellectually prior to their team's work, (2) actively *engage* in task-related discussions, and (3) help *manage* the team discussion process.

Encouraging Members' Pre-Class Preparation

Unfortunately, members of newly formed groups are not automatically motivated to devote time and energy to group-related tasks. Instead, they are likely to engage in what has been called "social loafing," that is, acting in their individual best interest even though they have been assigned to a group and have been asked to engage in tasks on behalf of the group (Latane, Williams, & Harkins, 1979). Although maintaining stable groups is essential, it clearly is not sufficient to eliminate (or even substantially reduce) social loafing. Managers and classroom teachers must proactively create conditions that promote members' commitment to the success of their team. These include framing tasks and assignments so that they promote high levels of member interaction, provide ongoing performance feedback, and use appropriate rewards.

Minimizing Social Loafing

There are three major approaches for reducing the social loafing that characterizes newly formed groups. The first two approaches address social issues and are very closely tied to whether or not individual and group or team performance are assessed and rewarded (see Table 4.2). One of these approaches has to do with creating posi-

TABLE 4.2

Summary of Empirical Research on the Impact of Performance Measurement and Reward Systems

Measurement/Reward System Characteristics	Impact on Team Members' Behavior	Conclusions Based on Research by:
• Members' Individual Contributions are Measured	Increased individual effort	Kerr & Bruun (1981); Williams, Harkin, & Latane (1981)
• Members' Individual Contributions are Rewarded	More and better quality member contributions	Schnake (1991)
• Collaborative Behavior is Measured and Rewarded	More cooperation and higher team performance	Hackman (1990)
• Members Anticipate External Evaluation of Group Performance	More and better quality member contributions	Harkins & Jackson (1985)
• Reward System Promotes Shared Fates and Goals	Increased member commitment to team	Brandon & Pratt (1999)
• Rewards Based on Group Performance	Increased effectiveness of team member interaction	Ancona & Caldwell (1992)
• Team Members Held Accountable for Actions	More careful analysis in discussing alternatives	Tetlock (1985, 1992)

tive and negative consequences for the degree to which individual members behave responsibly toward their team. Research has shown, for example, that members' motivation to contribute to the success of their team can be increased in three different ways. One is promoting the perception that individual performance is indispensable to group success (Kerr & Bruun, 1983). Another is measuring individual performance on tasks that are related to the success of their team (Kerr & Bruun, 1981; Williams et al., 1981). A final way is by setting goals and ensuring that there are negative consequences for individual nonperformance (Schnake, 1991).

The other socially based approach that influences responsible member behavior has to do with group members' impressions about the consequences of their team's success or failure. For example, four studies have found a direct link between reward systems and group functioning. One found that groups need to be rewarded for group performance to encourage group functioning (Ancona & Caldwell, 1992). Another study (Brandon & Pratt, 1999) found that shared fates and goals are critical for developing group identity. Finally, Tetlock conducted two studies (1985, 1992) in which he found that, when decision-making groups are held accountable for their actions, they consider relevant information and decision alternatives more carefully.

Creating Conditions that Foster Group Self-Management

Two other studies have also identified conditions that are related to members' motivation to spend time and effort to ensure that their team is successful. One is whether or not members anticipate that their team's performance will be evaluated by someone external to the team (Harkins & Jackson, 1985). The other is whether or not members view themselves as being in a competitive situation. That is, will their performance be evaluated in relation to other comparable teams (Kravitz & Waller, 1980)?

Thus, even when tasks are clearly appropriate for learning groups, they are likely to fail unless the assessment–reward (grading) system encourages collaborative task behavior (Hackman, 1990). Overall, these empirical studies suggest four practices that are likely to encourage responsible member behavior. Two are related to what is being measured. The other two are related to what "counts" (what is rewarded—or not rewarded). Specifically, members are more likely to be motivated to ensure that their team is successful when: (1) individual contributions are measured, (2) individual contributions count, (3) team performance is measured (especially in relation to other teams), and (4) team performance counts.

Taken together, these studies suggest that an effective grading and performance evaluation system should include mechanisms for measuring and rewarding both individual preparation for team work and for assessing and rewarding team performance. Without this kind of accountability, one of two problems will almost certainly occur in learning groups. First, when individuals are not prepared to contribute to their group's task, other students are forced to carry their load. And second, when only one or two members prepare for group work, most group discussions degenerate into social events (Michaelsen & McCord, 2000).

The Importance of Timely Feedback

Feedback is essential to learning of any kind. Thus, creating an assessment–evaluation system that includes mechanisms for measuring and rewarding both individual members' contributions to their team and team performance is only the first step toward creating conditions that promote responsible member behavior and learning. In one sense, the performance-and-reward system is the theory, but performance feedback is the practice. Thus, the next step in promoting team development and responsible member behavior is ensuring that members receive performance feedback so that they can learn by experiencing the consequences of their choices.

A number of empirical studies have documented the importance of performance feedback for promoting high levels of member motivation (see Table 4.3). For example, probably the most widely accepted models for assessing a job's motivational potential is whether or not the person performing the job will have access to timely feedback on how well he or she is doing (Hackman & Oldham, 1976, 1980). In addition, a number of studies on goal setting have found that timely performance feedback powerfully affects member motivation by influencing their choice of future personal goals (Locke, Shaw, Saar, & Latham, 1981).

Performance feedback is also important to the development of the group. For example, Zander (1971) reviewed a number of studies on goal setting and found that timely performance feedback powerfully affects member motivation by influencing

TABLE 4.3
Summary of Empirical Research on the Impact of Performance Feedback

Performance Feedback System Characteristics	Impact on Team Members' Behavior	Conclusions Based on Research by:
• The Work Itself Enables Members to Track Their Own Performance	Higher Member Motivation, Effort and Contribution	Hackman & Oldham (1976)
• Members Are Aware How Well They Are Performing	Members will select difficult but achievable *personal* performance goals	Locke, Shaw, Saar, & Latham (1981)
• Members Are Aware How Well Their Group/Team is Performing	Members will select difficult but achievable *team* performance goals	Zander (1971)
• Members Have Ongoing Access to Performance Feedback	Increased understanding of how to contribute individually and how to work effectively as a group/team	McGrath (1984, 1991) McGrath & Gruenfeld (1993), Gersick (1989, 1988), Hackman (1990)
• Members Receive Performance Feedback by Being Rewarded	Increased effectiveness of team member interaction	Ancona & Caldwell (1992)

their choice of future group goals. Performance feedback also helps members develop a clear understanding of how both their individual efforts and the way in which members work together affect their group's effectiveness (e.g., Gersick, 1988, 1989; Hackman, 1990; McGrath, 1984, 1991; McGrath & Gruenfeld, 1993). Similarly, performance feedback in the form of group rewards promotes effective group functioning (Ancona & Caldwell, 1992).

Taken together, these studies suggest that timely performance feedback does much more than aid learning. It is particularly important in a learning-group setting because it has a powerful impact on team development in two different ways. First, timely performance feedback increases individual members' motivation to invest time and effort on behalf of their group or team. Second, timely performance feedback provides members with data that enables them to learn to work together more effectively.

SUMMARY AND CONCLUSIONS

At the beginning of this chapter we identified three hurdles that groups must overcome in order to develop into high performance teams: (1) bringing adequate knowledge and skill to bear on the task, (2) employing task performance strategies that are appropriate to the work and to the setting in which it is being performed, and (3) motivating members to exert sufficient effort to accomplish the task at an acceptable level of performance (Hackman, 1990). In reviewing empirical literature related to these hurdles, we have discussed several key issues that instructors must address as they contemplate using learning groups in their classes (see Table 4.4).

The first of the issues identified in the literature focuses on the composition of the groups and falls in the category of the first of the hurdles outlined above. Of greatest significance in this area are data concerning the optimal size and diversity for

TABLE 4.4
Research-Supported Prescriptions for Developing Highly Effective Learning Groups

How large and how diverse should the groups be?
- At least 5; preferably 6 or 7 members
- As diverse as the class membership will allow

How should the groups be formed?
- By the instructor and in a manner that assures:
  - Equal diversity and skills across groups
  - Perceived fairness of the member allocation process

How long should group membership remain stable?
- Permanently (within the limits of normal school terms)

What kinds of group tasks/assignments are most effective?
- Assignments based on Joint (not Independent) tasks to:
  - Ensure content-related give-and-take discussions
  - Provide a basis for peer teaching/learning
  - Promote group development
- Too difficult for individuals, but challenging for groups
- Based on issues of inherent interest to students

What kind of performance/reward systems should be used?
- Must include measures of and rewards for:
  - Individual member contributions to their group
  - Group performance (especially vs. other groups)

How important is timely performance feedback?
- Essential for the development of:
  - High member motivation
  - Effective group functioning

individual groups as well as the methods used for forming groups. Empirical research reported herein suggests that groups should have at least five and preferably six or seven members and should be as diverse as the class membership will allow (see Table 4.4). The goal is to have groups large and diverse enough to contain members with the knowledge and skill to successfully complete the group assignments, but small enough to develop into a cohesive working unit.

With respect to the issue regarding the formation of groups, the data show that the instructor, not the students, should take responsibility for forming groups. When the instructor is the one making the decisions, there is greater likelihood that student assets and liabilities will be more evenly dispersed among the groups. Also, if the instructor makes group assignments based on known criteria, and especially if the process takes place in a "public" setting, students are less likely to be concerned about one or more groups having an unfair advantage.

The issues discussed earlier in of this review are those related to the second of the three hurdles set forth by Hackman (1990), that is, developing processes that promote active member participation. The emphasis here is an examination of factors that encourage members to contribute actively to the work of the group. Our survey of the literature reveals two important practices that encourage active member participation. One is maintaining a stable membership in the groups or teams. The other is using tasks that require member interaction. Research shows that multiple benefits result from members engaging in open give-and-take discussion as they work together to complete group assignments. For example, as group members become better acquainted, they become more aware of each other's assets and liabilities and more aware of how to use those to the best advantage. They also learn to trust one another more, which results in a greater willingness to share salient information. The combination of these behaviors results in a heightened desire (by members) to achieve group goals. The data also show that because these processes occur over time as the group matures, they have a powerful positive impact on the development of cohesiveness among group members.

When we look back at the previous section, which examines the last of Hackman's (1990) hurdles, that is, motivating members to exert sufficient effort to accomplish the task at an acceptable level of performance, we find the research to be quite straightforward. In regard to the characteristics of effective reward and performance feedback systems, the empirically based small-groups literature strongly supports two key practices. First, instructors should use a grading system that includes *measurement* and *rewards* for both individual members' contributions to their group and for the performance of the group as a whole—especially in relation to comparable groups. Second, instructors should create conditions in which students have as much *immediate feedback* as possible on both individual members' contributions to their group and on group performance.

While the data do not reveal a specific recipe for guaranteed success with groups, the findings presented here provide a great deal of guidance for developing and using learning teams effectively. The research on developing high-performance teams highlights a number of specific practices that, if applied individually, are likely to provide incremental improvements in learning-group effectiveness. Further, these same practices, if followed in combination, will greatly increase the probability of developing truly high-performance learning teams.

REFERENCES

Amason, A. C. (1996). Distinguishing the effects of functional and dysfunctional conflict on strategic decision making: Resolving a paradox for top management teams. *Academy of Management Journal 39*(1): 123–149.

Amason, A. C., & Schweiger, D. M. (1994). Resolving the paradox of conflict, strategic decision making and organizational performance. *International Journal of Conflict Management 5:* 239–253.

Ancona, D. G., & Caldwell, D. F. (1992). Demography and design: Predictors of new product team performance. *Organization Science 3:* 321–341.

Argote, L., & McGrath, J. E. (1993). Group processes in organizations: Continuity and change. In *International Review of Industrial and Organization Psychology.* Ed. C. L. Cooper. & I. T. Robertson, Vol. 8: 333–389. Chichester, UK: Wiley.

Arrow, H., & McGrath, J. E. (1993). Membership matters: How member change and continuity affect small group structure, process and performance. *Small Group Research 24:* 334–361.

Bales, R. F. (1950). *Interaction process analysis: A method for the study of small groups.* Cambridge, MA: Addison-Wesley.

Bies, R. J., & Shapiro, D. L. (1988). Voice and justification: Their influence on procedural fairness judgments. *Academy of Management Journal 31*(3): 676–685.

Birmingham, C., & Michaelsen, L. K. (1999). Conflict resolution in decision making teams: A longitudinal study. *Proceedings Midwest Academy of Management.* Chicago.

Brandon, D., & Pratt, M. G. (1999). Managing the formation of virtual team categories and prototypes by managing information: A SIT/SCT perspective. *Academy of Management Proceedings* D1–D6.

Bray, R. M., Kerr, N. L., & Atkin, R. S. (1978). Effects of group size, problem difficulty, and sex on group performance and member reactions. *Journal of Personality and Social Psychology 36:* 1224–1240.

Brickner, M. A., Harkins, S. G., & Ostrom, T. M. (1986). Effects of personal involvement: Thought provoking implications for social loafing. *Journal of Personality and Social Psychology 51*(4): 763–770.

Chatman, J. A., & Flynn, F. J. (2001). The influence of heterogeneity on the emergence and consequences of norms in work teams. *The Academy of Management Journal 44*(5): 956–974.

Davis, J. H., Kerr, N. L., Atkin, R. S., Holt, R., & Meek, D. (1975). The decision processes of 6- and12-person mock juries assigned unanimous and two-thirds majority rules. *Journal of Personality and Social Psychology 32:* 1–14.

Eisenstat, R. A., & Cohen, S. G. (1990). Summary: Top management groups. In *Groups that work (and those that don't): Creating conditions for effective teamwork.* Ed. J. R. Hackman. San Francisco: Jossey-Bass.

Ellis, D. G., & Fisher, B. A. (1975). Phases of conflict in small group development: A Markov analysis. *Human Communication Research 1:* 195–212.

Evans, C. R., & Dion, K. L. (1991). Group cohesion and performance: A meta analysis. *Small Group Research 22*(2): 175–186.

Evans, J. R. (1988). Team selection. *Social Science Journal 25:* 93–104.

Frank, F., & Anderson, L. R. (1971). Effects of task and group size upon group productivity and member satisfaction. *Sociometry 34:* 135–149.

Gersick, C. J. G. (1989). Making time: Predictable transitions in task groups. *Academy of Management Journal 32*(2): 274–310.

———. (1988). Time and transition in work teams: Toward a new model of group development. *Academy of Management Journal 31:* 9–41.

Gersick, C. J. G., & Hackman, J. R. (1990). Habitual routines in task-performing groups. *Organizational Behavior and Human Decision Processes 47*(1): 65–98.

Greenburg, J., & Baron, R. A. (2000). *Behavior in organizations.* 7th ed. Upper Saddle River, NJ: Prentice-Hall.

Griffin, J. (1985). Some problems of fairness. *Ethics 96:* 100–118.

Gruenfeld, D., Mannix, E. A., Williams, K. Y., & Neale, M. A. (1996). Group composition and decision making: How member familiarity and information distribution affect process and performance. *Organizational Behavior and Human Decision Processes 67:* 1–15.

Gruenfeld, D. H., & Hollingshead, A. B. (1993). Sociocognition in work groups: The evolution of group integrative complexity and its relation to task performance. *Small Group Research 24*(3): 383–405.

Gulati, R. (1995). Does familiarity breed trust? The implications of repeated ties for contractual choice in alliances. *Academy of Management Journal 38*(1): 85–112.

Hackman, J. R., ed. (1990). *Groups that work (and those that don't).* San Francisco: Jossey-Bass.

Hackman, J. R., & Oldham, G. R. (1976). Motivation through the design of work: Test of a theory. *Organizational Behavior and Human Performance 16:* 250–279.

———. (1980). *Work redesign.* Reading, MA: Addison-Wesley.

Hambrick, D. C., Davison, S. C., Snell, S. A., & Snow, C. C. (1998). When groups consist of multiple nationalities: Towards a new understanding of the implications. *Organization Studies 19*(2): 181–205.

Harkins S. G., & Jackson, J. M. (1985). The role of evaluation in eliminating social loafing. *Personality and Social Psychology Bulletin 11*(4): 457–465.

Harkins, S. G., & Petty, M. M. (1982). Effects of task difficulty and task uniqueness on social loafing. *Journal of Personality and Social Psychology 52*(2): 1214–1229.

Harrison, D. A., Price, K. H., & Bell, M. (1998). Beyond relational demography: Time and effects of surface- and deep-level diversity on work group cohesion. *Academy of Management Journal 41*(1): 96–107.

Innami, Ichiro. (1994). The quality of group decisions, group verbal behavior, and intervention. *Organizational Behavior and Human Decision Processes 60*(3): 409–431.

Jarvenpaa, S. L., Knoll, K., & Leidner, D. E. (1998). Is anybody out there? Antecedents of trust in global virtual teams. *Journal of Management Information Systems 14*(4): 229–264.

Jehn, K. (1994). Enhancing effectiveness: An investigation of advantages and disadvantages of value-based intragroup conflict. *International Journal of Conflict Management 5:* 223–238.

———. (1995). A multimethod examination of the benefits and detriments of intragroup conflict. *Administrative Science Quarterly 40:* 256–282.

———. (1997). A qualitative analysis of conflict types and dimensions in organizational groups. *Administrative Science Quarterly 42:* 530–557.

Jehn, K. A. (2000). The influence of proportional and perceptual conflict composition on team performance. *International Journal of Conflict Management 11*(1): 56 –74.

Jehn, K. A., & Mannix, E. A. (2001). The dynamic nature of conflict: A longitudinal study of intragroup conflict and group performance. *Academy of Management Journal 44*(2): 238.

Johnson, D. W., Johnson, R. T., Johnson, J., & Anderson, D. (1976). Effects of cooperative versus individualized instruction on student prosocial behavior, attitudes toward learning and achievement. *Journal of Educational Psychology 68*(4): 446–452.

Johnson, D. W., Johnson R. T., & Scott L. (1978). The effects of cooperation and individualized instruction on student attitudes and achievement. *Journal of Social Psychology 104:* 207–216.

Kerr, N. L., & Bruun, S. E. (1983). The dispensability of member effort and group motivation losses: Free-rider effects. *Journal of Personality and Social Psychology 44:* 78–94.

———. (1981). Ringlemann revisited: Alternative explanations for the social loafing effects. *Personality and Social Psychology Bulletin 7*(2): 224–231.

Knoll, K., & Jarvenpaa, S. L. (1995). Learning virtual team collaboration. *Hawaii International Conference on System Sciences Conference Proceedings,* 92–101.

Kowitz, A. C., & Knutson, T. J. (1980). *Decision making in small groups: The search for alternatives.* Boston: Allyn & Bacon.

Kravitz, D. A., & Waller, J. E. (1980). Effects of task interest and competition on social loafing. Paper presented at meeting of Academy of Management, Anaheim, CA.

Langfred, M. S. C. (1998). The importance of organizational context, II: An empirical test of work group cohesiveness and effectiveness in two governmental bureaucracies. *Public Administration Quarterly 21*(4): 465–486.

Latane, B., Williams, K. D., & Harkins, S. G. (1979). Many hands make light the work: The causes and consequences of social loafing. *Journal of Personality and Social Psychology 37:* 822–832.

Lawler, E. E. (1988). Substitutes for hierarchy. *Organizational Dynamics 17:* 4–15.

Lazarowitz R., Sjaram., S., & Steinberg, R. (1980). Classroom learning style and cooperative behavior of elementary school children. *Journal of Educational Psychology 72:* 97–104.

Leana, C. R. (1985). A partial test of Janis' Groupthink model: Effects of group cohesiveness and leader behavior on defective decision making. *Journal of Management 11*(1): 5–18.

Levine, J. M., & Moreland, R. L. (1990). Progress in small group research. *Annual Review of Psychology.* Ed. M. R. Rosenzweig & L. W. Porter. Vol. 41:585–634. Palo Alto: Highwire Press.

Likert, R. (1961). *New patterns of management.* New York: McGraw–Hill.

Locke, E. A., Shaw, K., Saar, L. M., & Latham, G. P. (1981). Goal setting and task performance:1969–1980. *Psychological Bulletin 90:* 125–152.

McAllister, D. J. (1995). Affect- and cognition-based trust as foundations for interpersonal cooperation in organizations. *Academy of Management Journal 9:* 494–504.

McGrath, J. E. (1984). *Groups: Interaction and performance.* Englewood Cliffs, NJ: Prentice-Hall.

———. (1991). Time, interaction and performance (TIP): A theory of groups. *Small Group Research 22:* 147–174.

McGrath, J. E., Arrow, H., Gruenfeld, D. H., Hollingshead, A. B., & O'Connor, K. M. (1993). Groups, task and technology: The effects of experience and change. *Small Group Research 24:* 406–420.

McGrath, J. E., & Gruenfeld, D. H. (1993). Toward a dynamic and systemic theory of groups: An integration of six temporally enriched perspectives. *The future of leadership research: Promise and perspective.* Ed. M. M. Chemers & R. Ayman. Orlando, FL: Academic Press.

Michaelsen, L. K., & McCord, M. H. (2000). Cases and groups: A winning combination? *MBAR Journal 1*(1): 5–16.

Michaelsen, L. K., Watson, W. E., & Black, R. H. (1989). A realistic test of individual versus group consensus decision making. *Journal of Applied Psychology 74*(5): 834–839.

Moreland, R. L., & Levine, J. M. (1988). Group dynamics over time: Development and socialization in small groups. In *The Social Psychology of Time: New perspectives.* Ed. J. E. McGrath. Newbury Park, CA: Sage, 151–181.

O'Connor, K., Gruenfeld, D., & McGrath, J. E. (1993). The experience and effects of conflict in continuing workgroups. *Small Group Research 24:* 362–382.

Priem, R. L., & Price, K. H. (1991). Process and outcome expectations for the dialectical inquiry, devil's advocacy, and consensus techniques of strategic decision making. *Group and Organization Studies 16:* 206–225.

Ross, W., & LaCroix, J. (1996). Multiple meanings of trust in negotiation theory and research. *International Journal of Conflict Management 7*(4): 314–360.

Saunders, C. S. (2000). Virtual teams: Piecing together the puzzle. *Framing the domains of IT management: Projecting the future . . . through the past.* Ed. R. W. Zmud. Cincinnati, OH: Pinnaflex Educational Resources, 29–50.

Scheidel, T. M., & Crowell, L. (1979). *Discussing and decoding: A deskbook for group leaders and members.* New York: Macmillan.

Schnake, M. (1991). Equity in effort: The sucker effect in co-acting groups. *Journal of Management 71:* 41–55.

Seashore, S. E. (1954). *Group cohesiveness in the industrial work group.* Ann Arbor: University of Michigan Press.

Shaw, M. E. (1981). *Group dynamics: The psychology of small group behaviors.* 3d ed. New York: McGraw-Hill.

Simmons, T. L., & Peterson, R. (2000). Task conflict and relationship conflict in top management teams: The pivotal role of intragroup trust. *Journal of Applied Psychology 85:* 102–111.

Tetlock, P. E. (1985). Accountability: The neglected social context of judgment and choice. In *Research in Organizational Behavior.* Ed. B. M. Staw & L. L. Cummings. Greenwich, CT: JAI Press.

———. (1992). The impact of accountability on judgment and choice: Toward a social contingency model. *Advances in Experimental Social Psychology 25:* 331–376.

Tubbs, M. E. (1986). Goal setting: A meta-analytic examination of the empirical evidence. *Journal of Applied Psychology 73*(3): 474–483.

Watson, W. E., Kumar, K., & Michaelsen, L. K. (1993). Cultural diversity's impact on group process and performance: Comparing homogeneous and culturally diverse task groups. *Academy of Management Journal 36*(3): 590–602.

Watson, W. E., Michaelsen, L. K., & Sharp, W. (1991). Member competence, group interaction, and group decision-making: A longitudinal study. *Journal of Applied Psychology 76*(6): 803–810.

Williams, K., Harkins, S., & Latane, B. (1981). Identifiability as a deterrent to social loafing: Two cheering experiments. *Journal of Personality and Social Psychology 40:* 303–311.

Williams, K. Y., & O'Reilly, C. A. (1998). Forty years of diversity research: A review. In *Research in Organizational Behavior.* Ed. B. M. Staw & L. L. Cummings. Vol. 20:33–140. Greenwich, CT: JAI Press.

Zalkind, S. S., & Costello, T. W. (1962). Perceptions: Some recent research and implications for administration. *Administrative Science Quarterly 9:* 218–235.

Zander, A. (1971). *Motives and goals in groups.* New York: Academic Press.

Ziller, R. C. (1957). Group size: A determinant of the quality and stability of group decisions. *Sociometry 20:* 165–173.

PART II

The Voices of Experience

One of the goals of writing this book is to demonstrate the versatility, power, and practicality of team-based learning. To show these characteristics, we have included ten chapters in this section of the book that we call "The Voices of Experience." These are chapters written by college teachers who have used team-based learning in a wide variety of situations.

During the past twenty years, Michaelsen and his colleagues have shared their experiences and insights on team-based learning in more than twenty-five journal articles. Michaelsen himself has conducted over 200 workshops at professional meetings and at institutions of higher education on five continents. As a result, we had literally hundreds of potential contributors and the most difficult part of putting together this section of the book was deciding which voices to include in the project and how those contributions should be framed.

Eventually we settled on a strategy of inviting a diverse set of contributors but asking each of them to respond to the same general set of writing guidelines. Consequently, this section on the Voices of Experience includes several kinds of diversity. Of course, there are representatives from many disciplines. In addition, there are teachers who have different levels of experience, from individuals with only a few years of teaching experience to people in the twilight of their career. The selection also includes multiple levels of expertise, from people who were desperate [at the time] for "anything that will work" to teachers who have won teaching awards based on their skills as lecturers. Our selection also includes teaching in a wide variety of class sizes, with different types of students, and in a range of cultural settings.

In each case, contributors were asked to include information on: (1) the context in which they were using team-based learning, (2) the specific teaching approach they used before team-based learning, (3) the reason they decided to try team-based learning, (4) what they did with team-based learning (e.g., including at least one example of a question, problem, or activity they gave to students to work on), and (5) what outcomes team-based learning produced for their students and for themselves.

All in all, we (the editors) were very impressed by the amazing set of ideas and stories they produced. Although each voice is unique in many ways, the overwhelming conclusion one receives from their experiences—taken as a whole—is that team-based learning will work in a wide variety of teaching situations, promotes powerful forms of student learning, and is truly a transforming way of teaching.

Nonetheless a reader might still ask: Why should I read a chapter about teaching that is in a discipline quite different from my own? If I teach accounting, for example, why should I read about how someone teaches chemistry or human relations?

We are quite confident that readers will find that these chapters all have a value that speaks well beyond the particular subject matter involved. If readers approach the chapters in Part II with an open and inquiring mind, they will almost certainly feel the excitement that the teacher and the students felt as a result of this kind of engagement with the material; they will be able to see the results of team-based learning implemented properly in multiple settings; and they will develop a fuller understanding of the principles necessary to make team-based learning work effectively in almost any setting.

CHAPTER 5

An Alternative to Lecturing in the Sciences

Frank J. Dinan

Despite winning several teaching awards as an outstanding lecturer, Dinan was concerned about continuing problems with poor student performance in his chemistry classes. After attending a workshop and learning about team-based learning, he decided to give it a try. He found the results extremely satisfying: nearly perfect attendance, students coming to class well prepared, a significant reduction in the withdrawal and failure rate, an ability to cover more content, and significantly higher student performance on the final exam.

I first became aware of team-based learning during the summer of 1993 when I attended a case studies workshop conducted by Clyde (Kipp) Herreid. My goal was to learn about the case method of teaching, but I was totally unaware of team-based learning. Late in the workshop, we were told that on the following day we would be doing some work on an active-learning technique called team-based learning, and were given material to be read in preparation for that class. The assigned reading was one of Larry Michaelsen's publications describing the workings of team-based learning, and we were informed that we would have a reading quiz the following morning. So, although I had other plans for that evening, I reluctantly but dutifully read the paper to prepare for the quiz.

In class the following morning we formed groups and set out to answer the questions that Kipp had devised to test our knowledge of team-based learning. I greatly enjoyed working with my team and discussing the details of the method with them. I recall sitting in the workshop reflecting on how engrossing the team work had proven to be, and how the method had caused me to take time to read and prepare for today's class despite my other commitments. It was at that point that it occurred to me that team-based learning could potentially revolutionize the way I taught organic chemistry. My experiences that day led me to see that team-based learning had the potential to deal with many of the problems that today's students encounter in physical science courses taught by the lecture method.

At that time I had taught organic chemistry for twenty-five years at Canisius College. I had won a number of teaching awards, and was generally thought of as a successful teacher. In recent years, however, I had sensed a definite decline in the effectiveness of the lecture method in my courses. Student attendance was not as consistently high as it had been, and, despite my best efforts at "clarifying" the material presented in my lectures, the results on examinations were often disappointing to me. Combined student withdrawal and failure rates were also higher than I found acceptable, about 15 to 20 percent. My response to this situation was to work harder and harder at making my lectures clearer and more entertaining, but nothing that I did seemed to have any positive effect. Although my student evaluations remained good, I suspected that the evaluations may have become a better measure of the effort that I put into making my lectures entertaining than to their effectiveness in teaching organic chemistry. My colleagues' frequent complaints about "today's students" and the disappointingly high student withdrawal and failure rates that characterized their courses indicated that I was not alone in these perceptions.

My misgivings with the traditional lecture method were further enhanced upon reading Sheila Tobias' article, "They're Not Dumb, They're Different" (1990). Tobias documented the disaffection that many capable students feel with the passive role that the lecture method imposes on them in introductory physical science courses. Her work demonstrated that many intelligent students taking lecture-based physical science courses compare their experiences in these courses unfavorably to the more interactive teaching methods frequently used in the social sciences and liberal arts. This comparison, Tobias demonstrated, leads many of these students to desert the physical sciences in large numbers. Because the attrition rate for students majoring in the physical sciences, both at Canisius College and nationally, is very high, Tobias's findings forcefully caught my attention.

At about this same time, the results obtained in a study conducted at Arizona State University (Birk & Foster, 1993), also strongly predisposed me to consider alternative teaching methodologies. This extensive study was carried out over several years, and concentrated on evaluating the effectiveness of the lecture format in teaching chemistry courses. Among the main conclusions drawn were these: (1) the degree of learning that occurs in a chemistry course taught by the lecture method is independent of the lecturer, and (2) attendance at lectures had only a marginal effect on a student's performance in the course.

Together, these findings further undermined my confidence in the adequacy of lecture as an effective teaching method in the natural sciences, and prompted my interest in team-based learning as a potentially more effective teaching methodology. The basic elements of team-based learning seemed well suited to the teaching of chemistry, and I set out to tailor the method to meet the specific needs of my organic chemistry course.

Modifications had to be made to fit team-based learning to the specific demands of teaching organic chemistry, and to fit the situation that exists at Canisius College. Organic classes at Canisius range in size from forty to sixty students, and meet four times per week. Three of these classes are fifty minutes long and are termed lecture periods. The fourth class, a recitation period, is seventy-five minutes long and is used to review problems assigned during the previous several classes. The students taking organic chemistry are mainly sophomores majoring in the physical sciences, usually chemistry, biochemistry, or biology. For the most part, they are bright, highly motivated young people who plan to pursue graduate training in either the physical sciences or some area of the health sciences.

When teaching organic chemistry, it is traditional to rely heavily on the text as a primary information source. Our students are normally urged to read the text carefully, but of course, many do not do so. Often this is true because the professor, during his or her lecture presentation, spends the class time attempting to organize and clarify the text's information for the students. Thus, students who have read the text may find the lecture dull and repetitive, and those who have not done the reading often have difficulty following the condensed lecture's content. So, with these thoughts in mind, I set out to modify Michaelsen's basic team-based learning method to suit it to teaching organic chemistry.

The modified team-based learning method that resulted focuses on the efficient use of small groups in the teaching of high-content subjects, such as organic chemistry and general chemistry, that are typical of the physical sciences. This method utilizes many of the elements of the team-based learning method that Michaelsen originally developed, and the highlights of its operation are described below.

On the first day of class, I announce the composition of the four- or five-person permanent teams in which the students will work for the remainder of the semester. The goal that I seek in structuring the teams is to obtain the maximum possible diversity within the teams in terms of race, gender, and academic ability. To accomplish this, I use student academic performance data, principally grades obtained in previous chemistry courses, to assure that each group will have a wide distribution of academic abilities. My experience indicates that this is a highly effective manner by which to form teams. The variation in race, gender, and academic ability is intended to reflect the experiences that await the students when they enter today's "real world" and to help them to learn to deal with the wide range of people, personalities and abilities that they will surely encounter in that world.

While the newly formed teams are carrying out some get-acquainted exercises— for example, sharing common work experiences, places they have visited, favorite foods, and so on—a photo is taken of each team. The students write their names under their pictures, and indicate what they prefer to be called in class. This allows the instructor to correlate student names and faces very quickly, and facilitates a congenial class atmosphere. The team photos are also circulated throughout the class and posted so that the students can quickly learn each other's names. Additionally, each team is asked to decide on a team name, one that they feel represents some aspect of their collective personalities. These exercises are helpful in building an open, friendly classroom atmosphere, which I have found greatly minimizes student anxiety. Anxiety levels can often be very high at the beginning of any new course, and our experience indicates this can be a debilitating problem for many beginning chemistry students.

On the second day of class, I describe the grading system to be used in the course. I stress that the team-based learning system is designed to reward both individual and group achievement. Working in their groups, the class then decides, within limits set by the instructor, the relative weights they wish to assign to the three components of the grading scheme: group, individual, and peer evaluation grades. The allowed limits are such that the individual component of the grading scheme represents at least three-quarters of each student's grade. This process has proven to be a very effective team-building exercise, and one that shows the students that they have a voice in the equity of the course's operation.

The text used in a chemistry course taught by team-based learning must be clearly written and readable by the students with only occasional assistance. Fortunately, several high-quality organic chemistry texts are available that meet these criteria. I am currently using Solomons and Fryhle's *Organic Chemistry*, 7th Edition (1998). The text is divided into segments that can be covered in one class; normally, this is about one-third of a text chapter. A learning guide is then prepared for each of these single-class segments. The guide specifies exactly how the students are to prepare for a class; it lists the text material to be read, that which is to be omitted, and the specific problems to be done in preparation for the next class. It may also include brief comments about the relative importance of the assigned materials and some of the instructor's tips on dealing with the material in an effective manner. The learning guide for a class is normally distributed to the students at least two days before the class meets.

Each class meeting, except for the recitation classes, is a team-based learning class. The class begins with a reading quiz that is focused on several aspects of the text's content that have been specified in the learning guide. A reading quiz generally consists of three short-answer or multiple-choice questions. It is printed in large, boldface type and is projected for viewing using an overhead projector. Student answers to the reading quizzes may be entered and graded using Scantron sheets or other forms designed for this purpose. Approximately thirty reading quizzes are given over the course of a semester, and the percentage score obtained by each student on these quizzes is counted as one of four hourly examination grades. The entire reading quiz procedure generally consumes less than five minutes of class time.

I have always had an undergraduate student assistant in my organic chemistry team-based learning classes. In recent years this has been a student who has completed this course within the past year or two, one whom I judge has the proper combination of knowledge and personality to help me in my work with the teams. The student assistant grades the collected reading quiz responses while I am reviewing the reading quiz and its answers for the class. Every student assistant that I have had so far has gone on to graduate school in chemistry, and has done an outstanding job on his or her preliminary examinations in organic chemistry. This is an unanticipated, but real, benefit of our team-based learning method.

I have found that the combined use of reading quizzes and learning guides results in virtually every student arriving in class well prepared. At the suggestion of one of my colleagues, I now allow my students to use the notes that they have prepared while reading the material prescribed in the learning guide during the reading quiz. This practice results in the students taking extensive, careful notes while they are reading the assigned text material. The small investment of time that is required to give reading quizzes greatly leverages the available class time by assuring and rewarding good student preparation for class.

Upon completion of the reading quiz, each of the teams is given a problem set based on the learning guide for that class. A typical problem set, which I call a "ChemDo," consists of three or four problems dealing with the more difficult or problematic material assigned in the learning guide for that class. Although the problems are designed to be challenging for the teams, care must be taken to insure that they are not overwhelmingly difficult. The problems in a ChemDo are also designed to increase in difficulty as the students move through them. For example, a ChemDo might begin by asking the teams to clarify and explain some of the major concepts dealt with in the learning guide. The next question might require applications of these concepts to specific problems, and the ChemDo might conclude with a problem that requires the teams to integrate the material in the current learning guide with previously covered course material. A specific example of ChemDo design follows.

One of the ChemDos that is used in my organic course deals with the concept of aromaticity. It begins by asking the teams to clearly explain and define the meaning of the terms "aromatic," "nonaromatic," and "anti-aromatic." The ChemDo next asks the teams to illustrate how these concepts apply to specific molecules. To do this, the teams are required to use the polygon-and-circle method to determine the number and relative energies of the molecular orbital present in these molecules, and to show how electrons are distributed in each of the molecules. They must then use this information to decide whether each of the example molecules is aromatic, nonaromatic, or anti-aromatic.

At the end of class, each team submits one copy of the ChemDo completed that day for grading. To keep my work at a manageable level, I arbitrarily select only one of the (usually) three ChemDo questions for grading. ChemDos are graded on a one-to-four scale, and the resulting grade is awarded to all of those members of the submitting team that were present in class that day. Note that on missing a class, students must not only explain their absence to their team members, but they also miss the course points that can be gained from the day's reading quiz and ChemDo.

Any ChemDo question or its answer can be challenged by a team if the members feel that they have a sound basis for doing so. A question can be challenged as not being appropriate for the day's learning guide, and any one of my answers to the ChemDo questions can be successfully challenged if the team can support its challenge with a specific reference from the text. The team that has initiated a successful challenge is automatically awarded the maximum grade of four for the ChemDo, plus a bonus point. This practice prompts the students to closely scrutinize each ChemDo's content and the answers that I have given.

Three one-hour examinations are given in each semester of the course. These examinations are taken by individuals first, and then by the teams. To insure individual accountability, individual examination scores are weighted more heavily than are group scores, usually by a ratio of four or five to one. Answers to the examination questions are also subject to the challenge process described earlier.

The combination of daily reading quizzes which, in total, count as an hour examination, and peer pressure to be present to support the team's ChemDo efforts in class, result in nearly perfect attendance. This is a remarkable improvement over the attendance rate that was characteristic of my pre-team-based learning classes when absence rates of ten to fifteen percent were common.

Our experience clearly shows that once a team-based learning class is underway, the teams motivate attendance and preparation for class, and afford learning support to their members. The resulting positive atmosphere builds student connectivity and tends to minimize feelings of alienation and marginality. This may be the single factor that is most responsible for the low attrition rates that characterize these classes. Team-based learning students also quickly come to recognize how important good communication skills and interpersonal relationships are to their success. Most students tend to improve their skills in these areas throughout the course.

Our six years of team-based learning teaching has shown that this method can be very rewarding for the instructor as well. It is a joy to watch as students come to class regularly, arrive on time (usually early), and generally behave as professionals who are responsible for their own learning. Discussions within the learning teams are a pleasure to hear; they quickly focus on the material specified in the learning guide for that class, and are conducted at a high level of intensity. It is very satisfying to watch as a student support community grows and strengthens as the course progresses.

However, even given all of these positive features of our application of team-based learning, the method would be of no real value unless it resulted in effective instruction in the discipline. This aspect of the method has been carefully investigated. Our evaluation of the effectiveness of team-based learning in organic and general chemistry is based on six years of experience with the method, and encompasses both its cognitive and affective dimensions. Some of the conclusions that we have reached are described below.

Quantitative evaluations of our students' attitudes toward their team-based learning experience over a six-year period have afforded the following results:

- 95% of students feel that team-based learning builds better relationships among students than does the lecture method.
- 83% of students feel that team-based learning is a better way to learn organic chemistry than is the lecture method.
- 78% of students feel that team-based learning requires more consistent work than does the lecture method.
- 90% of students feel responsible to prepare for each class as well as possible.

- 93% of students feel responsible to their teams to be present in class everyday.
- Only 16% of students report that they learn chemistry better with the lecture method than they do with team-based learning.

The coverage of content is always a concern in chemistry courses because many of our students will take national qualifying examinations for graduate and professional schools. These examinations assume that the students taking them have been exposed to a wide range of content. Our experience with this team-based learning method has demonstrated that about ten to fifteen percent more course material can be covered using team-based learning than is feasible using the lecture method. It is frequently a problem for an instructor using the lecture method to keep up with another using team-based learning. This, I believe, results from the more thorough preparation for class that team-based learning requires of its students.

A major concern about the effectiveness of team-based learning is how well students learn organic chemistry when using this method. To investigate this question, results obtained on common, objective final examinations taken by both team-based learning and lecture students have been compared. These studies showed that the team-based learning classes consistently obtain statistically significant higher mean and average grades than do the lecture students. Over a period of five years, the team-based learning student performance on comprehensive, objective final examinations has averaged about five percent higher than that of the lecture students. These data are significant at the 95 percent confidence level.

One last consideration favoring team-based learning over the lecture method is student retention. Here, we have found team-based learning to be far superior to lecture. Combined student withdrawal and failure rates due to all causes over the two semesters of organic chemistry lecture courses at Canisius College historically run about 17 percent. The average combined withdrawal and failure rate in team-based learning organic chemistry classes taught over the past six years is less than 5 percent, and in one year was actually zero.

To put the academic performance of team-based learning students versus lecture students on common final examinations in better perspective, the difference in retention rates between lecture and team-based learning classes should be considered. In the latter, due to the higher student retention rates described, students who would have long since withdrawn from a lecture class generally finish the team-based learning class. Therefore, they take the final examination. So team-based learning student performances on the final examinations are actually more impressive than they seem at first glance because many of the academically weaker students in the team-based learning classes do take that examination, while those students often withdraw from lecture classes before taking the final examination. Without this effect, it is reasonable to assume that the difference in performance between team-based learning and lecture classes would be even greater.

I should note that, although I do not normally teach general chemistry, a freshman course, I did do so once four years ago to check the effectiveness of our modified team-based learning method in that introductory level course. The results that I obtained were closely comparable to those that I have described here for the organic chemistry course. A number of the students, now seniors, who were present in that general chemistry class often comment favorably on their experiences in that course whenever we meet. They recall with special fondness the closeness and friendships that developed during that course that still survive today.

In summary, team-based learning is an effective method for teaching introductory level chemistry courses. It is involving, active, effective, and leads to higher student success rates than does the lecture method. It is also highly rewarding to the instructor. The student–instructor relationship is altered remarkably for the better. Instead of functioning as a lecturer and evaluator of the student's learning, the instructor becomes a coach who is part of a team that is there to help smooth out the rough parts on the road leading to their success. This change in role is frequently noted in comments made on student course evaluations, where satisfaction rates consistently run above the 90-percent level.

Based on the experience that we have gained over the past seven years, it seems evident that suitably modified team-based learning courses could also be used very effectively in other introductory-level science and mathematics courses. Student evaluations of their team-based learning chemistry classes strongly indicate they would like to use team-based learning in other science and mathematics courses.

REFERENCES

Birk, J. P., & Foster, J. (1993). The importance of lecture in general chemistry course performance. *Journal of Chemical Education 70:* 180–182.

Solomons, T. W., & Fryhle, C. B. (1998). *Organic chemistry.* 7th ed. New York: John Wiley & Sons.

Tobias, S. (1990). They're not dumb. They're different: A new "tier of talent" for science. *Change 22*(4): 11–30.

CHAPTER 6

Using Case Studies in Science—And Still "Covering the Content"

Clyde Freeman Herreid

Many professors worry about shifting to small groups and other forms of active learning because of a fear they will not be able to cover as much content. Herreid used case studies with team-based learning and found his students learned as much or more, and comments on why this was so.

In the summer of 1992, I was invited to come to Vanderbilt University and give a lecture on the art of teaching. They were having a faculty colloquium, an annual event hosted by their Office of Teaching Effectiveness. They had invited me to lecture on how to lecture. I entitled my talk "The Ten Commandments." I am sure they thought they were getting something divinely inspired. Not willing to dissuade them of their fantasy, I went calling.

I gave my presentation to a large and generous audience. Not long afterward, I found myself seated at lunch with another presenter who was scheduled to speak in the afternoon on something called "team-based learning." In our brief exchange I found out that Larry Michaelsen had given up lecturing and was enthralled with a new method of presenting material that was a cross between collaborative learning and mastery teaching. He did not attend my lecture; I suppose it would have been antithetical to his newfound wisdom.

For years I had been looking for alternative forms of teaching, reasoning that I had exhausted the nuances of the lecture method and was ready to move on. I was mid-career and still found many students failing my classes. They complimented me on my presentations, yet there was always an eternal stream of students coming to office hours complaining that they did not understand why they could not absorb the material and perform better on the tests. They looked like intelligent students; they sounded like intelligent students; they said everything was clear to them when they heard the lecture; and yet, they were failing. Indeed, what was the problem? Could it be the lecture method itself?

Team-based learning sounded as if it might be the antidote. I attended the afternoon session and I felt as though the scales had fallen from my eyes. I rushed home to Buffalo determined to try out the method immediately. I had a course called "Scientific Inquiry" that was scheduled to begin in a few weeks; its purpose was to show nonscientists how science really works. The course was a new addition to our State University of New York at Buffalo curriculum and was required for general education credit. The basis for the course was Case Method Teaching. I had never tried using case studies before but had become convinced by Bill Welty of Pace University that this style of instruction might be a solution to my dissatisfaction with lecturing. When I heard of team-based learning it seemed that I could combine the two methods into a perfect medley.

At this same time, my son was teaching a course in informal logic for the first time as a graduate student in the Department of Philosophy at Buffalo and he also became enthused about team-based learning when he heard of my trip to Vanderbilt. He decided to use the method in his course. Our experiences turned out to be radically different. Although my course went smoothly one week after the other, he had problem after problem using team-based learning. Students continually challenged him in the use of this novel method.

What was the difference between us? I will return to this topic at the end of the chapter, but for the moment let me turn to what I have learned over the past seven years about using the method in science courses, especially in my field of biology. Let us begin by taking a look at one of my initial concerns: "Could I possibly cover all of the content?" Then we'll move on to examples in which I have successfully used team-based learning, how students responded to this method, and how I am now living happily ever after.

CONCERNS ABOUT COVERING THE CONTENT

A couple of years ago I wrote an article entitled "Why isn't cooperative learning used to teach science?" (Herreid, 1998). I listed at least a dozen barriers that faculty, students, and administrators need to surmount if the method is to be successful. None are unique to the sciences, but the problem that most science faculty cite as their biggest stumbling block is the question of content. They argue that cooperative methods always slow down the process of learning. They say they cannot cover as much material: "It's all right for the people in the humanities or social sciences to do it, but we can't afford to cut back on the content. We have other courses that follow this one that depend upon this knowledge and we have national standards to meet."

There is some truth to this claim for some styles of cooperative learning, such as Problem-Based Learning (PBL). Not as much subject matter can be covered, but the learning is much deeper. What good is it if a faculty member covers the material and the students do not remember it?

More to the point, team-based learning is an exception because it does permit the coverage of the same amount of material as a normal lecture course. I have no difficulty covering exactly the same subjects to the same extent in my summer team-based learning class as during the fall lecture course. And I have the added luxury of teaching several wonderful evolution cases. It is significant to note that Frank Dinan, writing in his section of this book, and in an earlier paper (Dinan & Frydrychowski, 1995), reports that he has been able to cover even more material using team-based learning in his chemistry courses than when he used the traditional lecture method— and students received higher grades. So team-based learning is ideal for the sciences in which content is the issue.

EXAMPLES OF WHERE I CURRENTLY USE TEAM-BASED LEARNING

I use team-based learning whenever I have a small class. This means that I use it to teach my evolutionary biology course in the summer when I have only two dozen students. This is a course designed for freshmen, although many upper-division students take it as well. There is no occasion for me to use this method during the normal fall semester, when I teach this course to 500 students in a fixed-seat amphitheater. The best I can do in that situation is to do some interactive lecturing. The other setting in which I use team-based learning regularly is in honors seminars, in which, again, I teach about two dozen students.

The largest courses in which I have used team-based learning were an honors colloquium with 100 students, and a scientific inquiry course for seventy students. I found the latter two experiences workable but frustrating because I could not deal well with the application part of the method, when I give out case studies or problems for the groups to solve. I simply cannot be everywhere to ask questions and probe for answers. Similarly, people using problem-based learning, in which permanent teams are established, also find they cannot keep track of the group work during their case teaching without the use of tutors as a central part of each of the teams. Yet, I hasten to add that I have heard of instructors who have successfully used team-based learning in classes with up to 280 students. However, it is essential in larger classes that the application phase of team-based learning be especially well designed so that students cannot simply divide up the work load. The assignment must require that students work cooperatively to complete the tasks.

WHAT KINDS OF PROJECTS DO I ASSIGN IN
TEAM-BASED LEARNING?

Typically, the assignments I use in team-based learning are case studies. I have published many of these in *The Journal of College Science Teaching* as well as on the

Web page for our National Center for Case Study Teaching in Science, supported by the National Science Foundation and the Pew Charitable Trusts: http://ublib. buffalo.edu/libraries/projects/cases/case.html.

Most of my cases extend for several class periods. Part of the case is presented on each day and the students are provided time between classes to look up material in the literature or on the Internet. When they reconvene, they pool their resources, try to solve problems, and are given another piece of the case. This follows the classic PBL strategy. For example, in my evolutionary biology course, I have one case that deals with the discovery of the first fossil bird, *Archaeopteryx*, and the evolution of flight. Other cases deal with the importance of the Galapagos Islands in the process of speciation, the possibility of life on Mars, and human evolution. All of these cases are on our website, along with detailed teaching notes explaining exactly how I handle them in the classroom.

To give you a flavor of these cases and how they fit into a course structure, let me walk you through the Galapagos case. I teach this about halfway through the summer course in evolutionary biology, in which class periods are two-and-a-half hours long. There is a reading assignment in the textbook for each day. I start each class briefly answering any questions from the students about the reading material. This is followed by the usual team-based learning Readiness Assessment Test (RAT), grading with a Scantron, and written appeals to ensure that students are familiar with key concepts. Then we take a brief break (after all, the classes are long). When the students return, it is on to the case.

The Galapagos case takes up part of four class periods; that is a lot of time, but it is worth it because of its importance in covering many of the principles of evolution. On day 1, I give out the first part of the case, which involves a graduate student named "Kate," who is considering what her research topic should be and musing on the history of the islands. There are many questions embedded in the piece that must be answered by the groups. Following the typical problem-based learning model, the students identify the learning issues and then subdivide the work so that when they leave class they know what to search for.

On day two, after the RAT exercise, the students share information with their team members. As a group, they must turn in a written set of answers to key questions about the formation and colonization of the islands by the flora and fauna. They are then given the second part of the case, which involves "Kate" talking to the director of the Darwin Research Station as he tells her about speciation problems. Again, the students ferret out the learning issues, subdivide the workload and leave class to search for the answers to their questions.

On day three, after they have shared their information and answered the key questions, they get part three of the case and read it. Here is a new wrinkle based on a real incident: Kate is caught in a crisis. Sea cucumber fishermen who have had a running argument with the government of Ecuador have taken over the Darwin Research Station and are holding scientists hostage along with a lab colony of endangered Galapagos tortoises. Now the students are told that each group must take on the role of one of the stakeholders in the controversy: fishermen, tourists, scientists, store owners, conservationists, and Ecuadorian politicians. Each group must outline its demands and develop a negotiating position on how to deal with the question of accessibility to the unique islands.

On day four, I give the groups thirty minutes to clarify their positions. Then I form negotiating teams, splitting up the group members. Each negotiating team has a politician in charge and includes a fisherman, store owner, scientist, and conservationist. The groups are all charged to draft a compromise policy statement that would form the basis for a law governing the islands; each member must be faithful to his own constituency yet must be committed to devising an equitable settlement. The policy document must be outlined by the end of the period and the politician must write it out in detail for the next class. The other members of the group individually must write out an analysis of Kate's research options in light of the crisis, which jeopardizes her thesis work.

Turning to another course, scientific inquiry, in which the purpose of the class is to have students understand how scientists really go about their work, human foibles and all, I follow the usual team-based learning approach with RATs, and so on. Again, I use cases involving contentious issues such as DNA fingerprinting, AIDS, and the Tuskegee syphilis experiments. But first, so that students understand the background of the scientific enterprise, I have them read an essay on the ethics and canons of science developed by the National Academy of Sciences entitled "On Being A Scientist." After a RAT on the reading, I give them their first application exercise. I ask the teams to develop a list of "commandments" describing what is appropriate and inappropriate behavior on the part of scientists. In thirty minutes they must develop at least thirty statements that begin with either "Thou shalt" or "Thou shalt not." For example, "Thou shalt repeat experiments," and "Thou shalt not plagiarize." The purpose of the list, which they hand in for my evaluation and criticism, is to solidify in their minds what ethical standards scientists must meet daily in their work. Then, to show how the scientific enterprise really functions, I have them read reports and articles about the cold fusion affair for the next class period. On the basis of the reading, in the ensuing class the groups must evaluate the problematic behavior of the scientists who claimed that they had discovered cold fusion. I have the teams rank on a scale of 1 to 10 how Professors Pons and Fleishman lived up to each of the standards of science the students had previously described in their commandments. Teams finish the evaluation with a brief written summary of their overall assessment of the scientists' behavior.

Another very effective application approach that I have used has been to have students develop lesson plans for kindergarten through twelfth-grade students. This is the requirement that I made for students taking my "Science and the Paranormal" course. The purpose of this course is to develop critical thinking skills in students by asking them to analyze extraordinary scientific and pseudoscientific claims. Student teams had to examine one paranormal phenomenon such as pyramid power, ghosts, hypnotism, and so forth. They had to research it and develop a lesson plan with activities for a K–12 classroom with the purpose of sharpening these students' critical thinking skills. Teams had to give an oral report to the class on their subject, turn in a written lesson plan, teach it to a K–12 class, prepare a poster for display in the library, and develop a website for a national skeptics' organization, the Committee for the

Scientific Investigation of Claims of the Paranormal. By the time the teams had finished the project, they had an excellent grasp of the nature of "evidence" for various paranormal claims. They also had developed a healthy skepticism of the media and learned one of the fundamental tenets of science: "Extraordinary claims require extraordinary proof." Just as importantly, they produced work that could be used by instructors in classrooms across the country.

GRADES AND PEER EVALUATIONS

I think peer evaluations are essential if we expect students to take group work seriously. Many students have worked in groups somewhere along the line, and frequently have had an awful experience. This is especially true for good students. The use of peer evaluations not only serves as an encouragement for all students to contribute their fair share, but can serve as a remedy for any misbehaving team members. The good students will get their just reward for the extra work they put in and the laggards will get their just desserts.

In setting up my grading schemes, I have found that individual scores should be worth about 75 percent of the grade and group work 25 percent. I have experimented with other strategies, such as permitting the students to collectively decide at the beginning of the course to set the grade proportions for the semester, but I have found that grade inflation sets in because group grades are typically higher than individual scores. A way to compensate for this is to shift the grading curve upward because the conventional 90 percent-equals-an-"A" is no longer appropriate. However, I have found that such an upward curve shift causes more dissension than it is worth. I solve the problem by a 75 percent-to-25 percent split, which keeps the grades more in line with expectations.

I use peer evaluations as a modifier of the group work score. Each student must evaluate his team mates anonymously using a numerical scale at the end of the course. If there are, say, five individuals in a group, they each have forty points to distribute to their team mates. In a group that is functioning perfectly, each person should receive an average score of ten points. Any student receiving an average of ten will receive all the points his team has earned for group work. On the other hand, if he receives an eight, he will receive only 80 percent of the group score. I have also set a lower limit on the peer evaluation score that a student can obtain. That is, if a student receives less than an average of seven from his teammates, I will fail him regardless of his individual or group score. I give them fair warning of this rule in the syllabus. Originally, I devised this scheme because our school has a regulation that allows students to take some of their courses on a pass-or-fail basis. Students choosing this option invariably did not contribute to their groups, expecting to slide by with a pass and crippling their groups in the process. I created the rule to stop this behavior. I have continued using this grading rule even in courses in which the pass-or-fail option does not exist, because it prevents any student from coasting through the course satisfied with a "C" or "D" effort. This strategy has almost always stopped lazy behavior.

WHAT KINDS OF RESPONSES DO STUDENTS HAVE TO TEAM-BASED LEARNING?

Whenever I have done evaluations of team-based learning and other cooperative strategies in which we set up permanent groups, invariably students say the thing they liked best about the class was working in groups. Most even enjoyed taking examinations with one another. Clearly, however, whenever people are thrown together, it takes time to adjust. Groups pass through a series of stages that have been described as "forming, storming, norming and performing." I believe that it takes at least a third to a half of a semester before students are comfortable with the method.

The use of peer evaluations tends to make them work harder at getting along. I always have the groups do a practice peer evaluation about a third of the way into the semester. By this time the groups have been together long enough for any interpersonal problems that exist to be evident. I have them turn in their practice peer evaluations to me and I tally the individual scores. At the next class period I hand students their scores with the comment that anybody that does not like their score needs to correct the situation by asking their group what they can do to improve the situation. In addition, I may have to take some people aside and have a conversation with them about their work. This usually sets matters right. Recalcitrant students getting low peer evaluation scores generally make amends rapidly.

I am often asked how frequently groups have problems in getting along (Herreid, 1999). Over the years I have queried hundreds of faculty who have attended workshops I have given on collaborative learning. The average answer seems to be that around 15–20 percent have difficulties, and that is my experience as well. Nonetheless, I have been able to fix virtually all of these problems by using practice peer evaluations and by talking to the students involved. Additionally, I find it useful to have the groups evaluate their own progress in team work. This is especially valuable during the early days of the course. To do this, I might ask them to write a list of characteristics that identify good and poor team members; this starts a little introspection about their own behavior. Alternatively, I might hand out profiles of fictional students and ask the groups what kind of peer evaluation they would give to these individuals. Or I might ask them to use a numerical scale and to rank how well their group is performing and ask what they could do as individuals to improve the team's work. All of these techniques make the students aware of how individual performances can be improved to produce a better group project.

WHAT ARE THE OUTCOMES OF TEAM-BASED LEARNING?

First, I notice a dramatic difference in student attendance in classes using team-based learning or any other type of collaborative learning in which permanent teams are used. At my institution, the average attendance when the lecture method is used may fall to 50 percent. In contrast, collaborative learning strategies produce an attendance of about 95 percent. The students tell me there are several reasons for this:

(1) the in-class RATs determine a large part of their grade, so they can't afford to miss them; (2) group projects are done in class and figure significantly in their grade; and (3) most important, they feel that they cannot let their team mates down. This is not only because I use peer evaluation, but also because once groups have bonded, the students realize their absence hurts their new friends.

Second, the grades in the course are always higher than during the normal year when the lecture method is used. With team-based learning, most of the grades are "As" and "Bs." Part of the reason is that a significant portion of the grade comes from group work and the groups usually produce higher scores on quizzes and projects than individuals. Additionally, students work much harder at grasping the material, and retain it better once they have to work on their own to digest the reading and have to apply the general principles they have learned to real life problems. They cannot escape the work load. It is relentless. In normal lecture-based classes, students can remain passive, hidden throughout the semester. This is impossible to do in team-based learning. They must keep up with the work or everyone will know it. It is no wonder the grades are better.

HINTS FOR USING TEAM-BASED LEARNING

I have often been asked by faculty how much time it takes to prepare for a team-based learning class. My answer is that if you are devising a new course, then you will need to put in the same amount of effort to prepare either the lectures or team-based learning material. There is a huge investment of time required either way. On the other hand, if you have been teaching a lecture course for years and have the bulk of the work done, then there is a large extra investment of time needed to convert to team-based learning. You must create RATs and applications for every class. Lots of teachers understandably balk at this. Furthermore, you might even have to create original written material for the students to read. Text book readings are not designed for teaching using this approach. When using the lecture method, we are apt to give assigned readings in almost a casual way, more as an enrichment than as a central part of the learning. The content or the quality of the chapters doesn't necessarily have to be right on target. In contrast, in team-based learning, in which the students must get everything from their reading materials, such an approach will not work. As a result, many of us find we must write our own text material to get the job done right or at least we must write study guides to aid the students as they wade through a morass of text material. This takes a lot of time.

Fortunately, there are some helpful ways to survive without the heroic effort of rewriting the text. In evolutionary biology, I use a commercial text book. Consequently, I take special care to provide a detailed list of important key points that the students must know in the assigned reading. For each chapter I give them a printed list with three columns. Its headings read: "Must Know," "Good to Know," and "Nice to Know." Under each heading I list the appropriate key words and concepts, depending on their level of importance. Students pay close attention to these helpful signposts while doing their reading. I also place the lists on my course website, where students may take practice quizzes on the reading. In a similar fashion, I have heard of a physics instructor who produces an audiotape reading guide for his text that the students listen to at the start of their reading and study sessions, and a statistics professor who uses Web-based problem walk-through examples in his course. These aids are always helpful in any course, but particularly valuable when there are no lectures. Naturally, these guides have the added advantage that the students see that you really are earning your salary (something they are not always sure about when they see you standing by as they work feverishly in their groups).

Finally, let us turn to the problem(s) that bedeviled my son in his one and only foray into team-based learning. First, let me say that my son seemed like a natural for team-based learning. His undergraduate schooling was at St. Johns College where all of the classes were seminars. He had the patience of Job in helping students. Furthermore, he did not covet the lecture platform, nor was he concerned about relinquishing power in the classroom. He had no apparent barriers to a successful team-based learning experience. What was it then?

I think it was his lack of experience in the classroom. Here he was, a new instructor trying out a new method never seen before by him or his students. Not only was he facing the task of dealing with a new teaching style in which he had to give up a lot of authority to the students, but he did not have the depth of experience in dealing with the normal classroom problems. As a graduate student, he did not have the stature of a professor, nor was he considered by them a seasoned veteran. He did not have ready responses to such age-old questions as "I wasn't able to finish my homework. May I have an extension?" Or, "I have a conflict with the test time. May I take the test on another day?" Or, "What can I do for extra credit?" and "Are you going to curve the grades?" His uncertainty in how to deal with these problems as well as team-based learning produced an anxiety in him as well as in his students. He was vulnerable to attack by the students, who were not accustomed to working in groups and didn't know what group grading, individual grading, or peer evaluation were all about. His was a disastrous experience, and he has never tried to teach with team-based learning again.

It is not always that way with beginning teachers. I know of several young assistant  so captivated by team-based learning that they immediately hod—successfully. It clearly depends on the person and the circ- variable seems to be how comfortable the instructor is in being lents. There are veteran teachers who cannot abide it and there Still, the bottom line is that I do think inexperienced teachers task in instituting team-based learning. They should be espe- pting it if they are in a school that is not tolerant of novel teach- depends on a high productivity in research.

IS TEAM-BASED LEARNING WORTH THE EFFORT?

The answer to whether team-based learning is worth the effort is obviously "yes" in my case. One great benefit for me in using team-based learning, or any other collaborative learning strategy, is that I get to know my students extraordinarily well. In a lecture course, I see the students sitting there taking notes as I pontificate on weighty matters. I assume all is well. I am doing a good job. All is right with the world. Then comes the exam. There are all those "Fs" and "Ds." Well, I think, it was their fault: they were lazy or stupid. And yet?

In lecture classes, I generally did not see students as individuals. They were simply there—as an audience. All of this changed the moment I started using team-based learning. While students are working on their projects, I have plenty of time to observe every nuance of their interactions with the material and with each other. The openness of the classroom is much like a second-grade class in which a certain amount of chaos reigns. Students have less hesitancy to ask me questions or to approach me as a human being rather than as an authority figure. Not surprisingly, I get to know them; most are neither stupid nor lazy.

I began to have real fun in the classroom again. And that was not all.
There were the better grades.
The better retention.
And they liked it—
a whole lot.
So did I.

REFERENCES

Dinan, F., & Frydrychowski, V. A. (1995). A team learning method for organic chemistry. *Journal of Chemistry Education 72:* 429–431.

Herreid, C. F. (1999). The bee and the groundhog: Lessons in cooperative learning—troubles with groups. *Journal of College Science Teaching 28*(4):226–228.

———. (1998). Why isn't cooperative learning used to teach science? *Bioscience 48:* 553–559.

CHAPTER 7

Working with Nontraditional and Underprepared Students in Health Education

Patricia Goodson

Team-based learning calls for students to gain their first introduction to the content on their own, through reading assignments. Contrary to what one might expect, Goodson found that team-based learning enhanced the ability of nontraditional and underprepared students to learn on their own.

My first exposure to team-based learning was at a workshop conducted by Dr. Larry Michaelsen at the University of Texas at San Antonio (UTSA) in 1997. The Teaching and Learning Center sponsored this workshop as an effort to motivate and equip professors to undertake new strategies that would motivate learning, contribute to student retention, and nourish professors' enthusiasm for teaching.

At the time, I was teaching in the Division of Education in the College of Social and Behavioral Sciences, and my area was health promotion. I taught two undergraduate classes: understanding human sexuality, and survey of human disease. My classes averaged forty students with many being nontraditional, and of Hispanic descent. While 44.2 percent of UTSA students range in age from 17 to 22 years, 31.4 percent are aged 23–29, and 24.4 percent are thirty years old or older. More than 42 percent of UTSA students are Hispanic, and more than 50 percent are from groups underrepresented in higher education (http://www.utsa.edu).

Before using team-based learning, I applied a mixture of lecture and group discussion formats to my classes with a reasonable degree of success, as measured by formal student evaluations. While successful by institutional standards, I had mixed feelings regarding my teaching experience and felt there was something absent from my achievements. Students had difficulty engaging in the lectures and asked very few questions; furthermore, only a small number of students read the required background texts, making class discussions drag and lack interest, even when the debates were over controversial topics.

This discontent with the lecture-and-discussion format motivated my participation in Dr. Michaelsen's workshop. I must confess, however, that during the workshop I was very skeptical for two specific reasons. First, as a student I had taken part in group assignments and, invariably, I would be the one doing all the work and getting the good grade for the entire group.

The second reason for my skepticism was much more involved and was shared by my colleagues. Our concern centered around the fact that, with team-based learning, students must read and master basic content before lecturing and testing. These concerns are heightened when students are bilingual or come from minority ethnic groups for whom English is a second language, a situation that was prevalent in all of my classes. My fellow faculty members and I had reservations that, because of potential difficulties with reading, not even the basic content would get covered, much less any additional material. Nevertheless, the experience of going through the nuts and bolts of the team-based learning process in that first workshop (I later attended a second, follow-up session, also sponsored by the Teaching and Learning Center), convinced me that there was enough potential in the strategy to be worth trying a few of its elements in a class that was already under way.

My first attempt consisted of modifying the ten-question, multiple-choice quiz I gave the class each time we had a topic for debate or discussion. Normally, I would have the ten questions on an overhead transparency. Students would write their answers on paper to turn in to me, and then we would discuss the issue. I modified this process by asking them to answer the ten questions individually, then answer the same ten questions as a group (I had assigned them to small groups at the beginning of the semester for a research project). When all groups were finished, I opened the discussion to the whole class, going over each of the questions on the quiz while students graded each other's answers.

The immediate results stunned me: these students, once so detached from the topics they were debating, were now actively engaged, defending their points of view, listening to others, wanting to be heard. The whole-class discussion afterwards was equally dynamic, and I confess I was very surprised. A few minutes before the end of that class, I asked students to provide feedback on how they liked doing their quiz in this individual–group format. The answers also surprised me. They "just loved" learning from each other and voted for the continuation of this process. The student responses were foreign to me because I never enjoyed peer learning when I was a student; I thought I was paying to hear the professors teach; I could get peer education without going to school.

Given the success of my first attempt, I partially reformatted both the sexuality and the disease classes that same semester to include individual and group quizzes with immediate feedback. I wasn't ready just yet to restructure my classes entirely into a team-based learning approach. I was afraid of the risk involved: attempting this new strategy could significantly affect my teaching evaluations. Due to my group experiences as a student, I knew there would always be someone who would not feel comfortable with the approach and would think that the teacher was not teaching.

As I struggled with whether I should develop at least one of my classes into a full-blown team-based learning format, I consulted with Dr. Mike Ryan, director of the Teaching and Learning Center. His support was instrumental in helping me become increasingly comfortable with, and confident of, what I was doing. My comfort and confidence developed slowly, based on what I was experiencing in the classes in which I was using pieces of the process. Students were more motivated and engaged (even during the lectures). There was more in-class participation (even from nonnative speakers) during debates and discussions. There was also more reading of assigned texts before class, because students knew they would be required to discuss the issues with their teammates and did not want to "let their colleagues down," as one student stated. In addition to what I could personally observe and appreciate, students' feedback on their experience coupled with strong support from the Teaching and Learning Center encouraged me to try the whole procedure, at least in one class. If there was one important lesson I learned at this time, it was this: when trying team-based learning for the first time, it is important to be surrounded by a support system of some kind.

TEACHING PROCESS USED

In the spring of 1998, while still teaching at UTSA, I decided to restructure my human sexuality class entirely into a team-based learning approach. Most of the procedures and steps outlined here are still in place, although I am now at Texas A&M University in the Department of Health and Kinesiology.

In the human sexuality class (ranging in size from 40 to 95 undergraduates), students are placed in small groups of five to six persons each, based on their scores on a test of attitudes toward sexuality. Because one of my goals for the class is for students to develop critical thinking skills about matters related to human sexuality as well as a respectful attitude toward others' opinions, each group represents a true mix of scores and of different viewpoints, which invariably accounts for very lively discussions and intricate consensus-building dynamics.

The course includes an individual and group Readiness Assessment Test (RAT) each time a new unit is introduced. New topics are covered almost every week, so my course tends to have a large number of RATs. After a few conceptual units are presented in the course (every 3–4 weeks), the groups complete an assignment that integrates concepts from multiple units. This typically consists of a problem-solving or analytical task to which they must apply the basic content covered in class up to that point. I maintain an individual midterm exam, but I usually have the final exam as a group activity in which the groups are asked to select a target audience and topic, then develop a sexuality pamphlet with pertinent and useful information. Here, students are encouraged to be creative and artistic, in addition to scientifically and theoretically accurate.

The class schedule consists of two weekly sessions of one hour and fifteen minutes each. I usually use the first session in the week for the RAT. The time students spend on individual and group test-taking varies by topic, but normally ranges from twenty to thirty minutes. Going over each question clarifying doubts and announcing the "correct" answer requires me to spend, in the entire procedure (individual and group tests, and appeals), approximately forty-five to sixty minutes (once again, depending on the topic covered). I usually spend the fifteen to thirty minutes that are left answering related questions and, most of the time, bringing in recent findings, current events and alternative perspectives not covered by the students' textbook. When a group application activity is scheduled, I usually reserve an entire class period for this (75 minutes) and try to plan the activity accordingly. It is important that groups have enough time to complete the activity, but it is equally important to schedule intergroup and whole-class discussions. Depending on the size of the class, I generally reserve fifteen to thirty minutes for intergroup sharing.

Not only has the time allocation of my daily sessions changed quite markedly (because I spend less time lecturing), but my role in the classroom with the team-based learning approach has also changed significantly: I have become the facilitator, the enabler, as students learn to become responsible for their own learning. While in class, I walk among the groups as they are working on application group activities or group discussions. This gives me an opportunity to observe and interact more closely with each of the groups and their individual members. Such an opportunity to relate more closely with students during their learning process is something I never had while only lecturing.

My greatest fear in making the transition to team-based learning (and that of many faculty peers as well) was that students would be unable or unwilling to read and master basic content without lectures. In particular, I was worried about students who come from minority ethnic groups for which English is a second language. Because of their potential difficulties with reading, I had little confidence that even the basic content would get covered, much less any additional material.

Fortunately, my fears about the value of pre-class reading for ensuring content coverage turned out to be totally unfounded. After a couple of weeks into the team-based learning strategy, students learn that if they are struggling with basic content, they can readily rely on their group as a source of help. Many times I have had the experience of coming early to a classroom and finding students discussing the topic that will be covered that day in the RAT, together, as a group—helping each other understand the material. Because I can now expect students to master the basic content on their own, I can actually cover more content than when I spent all my time lecturing. Even after I spend time clarifying doubts and correcting misunderstandings, I have extra classroom time to go beyond what is presented in the textbook.

I have also seen benefits for other students with special needs. At the beginning of courses, I have had a few students express considerable anxiety about the procedures because they have been diagnosed with a learning disability such as attention deficit disorder (ADD) or test-taking anxiety. With these students my tactic (which so far has worked every time) has been to ask them to "hang in there" for a couple of RATs and then, later, let me know how they are feeling and performing. I have never had any of these students return to express concerns, and their grades have always been satisfactory. In fact, one student with ADD told me she "loved" the strategy because she didn't have to sit and listen to a seventy-five-minute lecture, which she invariably sees as a torturous experience.

One of the key components of team-based learning is the application of basic knowledge, in groups, to new and diverse situations. For me, developing good application-focused activities and assignments still remains one of the most challenging aspects of the whole procedure. In the area of human sexuality, finding real-life problems and situations for analyses is perhaps the easiest step with one just needing to open a national or local newspaper to find a year's worth of problems to be solved or debated.

For instance, it was time for an application activity with my sexuality class in the spring of 1998, when the local newspaper published a piece entitled "Agency says ex-teacher, boy resumed sex relations." The article reported on the nationally famous case of the middle-school female teacher who had sex with one of her male pupils (and became pregnant) in 1996. The teacher was indicted and pleaded guilty to two counts of child rape; she was imprisoned but released early. The 1998 account described how the teacher had violated the early release terms (which included a ban on all contact with juveniles) and had been caught together with her male pupil, apparently prepared to flee the country. The newspaper story said the couple had resumed a sexual relationship (the boy was 14 years old at the time; the teacher, 35).

Based on this story, I developed an activity for the class. Here are the instructions that accompanied a copy of the newspaper story, provided to each group:

1. Considering that the legal age of consent in Washington state is 16 (for sexual intercourse), how would you rule in this case if you were the presiding judge (is the teacher guilty of rape?). What is the rationale for your decision?
2. If you were not the judge, but a state legislator, would this case lead you to reconsider or reexamine the state's rape laws? Why? Why not?

I give students twenty minutes to choose their verdict and answer the second question. During the remainder of the class period, groups report on their positions and rationale to the whole class.

This activity is an example of a task that works well because the topic is timely and the students are required to reach a decision or a choice through group consensus. While I have learned that activities that require students to reach a group consensus and choose an alternative or decide between options tend to foster group cohesiveness and facilitate learning, I have also learned that using topics that are current and relevant to students facilitates engagement and motivation for discussion.

Although many of my application group activities are timely and are, therefore, used only once, many are timeless due to the perennial nature of the topics. An example of the latter type, which I use almost every semester, involves the scenarios posted on the SIECUS (Sexuality Information and Education Council of the United

States) website concerning sexuality education (www.siecus.org). One of the website's sections entitled "Oh, no! What do I do now?" presents small vignettes that generate interesting discussions about how to handle specific sexual situations or questions presented by children. I present some of the vignettes, along with an example of the task, to the groups. This is the set of instructions I provide:

APPLICATION GROUP ACTIVITY
Adapted from www.siecus.org

Consider the following scenarios:

Scene A: A father enters his four-year-old son's room and finds him changing the diaper on the baby doll belonging to his playmate Mary. He asks: "Will you buy me a baby doll like this?"

Scene B: A mother notices her five-year-old son pulling on his penis while watching television right before bedtime.

Discuss the questions below with your group and provide the answers on a separate sheet of paper (do not forget your group number on that sheet).

For each of the scenes above, answer the following questions:

1. Why is he/she doing that ? (list 3 reasons for each scene)
2. What are some responses the parents in these scenarios could have? (list 3 for each scene)
3. What messages are each of the responses you listed above, sending to the child? (list one message per response)
4. List one reason for each of the possible responses the parents may have (why would the parent respond that way?)

Try to balance responses: suggest some responses that you think are negative, as well as positive ones.

Example: A mother walks into her son's bedroom and finds him being examined by his friend Tammy. He has his clothes off and she is listening to his heart with a toy stethoscope.

1. Why is he/she doing that?
    a. The children may be curious about each other's bodies.
    b. They may be imitating what happens in the doctor's office.
2. Responses and Messages
    a. "Put your clothes on, right now! I never want to see this again!"
    Message: The children are bad; this can be done but away from mother's sight.
    b. "Tammy, put your clothes on and go home right now!"
    Message: Tammy is bad and it's her fault.
3. Reasons for responses:
    a. Parent is embarrassed and angry because she doesn't know what to do or say. Was taught that nudity is "dirty."
    b. Parent views other children as threats to her child's development.

OUTCOMES

I have not yet measured the impact of team-based learning on my students' learning. Their grades have been somewhat inflated, not due to the team-based learning process itself, but to my purposefully structuring their learning experience to become a successful one. Even though I do not have comparable measures of student performance because I changed all my tests when I began using team-based learning, my overall impression is that team-based learning students do better in their midterm and final exams (when I give individual finals) than the students who are not exposed to this strategy. At the end of the semester in one of my present graduate classes (an introduction-to-research-type class), I give students an exercise that has been especially gratifying. I tell them they will be retaking—as a kind of final exam—all of their old RATs since the beginning of the semester (all at once; usually a 100-question test). The exercise is worth nothing in terms of a grade. I tell them to take it without studying or preparing—only as a personal challenge and a measure of how much they were able to retain during the semester. All students score a B (80%) or higher on this test (even if their individual scores had been lower, during the semester). Students are surprised at how much they are able to recall and I, of course, am very pleased with how the exercise accomplishes at least two immediate goals: that of testing their knowledge, and that of reinforcing that they did, in fact, learn something.

Although I do not have objective measures of the impact on learning, I have systematically collected data on students' perceptions of the team-based learning process across five semesters of using it at UTSA (I am still in the process of collecting data at Texas A&M). At the end of each course, I ask students to fill out an evaluation form composed of ten questions with responses on a seven-point Likert-type scale, and two open-ended questions asking for three positive and three negative aspects of their experience with team-based learning in the sexuality class.

Results for the ten questions indicate that students view team-based learning very favorably and think this strategy would be helpful in other classes (higher scores mean more favorable attitudes). The question exhibiting the lowest mean score is the one related to keeping friendships made in the class (M = 4.38, sd = 1.71 [M = mean; sd = standard deviation]). These results are probably confounded by responses from students in summer classes, because these classes often pool students from several divisions across UTSA. The item with the largest mean score was "How valuable do you think a team-based learning approach would be for some of your other classes at UTSA?" (M = 6.40; sd = 5.23). Even though the mean score for "How compatible is team-based learning with your personal learning style" was lower (M = 5.42; sd = 1.44), in tandem, both mean scores support the hypothesis that most students appreciate the strategy and feel they could benefit from the technique if it were applied to other courses (Table 7.1 summarizes the responses to the ten questions, presenting students' mean scores and standard deviations).

For the open-ended questions, the three most frequently cited positive aspects of team-based learning for my students were: (1) exposure to different opinions and points of view; (2) collaboration in the process of learning by having students help

TABLE 7.1
UTSA Students' Reactions to Team-Based Learning*

Item	Question	Percentage Responses			M	sd
		% 1-2	% 3-5	% 6-7		
1.	Do you find that a team learning strategy has more or fewer advantages than the traditional "lecture, mid-term and final exams" approach? (1=Fewer advantages; 7=More	–	20.4	79.6	6.10	1.06
2.	How stressful did you perceive the individual RATs to be, in this class? (1=Very stressful; 7=Not stressful at all)	6.1	52.5	41.4	4.88	1.38
3.	How stressful did you perceive the GRATs to be, in this class? (1=Very stressful; 7=Not stressful at all)	2.0	27.1	70.9	5.77	1.28
4.	How compatible is team learning with your personal learning style (in other words, does a leam learning strategy match your way of learning)? (1=Not compatible at all; 7=Extremely compatible)	6.1	38.8	55.1	5.42	1.44
5.	How likely are you to keep some of the friendships you made made in your group, outside of this class? (1=Not likely at all; 7=Extremely likely)	18.5	49.9	31.4	4.38	1.71
6.	In terms of managing day-to-day activities in class (such as handing out tests, grades, etc.), how complicated did you think team learning was? (1=Extremely complicated; 7=Not complicated at all)	2.5	15.8	81.6	6.20	1.20
7.	How valuable do you think a team learning approach would be for some of your other classes at UTSA? (1=Not valuable at all; 7=Extremely valuable)	3.5	20.0	76.2	6.40	5.23
8.	How satisfied were you with the amount of learning you gained in this class? (1=Not at all satisfied; 7=Extremely satisfied)	2.0	21.8	75.8	6.02	1.18
9.	Overall, how would you rate your experience in this class? (1=Terrible; 7= Excellent)	0.5	20.4	78.4	6.08	1.06
10.	How likely are you to recommend this class to other students? (1=Not at all likely; 7=Extremely likely)	0.5	15.3	84.0	6.38	0.99

* From 194-196 students in five classes.

each other understand the subject; and (3) increase in interaction among students. I was not surprised by these findings, considering that UTSA is characterized as a commuter campus, and students often complain about coming in and out of classes without ever talking to anyone (especially in large classes).

The most frequently mentioned negative aspects of the strategy were: (1) members who do not participate; (2) group consensus is difficult; and (3) dependence on other team members for the grade. While 23 students (N = 171) mentioned that there were no negative aspects to team-based learning at all, eight responses indicated that students preferred lectures over group work. Some of these students mentioned that team-based learning "takes away from valuable lecture time," or they "preferred lecture before quizzes," or even (as one student mentioned) "I like classes where I can take a lot of notes!"

As a whole, the above data (even if instruments were not validated) provide a positive evaluation of the team-based learning process in the sexuality class. For the disease class, I have restructured the quizzes to include individual and group tests in addition to application group activities. Likewise, I have formatted all my graduate classes into a team-based learning approach, but have not collected systematic evaluations from them. More important, my "formal" student evaluations—the ones I feared might be negatively impacted—have only improved these five semesters.

Considering the high mean scores (representing positive attitudes) displayed in Table 7.1, and the positive features described in the open-ended questions, it appears that students appreciate team-based learning because of the richness in the viewpoints and the learning tasks they are able to experience within the classroom. A handful of students are, nevertheless, resistant to the process and perceive team-based learning as incompatible with their learning style.

I was very privileged to be in a department at UTSA that embraced the idea of team-based learning wholeheartedly. Many of my colleagues, due to my experience and with support from the Teaching and Learning Center, began to use aspects of team-based learning in their classes. It was very gratifying to see how much other professors enjoyed the strategy and how our health-promotion students were slowly becoming acculturated into a new way of learning.

Team-based learning has made the in-class learning experience much more engaging and active while enabling the practice of very important skills in health promotion generally—and particularly in human sexuality—such as communication, respect for others' opinions and values, trust, and collaboration for accomplishment of common goals. To hear students say that they are able to learn better and faster while retaining their knowledge for longer periods of time, coupled with making new friends and learning how to work in groups, is a precious reward for any professor. With team-based learning, this type of feedback becomes routine; with lecture-only learning, such comments are rare.

Overall, I would rate my experience with team-based learning as invaluable and extremely motivating. I am very satisfied with how the strategy fosters an atmosphere for collaboration among students, and between the students and me; I am gratified by the sense of excitement I feel when I see an entire class of students actively engaged (and enjoying) their learning task; I feel a strong sense of accomplishment when students come to me—many months after the end of a course—and mention, in great detail, specific discussions their groups had had and, thus, convey that they still remember what they learned.

Granted, implementing team-based learning was not an easy task at first. It takes time to prepare the RATs and GRATs, group folders, application group activities, appeals forms, and so on. I strongly doubt, however, that it takes more than the normal preparation expected for a new course. In addition to the time requirement, being willing to try a new teaching strategy and being willing to identify and correct unpredictable circumstances is, oftentimes, scary and challenging.

Nevertheless, when recalling the early days during which I struggled with the decision to re-format my classes, I remember a discussion I had with a professor who had recently begun using team-based learning at another institution. I had asked him, "Is it worth it?" and he answered, "You know, I don't think I can ever go back to lecture-style teaching!" His statement made a strong impression on me, and I became eager to test his claim. Now, if anyone would ask me about team-based learning, I wouldn't mind paraphrasing: "Me? How could I teach any other way?"

CHAPTER 8

A Dramatic Turnaround in a Classroom of Deaf Students

Melanie C. Nakaji

If you have wondered whether changing one's teaching strategy can make a significant difference, this story provides a powerful answer to that question. In extreme situations, it is sometimes possible to see the effect of differences more clearly. Melanie Nakaji was co-teaching a course for deaf students that was clearly headed "South." Students had developed a negative attitude and were under-performing in a major way. Baffled as to how to deal with this situation, the teachers heard about team-based learning and decided to start using it, even though they were already at midsemester. The impact and results were truly extraordinary.

My first exposure to team-based learning was at a workshop presented by Larry Michaelsen during the spring semester of 2001. Before the session was over, I was convinced that I should switch to team-based learning in a class I was currently teaching. Even though we were already halfway through the semester, I was so disappointed with the quality of student learning that I was willing to take the risk of totally restructuring my class. The results were absolutely astounding. Perhaps the most amazing part of all, however, is that the class was taught by a Deaf[1] instructor (myself), along with a hearing instructor (Julie Pludow), to a class of students who were also deaf or hard of hearing.

BACKGROUND

Regardless of a deaf individual's intelligence level and educational background, actively learning and participating in the classroom (whether mainstreamed or self-contained) poses a great hurdle. Although deaf students may have the benefit of accommodations such as an interpreter or a real-time captionist, they are still faced with the formidable challenge of assimilating into the predominant culture, that is, a "hearing" world. One of the difficulties they face is that English is their second language. The primary mode of communication for the majority of deaf people is American Sign Language (ASL). However, others communicate orally, use an English version of sign language, or total communication (i.e., they sign English and talk simultaneously). Still others rely on lip reading.

In addition to inherent limitations in available communications media, deaf students are often further disadvantaged by inadequacies in their formal education. Many deaf education programs in primary and secondary schools are based on a slower-paced curriculum that, although theoretically tailored to meet each individual's educational needs, rarely includes rigorous teaching of English, writing, or appropriate communication. As a result, the deaf are likely to lag behind their otherwise equally abled, hearing peers in two important ways, both of which affect their ability to succeed in college courses.

First of all, from a cognitive preparation standpoint, the deaf students' lower level of exposure to information of all kinds often translates into poor analytical and problem-solving skills. Second, from a social standpoint, deaf students tend to feel victimized by what they see as years of oppression from teachers, parents, and other authority figures (who are hearing) and tend to blame them for their own incompetence. Unfortunately, this predisposes many to take on a passive student role that further impedes their ability to succeed in their formal educational pursuits.

Regardless of whose fault it is, deaf students are usually not equipped with the fundamental reading and writing skills nor the cognitive capacity that a competitive post-secondary institution demands. As a result, the majority of deaf and hard-of-hearing students are forced to enroll in junior colleges because of their open-enrollment policies and the ready availability of remedial courses. For example, at San Diego Mesa College (the community college where I teach), the mean level of reading and writing skills for deaf students who are recent high school graduates ranges from 3.8 to 4.5 grade level equivalency. As a result, nearly all are required to complete a two-year developmental English class for the deaf taught through direct communication in ASL.

The class in which I first used team-based learning was a "college success" course entitled "Personal Growth 127." It is offered through Disabled Student Services and Programs, and is taught in ASL. That semester, the class was composed of one Deaf instructor (myself), a hearing instructor (Julie Pludow), and eight deaf or hard-of-hearing students, none of whom had scored high enough on the entrance exams to be able to bypass the developmental English class.

PERSONAL GROWTH 127: BEFORE TEAM-BASED LEARNING

Our first key decision in designing the course was deciding on appropriate reading materials. Based on past experience, we knew that struggling with a textbook that contained college-level vocabulary would be a frustrating and debilitating experience for deaf and hard-of-hearing students. Thus, instead of using a text, I attempted to compensate for our students' low reading skills by creating a course packet covering the same topics as ten different traditionally accepted college success textbooks. I simplified the information by eliminating the philosophical underpinnings and the background information, and converted abstract concepts into tangible, concrete ones. Instead of thirty-five to forty pages per chapter, I wrote succinct five- to ten-page chapters. I anticipated that tailoring students' reading materials would motivate students to read in advance so that they would be prepared to participate in class discussions.

For the first eight weeks of the sixteen-week semester, Julie and I adopted the traditional lecture-style format for the first hour of the class and planned to use the remaining thirty minutes as a lab. Seven of our eight students classified themselves as Deaf with a capital "D" and used ASL as their primary mode of communication. The remaining student, whom I shall call Bob, classified himself as deaf with a lower-case "d" and vacillated between using total communication, speaking, and signing English. Thus, in the "lecture" part of each class, I signed ASL for the seven Deaf students while Julie signed and spoke simultaneously in an attempt to accommodate Bob's communication needs. Unfortunately, our approach was not well received. Almost nothing worked out in the way we had planned and, by the middle of the term, we found ourselves facing a myriad of problems.

Many of our difficulties centered around communicating with Bob. Limitations in his residual hearing prevented him from consistently understanding oral communication, and his ASL skills were not sound enough to enable him to consistently understand either the lecture or the other students. Thus, communication misunderstandings frequently occurred between Bob, his Deaf peers, and me (as both instructor and a Deaf person). In fact, the other students, who were fluent ASL users, became so frustrated that they refused to even pay attention to the talkative, slow-signing, half-speaking Bob. To complicate communication problems even further, four of the Deaf students, who were concurrently enrolled in the developmental English class (mentioned earlier), formed a clique and distanced themselves from all of the Deaf students who had not yet taken the class.

These communication breakdowns had a heavy impact on student attitudes. The students rarely prepared for class, resisted participating in class discussions, relied on me to provide entertainment, and engaged in personal side conversations with each other during lectures. In addition, they frequently complained or argued about a wide variety of issues, including boredom, misunderstandings, and homework assignments.

Over time, students' poor social behavior (both with peers and instructors) became so much of a problem that it totally overwhelmed our efforts to create a positive learning environment. For example, instead of taking low grades in stride, their reactions included such things as overtly pouting during the class lecture, exploding and demanding a higher grade, and blaming me in a confrontational manner for not informing them of the expectations of the assignment. Their ASL side conversations during the lectures, which, unlike whispering, are discernible to everyone in the classroom, also grew to the point that it was impossible to keep the class focused on the topics we had planned to discuss. Further, even when I confronted students about their inappropriate social etiquette, nothing seemed to be changing for the better.

In an effort to better engage the students and bring order to the classroom, Julie and I had already made significant changes in the curriculum. First, in hopes of increasing student comprehension of core concepts, we reduced the amount of content covered in class. We erroneously assumed that, because of the reading and writing barriers faced by the students, we needed to provide a deeper explanation of important concepts. Based on that assumption, we scaled back to covering two chapters, instead of five, during the first half of the semester. To our dismay, student attitudes became even more negative and we were left with the prospect of having to cover the remaining six chapters in the final eight weeks of the term.

Even in the areas we were able to cover, students' work failed to meet our minimum expectations. For example, although students could correctly answer test questions requiring recall of key goal-setting concepts, when we engaged them in a goal-setting exercise that required applying the concepts, their best efforts consisted of incoherent thoughts scribbled on a piece of scratch paper. Similarly, students memorized what the words "time management" meant but could not construct a daily calendar for themselves.

By the time I was first exposed to team-based learning in late March, the semester was half over and we had not seen any improvements in either classroom behavior or cognitive development. Our primary goal for the deaf students—to understand that the way they behaved would directly affect their cognitive development—was clearly not being achieved, and Julie and I had clearly begun to lose hope for this unmotivated, uncooperative group of students.

INTRODUCTION OF TEAM-BASED LEARNING

The first week of April marked a new beginning for the class, for the students as well as for Julie and me. On this momentous day, I opened discussion with a few reflections about students' behaviors and attitudes and how their lack of motivation and preparation disappointed me. The serious demeanor of my sign language and facial expression changed to elation when I signed "Today is a new day! A day that will change the structure of our class for the remainder of the semester!" I am sure that my body language and use of movement demonstrated excitement as I continued to elucidate the changes regarding the overall structure of the class. My arms and hands signed furiously as I motioned students to sit together and formulate two groups. Students moved to their appointed chairs but sat in amazement and said nothing.

I started by giving an overview of team-based learning and explicitly told the students that they would have the primary responsibility for learning vocabulary words, reviewing the chapters, and working on individual assignments outside of class. Two students shrugged, turned their heads in a disapproving manner, then glanced back to me. The other students observed the spectacle unfolding before them, but in contrast seemed to be inspired or at least intrigued by the prospect of the new process.

I distributed a new syllabus and instructed the students to read, not skim, the information, and prepare for a practice individual Readiness Assessment Test (RAT) over the syllabus. One student threw his arms down and exclaimed, "Why are we changing the system?" Another student asked nonchalantly for sign language interpretation of the English sentence. Bob carefully perused the information, asking for clarification of concepts. The students had a variety of questions that I answered as well I could. I concluded by saying, "Try your best on the individual test. When you take the test with the groups, ask them for their opinion." Five minutes later, I informed students that it was time to start, then handed out the RAT.

In explaining how to fill out the test, I tried to communicate my enthusiasm about the three-point scoring system (see "Split Answers" in Appendix A, p. 229) through my expressive nonverbal communication. The students, however, became frustrated and confused about the allocation of points. One threw down his scoring sheet and said, "forget it" and the others nodded in agreement. I explained the process again and this time one student understood how the allocation of points was to her benefit. She waved her hands to get the others' attention and said (signed), "Listen, you can gamble on the answer . . ." and reinterpreted what I signed in a simpler manner. Suddenly, smiles and "yeahs!" replaced frowns and perplexed faces.

As students proceeded to take their first RAT, expressions of unfamiliarity with the content and structure of the test became evident. A few students struggled with the three-point system, others asked for meanings of words, and a few asked for the answers in an indirect way. But all of the students breathed a sigh of relief and felt they achieved a major accomplishment once they turned in their first RAT.

When it came time to retake the same test as a group, an assertive woman in Bob's group spoke up and clarified the goals of the test. She also suggested how the group should proceed in answering the questions. Meanwhile Bob, who did not understand the assertive woman's signs, needed help. He first turned to his voice interpreter (an interpreter that translates sign language into spoken English for predominately oral deaf students) for clarification but, because she was bound by general guidelines for ethical interpreting, she was precluded from inserting or repeating any information. Next, he turned to us and we responded with, "Ask your group for help and explanations of the system." Fortunately, the other fluent signers fulfilled their newly acquired responsibility for each other and explained the "how" of the process to Bob, using more gestural signs and accentuated mouthed words. Even though they did not realize it, they had started the process of integrating Bob as a contributing member of the team. Once Bob understood the basic premise of the team-based learning and how it applied to the group, the group proceeded to discuss how to reach a consensus in the event that there were discrepant answers.

As far as the other group was concerned (the group without Bob), they were dealing with a different kind of problem. In the beginning, they relied on one assertive female student to make the decisions for the group. The assertive student's female friend followed whatever she said. The two males in the group, one an introvert and the other an extrovert, did not partake in the discussion at all. The typical pattern was for the leader, the strong female student, to answer all of the questions on the group

RAT and then ask if the answers she wrote were acceptable to all. Later on, this early leader of the group was absent from class due to family crisis, and the other three team members were forced to become more active in completing their assignments.

POST–TEAM-BASED LEARNING

What Julie and I discovered from the new system truly amazed us. Instead of the students continuing in a passive student role, they embraced the opportunity to become actively involved in the learning process. In spite of the fact that their initial interactions were dominated by an assertive member, over time, members of both teams learned to strike a balance between speaking and listening. For example, although his poor communication skills clearly limited Bob's contributions to his team during their early work, his mature and respectful demeanor enabled him to gain credibility with each project. In fact, by the end of the semester, he had emerged as the lifeblood of his team. Once they began to communicate with him, the members of his team completely changed their attitudes toward Bob. They saw the value of, and were able to use, Bob's knowledge of the content, and his practical experience from his job at a drug and alcohol treatment program to help them achieve the primary goal of the class, that is, understanding how the content they were studying was relevant to their lives.

Julie and I also witnessed a dramatic improvement in the students' cognitive abilities. For example, for each application exercise, we instructed the students to create an engaging group activity, game, or presentation based on the information from the chapter. The creative group activities that the students presented to the class far exceeded our expectations. It was evident that they learned how to extrapolate the main ideas from the chapter and come up with appropriate examples. In addition, they clearly provided for individual students' learning needs. For example, they designed their group activities so that students had multiple opportunities to use key concepts. Students were also given opportunities to ask for clarification if needed. Further, the process of explaining concepts to each other clearly enabled team members to understand core concepts on a deeper, more meaningful level. Over time, students substituted simple signs with more visual signs and replaced simple explanations with poignant stories. The team members united and delivered effective and entertaining hands-on activities to the class.

One of the most beneficial aspects of the application-focused activities was being able to watch students demonstrate their understanding (or lack thereof). When they understood, they were happy and so were we. When something was unclear or misunderstood, we immediately knew what the problem was and could correct the concept. In most cases, their misunderstandings centered around wordy and abstract concepts needed for higher-level thinking and analytical skills. Once we understood the problem, we could resolve it by using a lower register of signs, that is, unequivocal pictorial-like signs and gestures. In fact, with our students, the majority of our opportunities to provide corrective instruction occurred as a result of the application exercises, not during the Readiness Assurance Process as we had expected. Further, I found that I could give the groups honest feedback that, although not always welcomed, seemed to prompt greater effort rather than hostility.

At the end of the semester, we had students complete a self-report questionnaire about their experience with the team-based approach. Judging from their responses, team-based learning clearly challenged the deaf students and gave them a number of incentives to learn and synthesize core concepts. In particular, many of the students focused on how the learning teams had aided their ability to work with others. Among their comments were, "the work in groups . . . gave me the courage to risk all of my work to benefit the group," "keeps the students motivated . . . helps us learn more and work with other students," "it's a weird test, but it will help me how to do a real good job with the group in my future," "learned to cooperate and don't give up—just go for it and try your best."

CONCLUSION

One of our greatest concerns in working with deaf students is the sheer magnitude of the task they will face in trying to fit into the hearing world. Very few hearing people have even a vague understanding of the Deaf culture and the issues that the deaf face. Based on what we observed as our students learned to work with each other, Julie and I are confident that our deaf students have a better understanding of what they need to excel in the hearing world. The group learning process provided our deaf students with numerous opportunities to hone their social, behavioral, and cognitive skills.

The use of learning teams changed the focus of our class from one of merely learning about personal growth ideas into a personal growth experience. In essence, it provided our Deaf students with a prelude to the "real world."

NOTE

1. Deaf with a capital "D" represents those individuals with a common cultural heritage including: language (ASL), values, norms, and behaviors that result from having a hearing loss. Deaf, with a lowercase "d," refers to individuals or groups who have a hearing loss but may or may not identify themselves with the Deaf culture.

CHAPTER 9

Overcoming Initial Mistakes
When Using Small Groups

G. Fred Streuling

Streuling tried small groups in his accounting classes and had a very negative experience. After learning better procedures for using team-based learning, he reversed the results. Both he and his students found great value in this approach to teaching.

At our institution, administrative duties are typically rotational assignments. In 1990, I was completing my second consecutive three-year term as the director of the School of Accountancy and Information Systems (SOAIS). By and large, I viewed it as a relief to finally get back into the classroom on a full-time basis, the real reason I had opted for a career as an academician in the first place. However, there was this nagging feeling that I had to start making changes in my approach to classroom instruction.

Prior to becoming an administrator, I had established a reputation as a good teacher. The students typically ranked me somewhere in the top twenty percent of the SOAIS faculty. So although I had achieved considerable success with my lecture-style approach, combined with a reasonably caring and friendly personality, I was troubled by the fact that many of my students were only passive participants in the learning process. Of course, the safe approach would be to continue what had brought me success in the past. Like most professors, I had not been trained as a classroom instructor. My entire pre-university education had been in German schools and was typically lecture-based. When I began my first full-time teaching position at the University of Texas in Austin, I simply tried to emulate the professors who I felt had left the most lasting impression on me. I knew very little about learning theory and what motivated individuals to learn. However, on April 1, 1990, the Accounting Education

Change Commission (AECC) issued an exposure draft on the "Objectives of Accounting Education." Among several suggestions, the draft included the following recommendations: "Students should be active participants in the learning process, not passive recipients of information. Working in groups should be encouraged. "[1] This statement appealed to me because during my college days I had been a member of an informal group for two consecutive semesters. We assembled each evening for the purpose of completing assignments for an intermediate accounting course that met daily. This experience had been extremely valuable to me in learning the concepts of accounting.

A FIRST ATTEMPT

As I prepared my syllabus in the fall of 1990 for my graduate course on Partnership Taxation, I included a group activity. I had previously arranged with six of the large accounting firms in Salt Lake City for student groups to contact them to obtain a factual situation related to a partnership tax problem. The group was to research the issues surrounding the fact situation and then reach definitive conclusions. The facts, issues, and conclusions were to be submitted in a single formal term paper, a copy of which would be shared with the accounting firm that had contributed the facts of the case. The groups were instructed to make an appointment with a respective representative of the firm they had been assigned to visit. For their appointment they were to dress professionally, and all members of the group had to be present for the meeting. I thought I had hit upon a rather unique project, well suited for a group project. However, at the conclusion of the semester, I received the lowest student evaluations I had ever received. Needless to say, I was devastated. I concluded that experimenting with groups was not in my best interest and that I should return to my former teaching methodology.

What had gone wrong? Later, when I became more informed and sophisticated in the use of groups or teams in the classroom, it became easy to identify all the "do nots" I had violated in my first attempt to use groups in the classroom. First, when forming the groups, I had allowed self-selection. The second mistake involved the type of project I assigned. Each group was required to create and submit a single, formal paper, usually considered by experts to be one of the least suitable group projects, because it lacks individual accountability. The third major mistake I committed was that all group members received the same grade for the group project, that is, the grade I assigned to the term paper. I made absolutely no allowance for the fact that some students had worked hard on the project while others had freeloaded. In other words, I provided no opportunities for group members to evaluate their peers' performances or non-performances. Subsequently, I also realized that I had committed a fourth mistake. Given the amount of time required to complete the group project, I had not allowed for sufficient weight for the project to influence the final course grade in a meaningful way. As a result, the students concluded that the group project was not really that important.

HELP IS ON THE WAY

After such a dismal failure with groups, I was ready to give up and return to my trusted lecture approach. Frankly, the experience had bruised my ego considerably. But as luck would have it, Professor Larry Michaelsen was invited to present a faculty workshop at Brigham Young University on the benefits of team-based learning. Subsequently, I had the opportunity to attend a second workshop presented by Professor Michaelsen and slowly began to recognize the potential and value of learning teams. It also became clear to me how inept I had been in my earlier efforts at utilizing groups or teams in a classroom setting, and the specific mistakes I had committed that had doomed me to failure.

CURRENT TEACHING ASSIGNMENT

My teaching responsibilities at Brigham Young University consist of one undergraduate course (approximately 80 students) and two graduate courses (approximately 30 and 20 students, respectively) in the areas of federal, state, and local taxation. As a rule, taxation is an area that is highly rule-intensive. Early in my career (in the 1970s), tax professors spent a lot of lecture time focusing on the specific rules found in the respective tax provisions. It has only been since the advent of the personal computer that tax professors have begun to focus more on the conceptual framework in the field of taxation, because many of the detailed rules could be programmed as a computer function. However, for purposes of innovative tax planning, a basic understanding of tax rules remains essential.

FORMING GROUPS OR TEAMS

The undergraduate course I teach each year, Junior Core for accounting majors, is multiple-section and team-taught. I share teaching responsibilities with three other instructors. The topics covered include financial accounting, managerial accounting, systems, auditing, leadership, and taxation. I am assigned to teach taxation in one of the four sections. The Junior Core consists of four eight-week terms, two during fall semester and two during winter semester. The topics related to taxation, the subject I instruct, are covered during the last two of the four eight-week terms. Because the course is team-taught, I do not have exclusive control over many of the administrative policies of the course.

Team work is definitely encouraged in the Junior Core. In fact, during the first week of the Junior Core, I have a specific assignment to present a module (3 hours) on group dynamics and team-based learning to all four sections of the Junior Core.

The formal process of introducing group dynamics at the beginning of the Junior Core has also served as a means of enhancing the integration of the team members into their respective teams. When teams have subsequently been changed, no formal attempts have been made to assimilate the students into their new teams. Consequently, we have found evidence that during later terms informal teams have developed which closely resemble the original teams of the first term.

The instructors form student teams randomly with five to six students per team. In the past, new teams have been formed at the beginning of each eight-week term. However, I convinced my colleagues that teams need to be together for at least the equivalent of a full semester to allow a team to bond and to reach its full potential as a team. Therefore, beginning with the fall 1999 semester, teams have only been changed once, at the beginning of the third of the four terms. At that time, another formal activity will be scheduled to enhance the bonding process of members with their new teams. Seating is assigned and arranged so that in-class team projects are workable. Each section of the course is composed of approximately ten to fourteen teams.

In my graduate courses I have complete control over all aspects of the course. Consequently, I form heterogeneous teams by distributing the assets and liabilities of the students as equally as possible. I consider the following attributes to be important assets: significant full-time work experience, internship experience, relevant prior course work, grade point average, and cultural background. Cultural background could just as well be considered a liability, especially when a problem with fluency in English exists. However, I consider it to be an asset, especially when international topics are part of the class curriculum.

A significant number of our students are married and nearly every semester a married couple is enrolled in one of my courses. I believe that placing a married or an engaged couple on the same team is a liability for intrateam relationships, because before the team has a chance to bond, a subteam has already been established. It can also create problems between spouses when they assume contradicting positions in a discussion. To avoid conflicts in the marriage, one of the spouses may be unwilling to openly express a true opinion, which ultimately hinders the full development of that spouse. Other similar relationships such as siblings or roommates receive similar treatment.

Another liability is a poor attitude toward teamwork. If I have students who express a dislike for teamwork, I try to place only one of them in any one group to avoid discouraging the entire team.

Some of the information regarding assets and liabilities (e.g., course work, grades, etc.) is readily available to me from administrative sources in the SOAIS office. To obtain the rest of the information, I use a survey form on the first day of the semester to acquire information regarding full-time work experience, internships, attitude toward team work, and so forth. The enrollment in my graduate courses allows me to form approximately four to six teams of five persons per team.

CURRENT APPLICATIONS OF TEAM-BASED LEARNING

I use individual and group Readiness Assurance Tests (RATs) extensively. In fact, I do not begin a new chapter or a new module without an individual and a group RAT. The topics covered on the RATs are taken from the reading assignments for a respective chapter or module. As a rule, the RATs consist of objective questions (e.g., true or false, or multiple choice). However, on occasion and especially in my graduate courses, I use short problem questions. For objective RATs, I make use of a Scantron machine to grade the individual tests while the teams retake the test as a group. When I use short problem questions, I try to structure the facts in such a way that the solution should be a short answer or a single dollar amount for each section of the question. This allows me to grade all individual tests quickly while the teams work on the group test. I have become very efficient in administrating the RATs. Whether I use an objective test or a short problem test, and regardless of the number of teams in the class, it rarely takes more than twenty-five minutes to complete the entire process, including the public comparison of group scores (never individual scores), recording the scores in the group folder, and completing written appeals.

After the RAT is completed, I typically give a brief lecture (2–3 minutes) on what I perceive to be the more complex portion of the material covered in the advance reading and the test. I also try to be responsive to specific issues and questions raised by my students. The students then apply the material to case studies. Case studies are team projects and in-class projects. I try very hard not to have them carry over as outside-of-class projects. Although this may happen occasionally, it is quite rare.

SAMPLE CASE STUDY FOR UNDERGRADUATE COURSE

The educational purpose of case studies is to develop in students several of the competencies necessary for success in the accounting profession. In addition to the technical competency of legally lowering a taxpayer's tax obligation, I have found that working cases during regularly scheduled class periods helps students to develop several "soft skills," such as presenting views in writing, and listening effectively, understanding and working effectively with groups of people, solving diverse and unstructured problems in unfamiliar settings, dealing effectively with imposed pressure, and resolving conflict. From a list of twenty-seven behavior-oriented competencies (soft skills) identified in a recent study (Deppe, Sonderegger, Stice, Clark, & Streuling, 1991), our Junior Core faculty has selected nine to emphasize as part of our classroom instruction.

The following case study requires two groups to negotiate a nontaxable exchange. Each team receives a set of facts. The instructor pairs each team that receives Case A with a predetermined Case B team. The facts are available two or three class periods prior to the period when the exchange is actually negotiated. The negotiation can be handled as either an in-class or out-of-class event. I have tried both with equal success. In preparation for the actual negotiation, the teams must engage in activities that teams usually do well, namely learning to understand the nontaxable exchange provisions, understanding the facts of the case assigned in light of those rules, and formulating a strategy for the negotiation process. The results of the negotiation must obviously be communicated to the instructor so an assessment can be made of the outcome. Transmitting the results through a single polished document is not what teams do best and is usually not recommended as an activity for teams. I have solved this dilemma by requiring each member of the team to send me a memo via email. The memo is graded from a group perspective (the technical outcome of the negotiation), and also given an individual score (the individual team member's ability to communicate).

NONTAXABLE EXCHANGES
NEGOTIATION PROBLEM
CASE A

You are employed by The Delta Manufacturing Company who owns a section of land near the Quail Creek residential development, an area that is not conducive for future business development. To sell the property would result in taxable income, something your company tries to avoid. Since expansion is definitely part of the long-range plan of your company, it has been suggested that the property be exchanged for like-kind property in a more suitable location.

As members of the real estate department, your group has been assigned to find appropriate replacement property that would fit the needs of your employer. During your search you have become acquainted with a shopping center developer (The Waterford Group), who owns two pieces of property that meet the specifications for future expansion, both in size and location. Since either location is acceptable to your employer, it has been decided to acquire one of the properties in an economically sound exchange and with minimal tax liability.

Facts and Figures:

The property owned by your company has been appraised by an independent professional appraiser at $90,000. The property was acquired approximately 4 years ago at a cost of $48,000, which is also its current tax basis. The Quail Creek Savings & Loan holds a $30,000 mortgage secured by the property you plan to exchange.

Assignment:

Your assignment is to contact the negotiation team from the Waterford Group and arrange the best possible deal for either property. Since the property is encumbered by a mortgage, you should assume that a new owner of the property assumes the mortgage. Also, you should keep in mind that your company has an unlimited amount of cash available in the event it becomes necessary to offer cash boot for either of the two properties.

NONTAXABLE EXCHANGES
NEGOTIATION PROBLEM
CASE B

You are employed by The Waterford Group (a shopping center developer) who owns two properties in an area which is more conducive for industrial development. To sell the properties would result in taxable income, something your company tries to avoid. Consequently, it is the policy of your company to exchange the properties for like-kind property in a more suitable location.

As members of the property acquisitions department, your group has been assigned to find appropriate replacement property that would be suitable for a future shopping center. During your search, you have become acquainted with representatives of the Delta Company's real estate department. Delta Company owns a section of land near the Quail Creek residential development that appears to have great promise, both in size and location. It has been decided to surrender one of the two properties your company now owns for the Quail Creek property in an economically sound exchange and with minimal tax liability.

Facts and Figures:

Both properties owned by your company have been appraised by an independent professional appraiser.

	Property X	Property Y
FMV	$150,000	$140,000
Basis	60,000	10,000
Mortgage (held by S&L)	110,000	30,000

Assignment:

Your assignment is to contact the negotiation team from the Delta Company and arrange the best possible deal for the Quail Creek property. Since the mortgages are secured by the respective properties, upon sale or exchange, they will be assumed by the new owner of the property. Also, you should keep in mind that your company has an unlimited amount of cash available in the event it becomes necessary to offer cash boot in addition to either of the two properties.

SAMPLE CASE STUDY FOR GRADUATE COURSE

I use a variety of cases in my graduate courses. Cases are categorized as objective–computational and subjective–informational. In my partnership taxation course, a typical objective–computational case study would be like the following.

PARTNERSHIP TAXATION
CLASS EXERCISE
FORMING A PARTNERSHIP—1

Franz has been operating a successful tax preparation service as a single proprietor. He feels it is time to expand but does not have the necessary cash. Currently he leases an office suite in a large high rise, but he feels it would be better for business if he could build his own building. At a monthly Rotary meeting he meets Gena, who has recently graduated from college and wants to go into the tax preparation business. A few years ago she inherited a tract of land from her grandfather which would be suitable for an office location. She also has some cash she can contribute to the business. By agreement, Franz and Gena form a partnership effective July 1, 2XXX, with Franz receiving a 60% capital interest and a 50% profit/loss interest. Gena receives a 40 % capital interest and a 50% profit/loss interest.

Franz contributes the following assets and liabilities:

	Basis
Cash	$15,000
Accounts receivables	$12,000

| Supplies | $ 2,000 |
| Office equipment | $11,000 |

The two partners agree that these assets have a FMV of $70,000, since the office equipment is considered to have a value of $41,000. Franz also transfers a loan from the Second Interstate Bank to the partnership with a remaining balance of $10,000 to the partnership.

Gena contributes the following assets and liabilities:

Gena's tract of land appraised at $90,000. She took out a $60,000 mortgage against the land to finance her education and the partnership will take the property subject to the mortgage. In addition, Gena will also contribute $10,000 in cash.

Since Gena inherited the land from her grandfather, her basis is the value of the land on the day her grandfather died. For estate tax purposes the land was considered to have a FMV of $10,000 on the day of his death.

1. Compute the gain or loss, if any, on the transfer of Franz' property and liabilities to the newly formed partnership.
2. Compute any gain or loss Gena must recognize on the transfer of her assets and liabilities to the newly formed partnership.
3. Compute Franz' basis in his partnership interest.
4. Compute Gena's basis in her partnership interest.
5. Compute any gain or loss the partnership must recognize on Gena's or Franz' transfer.
6. Compute the tax basis of the property in the hands of the partnership immediately after the transfer.
7. Prepare a partnership balance sheet immediately after the formation showing both basis and value.

The subjective–informational case studies would be similar to the following example

PARTNERSHIP TAXATION
CLASS EXERCISE—SEC. 761-2

Several years ago, Dick McEven and Gordon Ridd acquired property in Orem, Utah. The property was improved and five sales were made during the three previous years. Two of the five sales resulted from condemnation proceedings in which the city acquired land for the building of a power station and a park. For a number of years, Dick and Gordon had filed partnership returns under the name of D & G Development. However, on the advice of counsel, they discontinued the practice, and for the last four years each has reported his share of income and expenses on his individual tax return. Both Dick and Gordon elected individually to report the gain from the condemnation sale under Section 1033. Both found like-kind property. At no time did Dick and Gordon ever execute a partnership agreement. However, they did present themselves to others as partners, and each contributed a considerable amount of time to the project.

Your question:

What potential dangers do you detect in connection with these facts?

The first case teaches students to focus on the tax concepts surrounding the formation of a partnership and then literally compute the tax consequences of such a formation. Each student team works together to arrive at an acceptable solution. The second case requires students to identify tax issues which may create potential detrimental tax consequences for a taxpayer.

In both instances, all team members are required to participate and give input. In the process, they develop and hone some of the soft skills mentioned earlier.

STUDENT AND FACULTY REACTIONS
AND OBSERVED RESULTS

I did not convert to team-based learning "cold turkey"; rather, I eased into it. I started with the individual and group tests. Most students liked the tests from the outset. However, a significant number opposed the new approach and preferred the old method in which tests would focus on only subject matter that had previously been discussed in class. One student wrote in the comment section of the course evaluation, "I feel that we should be given the tests after the lecture because the book does not give clear examples and it is difficult to understand before it is lectured on."[2] As a result, for the next few semesters I discussed at the beginning of each semester the professional competency of "self learning" and how individuals joining a profession, including accounting, must be motivated for continued lifelong learning. The message eventually took hold and I began to receive positive responses in the vein of "I liked when we had group [sic] tests" (i.e., I came to class prepared every day). Another student wrote, "I gained a different perspective of tax and liked the group tests."

Once I became adept at and comfortable with the logistics of administering group tests, I ventured out and added team projects in lieu of lectures. As a result, students made the following kinds of comments:

The group learning approach was enjoyable. We had fun and were able to cover a lot of material.
I really appreciated how you used group work, tests and in-class assignments. I learned more through these means.
I really liked doing group problems in class. This helped me assess how well I understood what was taught.
The case work we do in class really helps me to tie in chapter concepts.

Originally I investigated the possibility of adopting team-based learning because I had significant concerns about apathy on the part of my students. I feel that I have made significant strides toward combating apathy with team-based learning; all I have to do is watch group members interact with one another when they are engaged in team projects (e.g., cases, group tests, etc.). In fact, some days I feel that I may have created the opposite problem. Occasionally the students are so involved in the project that it becomes difficult to reestablish control in the classroom so we can move on to another project.

My greatest initial challenge in adopting the team approach was my concern that I had to relinquish considerable lecture time. Intellectually I am now convinced that my students learn more and retain more information and usable knowledge through case studies than through my lectures. However, the temptation is always there to expand the mini-lecture into a maxi-lecture. I am getting better at it but could improve.

I have to admit that, early on, when I first started to experiment with team-based learning, there were times when I wondered if it would be worth the effort. Initially, it seemed that the logistical tasks in managing the class got in the way. But I promise the reader that eventually logistics become second nature. However, to make team-based learning a good experience for both the teacher and the students, the most time-consuming effort has to be directed toward preparing effective case studies. But case studies are not like tests; they have a long shelf life. Because many of the in-class case studies are not graded per se, they can be used again in future semesters. Once a significant number of case studies are in the inventory, only minor updating and editing becomes necessary. It appears to me now that my work load and stress level are significantly reduced when compared with the traditional lecture approach, because the responsibility of learning the rules and basic concepts has been shifted from the professor to the students. I no longer have to worry about being an interesting lecturer or entertainer to keep the class interesting. The focus is now on application and helping students during classroom time with the application process. The application process is much less formal than lecturing and occurs in a more relaxed environment.

SUMMARY COMMENTS

I am convinced that more of my students are now actively engaged in the learning process. Group cases force all team members to participate. It is actually a joy to observe team members interact with one another. In using the team approach, it is no longer possible for a student to attend class without making a contribution of some kind. I have also observed that attendance is much more stable. In my undergraduate classes, attendance averaged 97 percent in 1998 and 98 percent in 1999. Graduate students, who typically have a heavy travel schedule for job interviews, attended at an average rate of 95 percent (1998) and 96 percent (1999). Although I have no comparative data with the years when I used the straight lecture approach, anecdotal evidence seems to indicate that being a member of a team encourages students to be present avoid letting the group down.[3]

At this point in my academic career, I would not entertain the thought of returning to the old passive learning approach. My efforts have paid off in many respects. In 1997, I was asked by my colleagues to present a faculty lecture on team-based learning. Eight years ago, when we first started our AECC-funded Junior Core, we hired ad hoc professors from the organizational behavior department to present the lecture on small group dynamics to our students. My colleagues now trust my expertise in the area and have given that assignment to me. Also, periodically, some of my colleagues inquire about a specific concept related to team-based learning or the administration of RATs. This gives me the satisfaction and indication that more of my colleagues are venturing into the field of team-based learning. Because team-based learning has become a standard in my courses, I was given a special faculty award for outstanding innovation in the classroom. And, incidentally, my student evaluations have significantly improved, even beyond the level I was used to under the old lecture approach. Although I am close to the standard retirement age, I am really having fun again and I am actually looking forward to meeting my classes. Team-based learning has rejuvenated me to such a degree that I could teach forever.

NOTES

1. The Exposure Draft was later published by the AECC as Position Statement No. 1, September 1990. The quote appears on page 5.

2. For this section I reviewed the comment section of the course evaluations for specific remarks related to team teaching. Quotes noted in this section are a sampling of the comments students made.

3. I have regular interactions, usually during lunch, with my colleagues who also teach masters students in our tax program. A couple of years ago, two of them were complaining about one particular student who kept missing class. The same student was also enrolled in my class and assigned to a specific team. In my course he was a regular attendee.

REFERENCE

Deppe, L. A., Sonderegger, E. O., Stice, J. D., Clark, D. C., & Streuling, G. F. (1991). Emerging competencies for the practice of accounting. *Journal of Accounting Education 9*: 257–290.

CHAPTER 10

Creating Group Assignments that Teach Multiple Concepts in an Interdisciplinary Course Context

Laurie A. Lucas

More and more of our institutions are offering courses with an inter-disciplinary curriculum. These types of courses are greatly enhanced when students can learn multiple concepts in single group activities. Lucas shows how she did this while teaching a legal studies course in an interdisciplinary program.

I was first introduced to team-based learning while teaching legal studies at the University of Oklahoma as part of a team of instructors who developed the pilot version of an innovative program called the "Integrated Business Core" (IBC) (see Michaelsen, 1999). At that time (the course structure has since been slightly modified), IBC required the same set of beginning business majors to enroll in the same fifteen hours (five courses): business communication, the legal environment of business, management, and marketing, plus a practicum-style lab course. The goal was to integrate the courses in such a way that the students could begin to see how the course concepts, previously presented only as discrete units, overlapped. In addition to studying four key subjects, students were placed into thirty to thirty-five member "companies" in the lab course. Here they were required to plan, develop, and implement a real, one-semester business venture, and select a community service project to which they would donate any profits from the business and contribute some personal work time.

Larry Michaelsen inspired this curriculum innovation and was actively involved in its development. Since he had also developed the idea of team-based learning, it was not surprising that he advocated the use of this instructional strategy for IBC. To succeed in IBC's challenging environment, the students needed to understand not only the concepts in each individual course but also the connections between the concepts in the four courses. The theory in team-based learning is that the Readiness Assurance Process frees class time for the students to work on activities designed to apply course concepts and to give the students an opportunity to use what they are learning. For IBC, many of these activities also would be designed to help the students implement their business plans. Given the fit between the teaching method and the course structure, it was surprising how many of the instructors involved in the course, including myself, were reluctant to try team-based learning.

MY INITIAL RELUCTANCE

The basis of that reluctance was the belief that the course concepts tested in the RATs and the activities could not possibly include, and therefore reinforce, all of the course material. Most of the instructors used the traditional lecture format, and we all believed that if the information about the concepts and the examples did not come from us, there was no possibility of the students really understanding the material. Thus, the instructors felt that their courses would be compromised if they used this teaching method.

The structure of the course, however, soon made it apparent that IBC demanded an interdisciplinary approach and team-based learning allowed that to happen more easily than did lecturing. Given this fact, I decided to try the method in my legal studies course during my second semester in IBC. We held class in the same large room with chairs that the students could easily work in teams, with each company "owning" a section of the room. Because the same students enrolled in the same five courses, we were not limited to fifty or eighty-minute blocks of time (although we made sure each instructor had the required number of contact hours with students). We were also able to schedule large blocks of time to suit the needs of the instructors and to provide enough time to work activities that were interdisciplinary in nature, complex and relevant to the students' companies.

For example, during the initial stages of the IBC course, the students were asked to organize their companies and provide the instructors with documents such as a mission statement, an organizational chart, job descriptions for all positions, and a company handbook outlining the companies' policies. The company handbooks were required to include a program of progressive discipline, an incentive program, termination policy, meeting procedures, and company policies on discrimination and sexual harassment. Many of these requirements were being discussed in the students' legal studies and management courses, so the management instructor and I decided to design interdisciplinary activities to help demonstrate how the concepts they were studying might affect these documents and policies.

A TEAM ASSIGNMENT TO MEET A PARTICULAR
LEARNING CHALLENGE

Specifically, the management instructor wanted the students to be able to understand the concept of a bona fide occupational qualification (BFOQ) and how to use that concept to draft the job descriptions needed by the companies. In addition, she wanted the students to begin to appreciate how difficult a hiring decision can be when a manager is faced with applicants who have varied but equally valuable qualifications. As the legal studies instructor, I wanted the students to understand what a manager legally could consider when making hiring decisions, and the consequences for the manager when he or she fails to follow the law. Both of us wanted the students to understand that a manager's priorities may conflict with the legal environment. The hiring process also raises many ethical problems for discussion because many of these conflicts are in gray areas, easily manipulated by an unethical manager.

Given these desired outcomes, we designed a two-part activity related to a hiring decision. First, we required the teams to play a management role in which they were to hire a food server for Hooters Restaurant and specify the most important reason for their hiring decision on a form that we provided. Second, after they made their hiring decisions, we forced the teams to examine the same decision from a legal perspective. We accomplished this switch in roles by requiring them to decide which of the rejected applicants had the best chance of winning a hiring discrimination lawsuit based on the evidence presented, including each of the teams' stated reason for their hiring decision.

Almost all the students had had the previous experience of working at a fast food restaurant, or had patronized a Hooters Restaurant, or knew of Hooters Restaurant, so all of the students identified with the situation we presented. The closer the activity is to the students' own life experience, the more invested they will become in the activity and the better their understanding of the concepts applied. The legal concepts that were applied in the activity are listed in Table 10.1. The complexity of this activity allowed for the application of at least fourteen concepts, which helped alleviate my concerns about adequate coverage of material in an activity. It is possible to adequately apply and reinforce the students' understanding of the course concepts if the activities are carefully planned.

INCORPORATING MULTIPLE CONCEPTS
IN A LEARNING ACTIVITY

During the first part of the learning activity, the students were given a job description, some background on what qualifications the restaurant needed for the position, and the newspaper advertisement for the job. Because we supplied this information, we could manipulate its content to demonstrate the types of mistakes managers frequently make; these mistakes would provide the evidence the teams would later draw on to support their legal analysis. The advertisement we used read as follows:

Wanted: Girls who are attractive, extremely bouncy, energetic and very friendly to work as waitresses in the evening. Apply in person only at Hooters Restaurant between 2 pm and 4 pm. Applicants may be required to model a Hooters uniform. No phone calls please.

The essential job functions, however, required only an employee who could work in the evenings, take food and drink orders, ring up tabs, and handle a fast-paced

TABLE 10.1
14 Concepts Incorporated into One Team-Based Learning Activity

Concept Applied	Task
Administrative Agencies (EEOC)	Initiate or respond to EEOC complaint
Civil Rights Act of 1964 Title VII	Make a hiring decision
Protected Class	Understand legal implications of hiring decision
Discrimination Disparate Impact Disparate Treatment Reverse Discrimination Business Necessity Bona Fide Occupational Qualification Age Discrimination in Employment Act	Defend a hiring decision
Federal Question Jurisdiction Federal Diversity Jurisdiction Concurrent Jurisdiction	Class discussion of activity

environment. This advertisement has obvious problems given its clear preference for females ("girls" and "waitresses") and younger applicants ("girls"). The advertisement also raises issues for ethical discussion because it required applicants to apply in person, allowing the unethical manager to observe and consider the applicant's race, gender and age in the hiring decision. In addition, we supplied the teams with limited biographical information about four applicants for the position, including current and past employment experience, educational qualifications, and a reason for applying.

Deciding Whom to Hire

The teams were then asked to make their hiring decision within ten minutes. We told the students that most hiring decisions are made in the first few minutes of the interview, but the real purpose was to keep them from thinking about the legal consequences of their choice and to focus on the more realistic visceral response they may have to each applicant.

This biographical information may be presented in many ways, but I find it is easier to use an overhead with a small photo of each applicant and with each applicant's information listed beside the photo. It is realistic to include the photo because this job and these types of jobs frequently require the applicants to come to the restaurant and fill out an application. Regardless of how you convey the information, you have a lot of control over the particular legal consequences you would like to create. The students' choices are largely predictable, and, even if they were not, you can manipulate their choices by the applicant information you present.

For instance, we presented information on four applicants: three females and one male. The first female was white and attractive, but clearly over the age of forty; the second female was young, attractive, and African American; and the third female was young, attractive, and white. The male applicant was attractive and white and had comparable qualifications to the younger female applicants. Photos of both the younger female applicants showed them to be well-endowed, although the picture we chose for the white female was more provocative in an attempt to steer the teams to her application. If the teams were to choose the white female, this would allow for more discussion about why the older female, the African American female, and the white male were not chosen. The teams will usually choose one of the young women. Regardless of their choice, however, the other applicants' profiles should allow for some discussion about discrimination based on age, race, and gender.

To facilitate ethical discussion, the activity purposefully created stereotypes. For instance, the white female was blond with little employment experience, had a general equivalency diploma rather than a high school degree, and was majoring in a discipline that business students traditionally believe to be "easy," such as education. The older female applicant, unlike the other three applicants who were all college students, had only a high school degree, although we gave her many more years of directly relevant experience. The activity also purposefully attempted to break down stereotypes. For instance, the African American female had the best employment history of the three younger applicants (we did not want her to have as much direct experience as the older woman), was an honor student, and was majoring in an area business students traditionally believe to be "harder," such as engineering. The white male was presented as having comparable qualifications to the two younger women.

Deciding Whom to Defend

In a class with many teams, you should get some variation in the hiring decisions, but even if every team were to initially hire the same applicant, the chances are low that all teams would choose to defend the same rejected applicant. Because the class discussion will primarily focus on the teams' legal analysis, you should have the opportunity to discuss all possible bases for hiring discrimination. For example, with these facts, the activity may be used to discuss the purposes behind Title VII of the Civil Rights Act of 1964, and the Age Discrimination in Employment Act. (If one were to revise the applicant information to include a disabled, but otherwise qualified applicant, the Americans with Disabilities Act also may be discussed.) Forcing the students to evaluate the chances of success for each of the rejected applicants also allows for discussion about the legal concepts of discrimination, disparate impact, or disparate treatment, reverse discrimination, business necessity, and a bona fide occupational qualification. Finally, during the class discussion of the teams' choices, the instructor may discuss what the administrative process requires, and whether and in which court system the rejected applicant may file a lawsuit.

After using this activity for many years, I am still surprised by how few of the teams will choose the male applicant to defend in a lawsuit, even though he has the clearest case of discrimination (remember, he should be otherwise qualified for the position). This fact helps facilitate a discussion about a BFOQ and highlights the frequent conflict between the best managerial choice, given the needs of the particular business, and the legal environment. The activity also demonstrates to the students the difficulty of comparing employment qualifications. For instance, we gave the older woman fifteen years of experience as a food server, while the other applicants had only summer jobs as food servers or "related" experience in a service position. Are the younger women more qualified simply because they are college students, or because they fit the Hooters' image (the most frequently cited reason by the teams to support their hiring decision)? These are not easy questions to answer, and the difficulty the questions create for students helps them appreciate the ethical manager's dilemma.

A "Reality Check"

Underscoring the manager's dilemma is the fact that several male applicants did sue Hooters Restaurant for gender discrimination in the hiring process, and this should be discussed with the class. Hooters Restaurant is well-known for its "Hooters' Girls." The Hooters' Girls evoke the restaurant's gestalt, and for that reason, Hooters asserted a BFOQ defense, arguing that a male food server could not be qualified for the job. Although this debate allowed for some spirited discussion among the students, the seriousness of the issue was not lost on them: Hooters settled the case for $3.75 million, and agreed to create more gender-neutral positions like bartenders and hosts (*New York Times,* 1997).

EDUCATIONAL RESULTS

Despite instructor concerns that content may not be adequately covered by the use of activities (which are limited in scope) rather than lectures, these activities—if properly structured—can be more complex than one may expect. The activities also may be designed for use in one subject area, or, as outlined previously, for use in an interdisciplinary situation.

For example, an instructor could steer the class discussion or present the applicant information in the above activity to emphasize the manager's hiring dilemma rather than the possible legal consequences of the hiring choice. Either discussion, though, highlights the conflict between the manager's interests and the legal environment. Without the context provided by the activity, the conflict might not have been as meaningful to the students. Allowing the students to make the mistake themselves was what facilitated learning; the students should be more likely to remember the concepts used in the activity because they were forced to draw on those concepts to defend and to consider their own actions. Since every team's choice will allow for some discussion (the activity is structured so there is not a "correct" choice), students also were able to discuss their hiring decision freely and without fear of being ostracized.

In the context of the IBC program, this activity also was quite useful. The experience not only helped reinforce the concepts relevant to the students' legal studies and management courses, but also helped them draft the employment policies required for their employment handbook, which was part of their business communication and lab assignments. This ripple effect added value to the activity because the activity's utility was high for the students. The students may have started with a simple abstract concept such as "discrimination," but they ended up with work product that highlighted the relevancy of what they were learning in business communication, and resulted in a tangible company handbook. In the end, the students turned to the policies in their company handbooks many times during the semester as one problem after another emerged within their companies. This result mirrored the reality of the business environment and reinforced the relevant concepts more than anything I could have said to the students using a traditional lecture.

MY VIEWS OF TEAM-BASED LEARNING NOW

After a skeptical introduction to team-based learning, I would now highly recommend the method. While it is certainly not the only method available, it is one of the few that has anticipated and eliminated many of the problems associated with cooperative learning. In addition, I believe that the students, because the method demands that they become actively engaged with the material during the Readiness Assurance Process, learn the material as well as they would in a traditional lecture environment. The application activities provide a richer context for the students if only because they are working the problem rather than merely discussing the problem, thus requiring the use of their higher-order intellectual skills.

Students' Reactions

The students' reactions to team-based learning have largely been positive. One can observe the teams as they coalesce and see their confidence increase as they grow to trust each other's opinions and contributions to the team effort. This interaction alters the traditional classroom setting because it forces students of different backgrounds and interests to interact with one another. I have had more than one student confide in me that they did not think their team took their ideas seriously until the RATs or activities provided the evidence to their teammates that they could perform. Many students, particularly in the early stages of team development, have only their test scores to speak for them. Since everyone in the team knows how well everyone else is performing, a student's high (or low) performance cannot easily be ignored. Students who might never have contributed to team discussion, for whatever reason, become empowered by both their scores on the RATs and their ability to articulate reasons for their answers. This result rarely occurs during a lecture. In fact, students who contribute to lecture discussion are sometimes even dismissed by their peers as class "pets." This result is less likely using team-based learning because every student is participating in the same task. Even if there were no other benefits to team-based learning, I would probably advocate its use based on this observation alone. Part of learning is creating an intellectually open environment for the students so that they may share their ideas without fear of ridicule or rejection.

My Enjoyment of Teaching

I enjoy teaching using the team-based learning method because it frees class time for the more interesting application activities. Although I occasionally stray from the method—I may use lecture and activities or combine the RAP and activities with some question-and-answer sessions—I find that the students seem to enjoy the process the most when the RATs are included. This process does require some time, but I would probably spend the same amount of time preparing for a weekly lecture because my subject matter can change so rapidly.

In summary, I find that team-based learning is a solid teaching method that facilitates the development of critical thinking for the students, particularly if the activities used are relevant to their life experiences and are complex enough to allow for a rich class discussion. After almost ten years of teaching, I am no longer concerned that I personally cover every concept in class. I would rather find a way to help the students think critically about the law, business, and the world in which they find themselves. With those skills, they can look up the details.

REFERENCES

Hooters settles suit by men denied jobs. *New York Times,* 1 October 1997, p. 20.
Michaelsen, L. K. (1999). Integrating the core business curriculum: An experience-based solution. *Selections 15*(2): 9–17.

CHAPTER 11

Team-Based Learning in Large Classes

Larry K. Michaelsen

As class size continues to increase on many campuses, many continue to use and refine variations of the large lecture—with all its attendant problems of student passivity and anonymity. Another option is using an entirely different instructional strategy. Team-based learning is one of the few instructional strategies that is scalable, that is, that can be used effectively in large classes as well as in small classes. In this chapter, Michaelsen identifies what needs to be done when using team-based learning in large classes. When this is done, large classes, in fact, operate and feel much like small classes because students are neither passive nor anonymous.

Although active-learning approaches can produce a wide variety of positive learning outcomes, most of the published examples of successful applications have been in classes of twenty to forty students. Thus, an important question with respect to team-based learning (and any other active-learning approach) is, "Will this work in classes of 100 or more?" The answer with respect to team-based learning is an unqualified YES (See Michaelsen, 2002).

The basic problem presented by large classes is that they typically create two conditions that foster negative student attitudes and inhibit learning: student anonymity and passivity. In small classes, instructors generally know the majority of their students by name and class members interact with the instructor and with each other on a regular basis. However, as classes become larger, individual students are lost in a sea of faces, and a smaller and smaller proportion of class members are able to engage in discussions with either the instructor or each other.

Because of the virtual absence social interaction, students' only active involvement in large classes is limited to their engagement with the material being taught. As a result, most attempts to deal with the problems of large classes focus on changing the instructor's behavior in ways that help keep students' attention focused on the material (more exciting presentations, increased use of videos and demonstrations, etc.). Unfortunately, few instructors have the creativity and energy required to keep students actively focused on the content alone for any extended period of time. Further, even if the instructor requires (and monitors) attendance to ensure that students are at least exposed to the presentations, he or she has no way to hold students accountable for actively engaging with the material either before or during the class.

Team-based learning, by contrast, focuses on changing the social fabric of the learning environment (see Michaelsen, 2002). Because most of the class time is used for group work, the interaction patterns resemble a small class even though there may be several hundred students in the same room. Students: (1) have many opportunities to interact with each other and the instructor, (2) are explicitly accountable for being prepared for, and attending class, and (3) are motivated to do their part in completing the team assignments. In fact, by ensuring that a large number of students are prepared for and attending class, team-based learning actually turns some of the potentially negative characteristics of large classes into assets.

This chapter is designed to accomplish three objectives. One is to discuss why and how team-based learning eliminates many of the problems of large classes. Another is to highlight a few important keys to implementing team-based learning that are uniquely important in large classes. The third is to provide concrete examples that illustrate both why the adjustments are important and how they can be made.

COPING WITH THE PROBLEMS OF LARGE CLASSES

Some twenty years ago, I faced a challenge that had a profound impact on my thinking about teaching. The challenge occurred when, because of enrollment pressures, I was forced to triple the size of my primary course from 40 to 120 students. Based on my experience in smaller classes, I was convinced that group activities and assignments were an effective strategy for actively engaging students in learning to apply concepts rather than simply learning about them. As a result, I rejected the advice of my colleagues who advised turning the class into a series of lectures in favor of an approach that involved using the vast majority of class time for group work.

By the middle of the very first semester, it was apparent that the approach was working. In fact, it was working so well that it accomplished two things that I hadn't even anticipated. First, the students themselves perceived the large class setting as being far more beneficial than harmful (see Table 11.1). Second, the approach created several conditions that would enhance learning in any setting.

Twenty years and 1,400 learning teams later, I am firmly convinced that very few of the requirements for successfully implementing team-based learning are measurably affected by the size of the class. In large and small classes alike, the Readiness Assurance Process (individual test → team test → appeals → instructor feedback/input; see Chap-

TABLE 11.1
Can Large Classes be an Asset?

Students in five classes (n = 605) in which team learning was used were asked the question:

Which of the following most accurately describes the impact of the large size of the class on what you gained from thaing this course?

They answered as follows:

1.	*It helped more than it hurt.*	49%
2.	*It both helped and hurt (about equally).*	18%
3.	*It did not make much difference.*	24%
4.	*It hurt more than it helped.*	7%
5.	*It hurt a great deal.*	2%

ter 2) ensures that the vast majority of students will: (1) attend class, (2) be individually prepared for the in-class team work, and, most important for large classes, (3) learn to work effectively with little or no assistance from the instructor. In smaller classes, the instructor's physical presence often masks the negative impact of what is actually ineffective instructional practice. When we started using team-based learning for large classes, some of the lessons we learned during our first few semesters were a bit painful, but the large class setting actually helped refine our understanding of the factors that impact the development of effective learning teams. With over 100 students, several suboptimal procedures and marginally effective assignments that worked pretty well in smaller classes created a level of discontent that was impossible to ignore.

Over time, however, I have come to understand two keys that are essential to successfully using team-based learning in large classes and two other catalysts that will measurably facilitate the development of a positive "chemistry" in both the teams and the class as a whole. The two implementation keys are adapting to the physical environment (space, noise, etc.), and creating procedures and props to handle the mechanics of running the class (handing out and collecting materials, pacing the teams, providing feedback, etc.). The two catalysts are scheduling the classes in longer class periods and getting to know students by name.

IMPLEMENTATION KEY #1:
ADAPTING TO THE PHYSICAL ENVIRONMENT

In most cases, classrooms that are large enough to accommodate large classes have fixed, amphitheater-style seating. As a result, adapting to the physical environment generally involves four things. These are:

1. providing teams with a space that becomes their "home";
2. ensuring that team members are able and willing to arrange themselves so that members have eye contact with each other as they work;
3. providing access to the team space for both students and the instructor;
4. maintaining control over the noise level during total class discussions.

Providing Team Space

In large class settings, providing a permanent space for each team is important for three reasons. One is that having students know where they belong helps maintain a semblance of order in what otherwise seems like a chaotic situation relative to students' experience in traditional classes. The second reason for providing a permanent space for the teams is that having a home makes it easier for teams to develop an identity. Members know where they belong and other teams implicitly associate each of the teams with the space they occupy. Finally, having a permanent home provides teams with time to develop procedures for overcoming the limitations (e.g., seating configuration, difficulty seeing and/or hearing, etc.) inherent in the space to which they have been assigned.

Over the years, I have seen colleagues use a wide variety of methods for establishing a home for their newly formed teams. The most common is creating and posting a seating map or chart showing the teams' assigned location. Another effective method simply involves announcing that team members should congregate around pre-placed and numbered markers (I have seen everything from cloth flags to helium-filled balloons to large Styrofoam cups that were suspended from the ceiling).

Ensuring Eye Contact

Being able to have eye contact during the team work is critical to the development of effective, self-managed teams. In fact, the single most reliable way to monitor the progress in team development is to observe the degree to which members voluntarily position themselves so that they have eye contact with each other. If members fail to notice that a member is sitting outside the team, they are implicitly sending the message that input from that member is not needed or wanted. Further, if the instructor fails to call their attention to the potential problem, then it often becomes a self-fulfilling prophesy that produces resentment from both those who are being ignored and those who are inadvertently doing the ignoring.

Unfortunately, this is not an isolated problem. Students who are naturally outgoing tend to take charge and make it difficult for quieter members to provide input to the team. In large classes, which are often taught in rooms with seats in fixed rows in an amphitheater-type classroom, they often compound the problem by regularly sitting in the seats that are located near the center of the team space. As a result, it is important to help students learn to use their space to help, not hinder, full participation.

Ensuring that teams develop the practice of maintaining eye contact while they work often requires two steps. The first and most essential is giving them a space that makes it possible to have broad-based member contributions (i.e., as near as possible to sitting around a small, round table). Even in amphitheater-type classrooms, this can be done by assigning seats such that members on one row can turn around and face the rest of their team seated behind them. The other step is ensuring that students understand how important eye contact really is. My standard practice for teaching this important lesson involves having students physically move within their teams so that they experience the difference between central and peripheral seats while they are taking the second and third team Readiness Assessment Tests (RATs—see Chapter 2). About two or three minutes into the team phase of the second RAT, I break in and make an announcement like, "I've noticed that almost everyone is sitting in the same place as they were for RAT #1 (and they usually are). Just for fun, I'd like everyone to stand up and move two seats to the right *within* your team."

Although the procedure is simple, the impact is profound. With one intervention, most groups do a pretty good job of ensuring that members have eye contact without ever having been told to do so. If enough of the groups are still not managing their space very well, which sometimes happens in rooms with fixed seats, I will make a similar announcement on the third team RAT except that I have everyone shift two spaces to the left. If most of the groups are doing well, I focus on the groups that need help and have them shift spaces until they get the message.

Providing Access

Having access to the teams is important for both the instructor and the students. Access allows the instructor to listen in on team discussions so that he or she has a sense of when the teams need input and what kind to give them. The teams need access so that they can retrieve and hand in the materials that are related to the team assignments.

In many cases, seats are set far enough apart to provide access as the teams work. If not, then I recommend leaving vacant rows or seats between teams. With neither built-in access nor the possibility of vacant rows, the best bet is to make students aware of the situation and give the teams some class time to work with each other to solve the problem.

Controlling Noise

Surprisingly, noise can be either good or bad. When students are working on in-class team assignments, a high level of noise is actually helpful. The sound of other teams is a reminder of the importance of staying on task because students know that they will soon be held accountable for having accomplished something. In addition, noise promotes team development because it forces members to literally act like a team (i.e., get physically close together and listen attentively). On the other hand, when a teacher wants total class discussions, even a low level of background noise can be very disruptive. If students cannot hear, they cannot learn. Thus, to be effective in large classes, instructors must develop ways to move students from a "noise is necessary" mode into a "now it is time to listen" mode.

The key to managing the noise level in large classes is training students to move out of the team discussion mode to a class discussion mode. This generally involves two steps. First, the instructor has to provide a signal (holding up a hand and having class members do the same, whistling, dimming the lights, etc.) to alert students to wind down their team discussions. Second, no matter how long it takes, the instructor must wait until students are quiet before starting to talk. Further, in some large class settings (e.g., most large auditoriums) the instructor will need to restate some of the class members' comments, and a number of colleagues have found that they need to use portable microphones that can be passed from team to team.

IMPLEMENTATION KEY #2:
MANAGING CLASSROOM MECHANICS

Implementing team-based learning in large classes requires effectively handling five mechanical aspects of running a class. These are distributing and collecting materials, pacing team work, and providing timely feedback on the RATs, giving application-focused assignments and exams, and providing feedback about the value of team discussions as a means of accomplishing intellectual work.

Distributing and Collecting Materials

Even in very large, lecture-oriented classes, handing out and collecting materials is seldom a problem because the need so seldom arises. In most large classes, the only times that materials are even handed out are on the two or three days on which the instructor gives midterm and final exams. With team-based learning, however, each of the RATs (see Chapter 2) and most class activities require handing out materials and collecting students' work. In smaller classes, the instructor can simply hand out the materials with no noticeable loss of class time. In large classes, however, the same procedure can consume significant amounts of class time and remind students of the negative aspects of being in a large class.

A simple but effective way to dramatically reduce the material-handling time is by using team folders. Although this requires spending a few minutes before class to put a set of materials in each of the team folders, the payoff is well worth the effort. Except in really big classes (200+), you can hand out the folders to the teams in a few seconds and the teams will all be distributing the materials to their members all at the same time. Team folders are particularly helpful in managing the RATs. In all, I use team folders five times in managing each of the RATs. First, I pass out folders containing the tests and answer sheets. Second, teams collect their answer sheets in the folder, bring the folder to the front of the room and exchange it for a team answer sheet. Third, while students take the team RAT, I remove the answer sheets from the folder, put the folders in the catch tray of the test scorer and run the answer sheets through the scorer right back into the folder. Fourth, when teams finish their RAT, they scan their answer sheet and pick up the folder so they can distribute scored individual answer sheets. Fifth, after teams have completed their appeals and I've had a chance to provide additional input on troublesome questions, I have students use the folders to turn in their tests and answer sheets.

Pacing the Team Work

Pacing student work is one of the most difficult challenges of any active-learning approach. Team-based learning partially solves one aspect of the problem but creates another. The learning teams reduce the negative impact of individual variations in students' ability or levels of preparation. Although compensating for individual differences does require some class time, the net loss is minimal because both slower and faster students benefit from better-prepared students tutoring their peers (which they are more than willing to do). With team-based learning, however, the new challenge is finding ways to adjust to the normal variation between teams in their pace of work. And the bigger the class, the bigger the challenge.

A number of strategies can help with the task of proper pacing, all of which are dependent on giving students deadlines for completing their work that are clear and specific but still flexible. The single most useful strategy is starting with a deadline that you think is slightly less than the teams will need, listening in on the teams (so you can assess how they are progressing) and, adjusting "on the fly." Another useful strategy involves using the pace of the faster teams to create a deadline for the slower teams by using a "five (or some other)-minute rule." For example, I use a five-minute rule that covers both the individual and team RATs. I announce that, "You can start the team test as soon as you have turned in your folder containing the individual answer sheets and, when ____ teams (approximately a third of the teams) have completed their test, the remaining teams have five minutes to finish." Finally, whenever the opportunity arises, I schedule the team assignments at either the beginning of class (to enable slower teams the opportunity to get a head start if they so choose) or at the very end (so that faster teams can leave when they finish their work).

Providing Feedback on RATs

A very important key to using team-based learning effectively in large classes is to provide content-related feedback that is immediate, frequent, and discriminatory (i.e., enables learners to clearly distinguish between good and bad choices) (see Michaelsen, Black, & Fink, 1996, and Chapter 2 of this volume). This kind of feedback is essential to learning and retention, and it enables each team to compare its work to other similar teams, a task that is critical to the development of self-managed teams.

The RATs offer an opportunity for immediate and discriminatory feedback in a way that enables cross-team comparisons. The easiest way to provide immediate feedback on the RATs is to use multiple-choice questions with answer sheets that can be scored in class with a portable test-scoring machine. Even if there are several hundred students in the class, instructors can provide timely feedback on the individual tests by scoring them during the team test, and give immediate feedback on the team tests by having a team representative run their own answer sheet through the test scorer or using IF-AT answer sheets (see Appendix A, p. 227) which give feedback on a question-by-question basis. Providing cross-team comparisons is as simple as recording the team scores on an overhead transparency or on the blackboard. My observation is that this kind of timely feedback on the RATs is the single most powerful means available for ensuring that groups develop into learning teams.

Providing Feedback on Application-Focused Assignments and Exams

Providing immediate and discriminatory feedback on application-focused assignments in a way that enables cross-team comparisons is a more challenging task, but it can be done. Because of the number of teams involved, in large classes the key is creating efficient ways for teams to present the results of their work to each other. One part of the solution to this challenge is for the teacher to find some way for the team to report the results of their work in a simple form, even though the decisions usually involve complex concepts and information. Creating decision-based problems helps this process greatly (see Chapter 3 for more on this). The other part of the solution is to create mechanisms by which the teams can simultaneously report their decisions.

A good example of simple reports of complex team decisions comes from a recently retired colleague who, for a number of years, regularly used team-based learning in a financial management course of 275–290 students. The assignment was based on a case that he assigned on the day he gave a RAT to ensure that students were familiar with the pros and cons of buying versus renting versus leasing. At the beginning of the next class period, he gave each of his forty-five or so teams a legal-sized sheet of paper and a large felt-tip marker. He then announced that they were to act as a financial advisory team and that they had thirty-five minutes (of a seventy-minute class period) to develop a recommendation to buy, rent, or lease a fleet of trucks that were needed to fulfill the terms of a three-year contract. When the time had elapsed, he gave a signal and had the teams hold up their legal-sized sheet of paper on which teams had written a single word—buy, rent, or lease—to reveal their choice to the rest of the class. He then handed out portable microphones to a couple of teams who had taken each of the three positions and conducted a class discussion of the factors that influenced the decision.

By having the teams reach mutually exclusive but directly comparable decisions and represent their work in a simple form, he ensured they were explicitly and immediately accountable for their work. As a result, the teams were both prepared and motivated to challenge each others' decisions, and he had no trouble generating a vigorous class discussion in spite of the many adverse conditions presented by the large class and the awkward physical setting (a very large auditorium with fixed seating).

The importance of having simultaneous team reports is one of the lessons I learned the hard way. For many years, I had successfully used an experiential role play called the New Truck Dilemma (Maier, Solem, & Maier, 1975) to make the point that employees were more likely to cooperate and have positive attitudes if they are involved in making decisions that affect them. This role play simulates a situation in which a telephone repair supervisor is allotted a new truck and must decide on how to juggle truck assignments among the members of his or her crew. The effectiveness of the activity is directly related to students' conclusion of why individual drivers were satisfied or dissatisfied with the truck that they were assigned. The value of the activity is that it sets the stage for students to discover that their emotions can blind them to important insights about managing team decisions. This occurs because their intuitive conclusion that the key issue is the decision itself, that is, who gets what truck, is seldom consistent across multiple teams. Instead, the process of how the decision is made is more important than the actual decision (i.e., dissatisfaction is far more likely when the supervisor makes the decision than when the drivers actively participate in deciding how the trucks will be allocated among team members). Thus, using the New Truck Dilemma involves students in three separate steps: (1) engaging in the role play itself, (2) collecting and summarizing the data about what happened in each of the teams, and (3) discussing the implications of the data from the entire set of role-play teams.

The first time I used the New Truck Dilemma in a large class, I followed my normal procedures for running the role play, collecting and summarizing the results and, discussing their implications. Thus, I had all of the teams role play at the same time, then collected and recorded their results one at a time in one of the columns of an overhead transparency (see Figure 11.1 for a simplified version of the one I would typically use for six teams).

Although students were intensely engaged in the role-play itself, the data collection that followed was a near disaster. With twenty teams instead of six, my normal one-at-a-time reporting procedure produced two negative outcomes that, in combination, completely destroyed the value of the entire experience. One was that the repetitive nature of the teams' reports was so boring that students would not even keep quiet enough for either me or the rest of the class to hear what happened in the other teams. The other problem was that the reporting process took so long that we didn't have time to discuss the implications of what they had reported. I knew something would have to change.

The next time around, I still had all the teams role play at the same time but changed the way they reported their results. This time, I had the teams simultaneously record their own results on a strip of newsprint that contained the same data as one of the columns of the chart shown in Figure 11.1 and that was large enough so that each team's decisions could be seen by the entire class. Next, I had them bring their results to the front of the room where I taped them to the wall after having

FIGURE 11.1
New Truck Assignments to Drivers

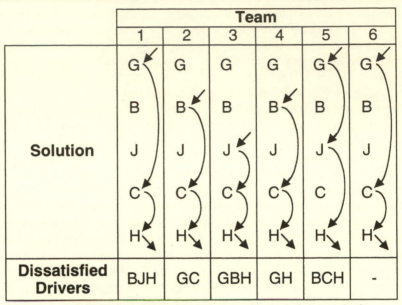

Solution	Team					
	1	2	3	4	5	6
	G	G	G	G	G	G
	B	B	B	B	B	B
	J	J	J	J	J	J
	C	C	C	C	C	C
	H	H	H	H	H	H
Dissatisfied Drivers	BJH	GC	GBH	GH	BCH	-

Notes: 1. Initials represent drivers' names (e.g. J=John or Jan)
         2. Arrows show truck moves:
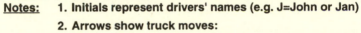
         G = driver receiving new or different truck
         H = old truck discarded

grouped them according to which driver had received the new truck. Then, I started the class discussion by asking, "Does anyone have any questions they would like to ask any of the other teams?"

The contrast between the first and second times I used the role play in a large class dramatically illustrated two important lessons about the value of simultaneous reporting. First, there was plenty of time for whole-class discussion because the teams were all creating their reports at the same time. The other lesson was that it actually set the stage for a much richer discussion than was typical in smaller classes. With twenty examples instead of six, there were multiple cases of counterintuitive results (i.e., examples of teams in which the same people ended up with the same trucks but with very different levels of satisfaction). For example, the sequential order of the results shown in Figure 11.1 hides the fact that two of the teams (1 and 6) reached exactly the same decision (i.e., G got the new truck, G's truck went to C, and C's went to H, and H's was discarded), yet there were three dissatisfied drivers in team 1, and no dissatisfied drivers in team 6. Second, because the newsprint strips were independent of each other, I could place the contrasting results side by side to ensure that students would discover which driver ended up with what trucks did not seem to have any effect on the levels of drivers' satisfaction. As a result, with no prompting from me, students raised a series of questions that led to the key conclusion that I wanted to bring out in the discussion (i.e., the way the decision is made is more important than the decision itself).

Providing Feedback about the Value of Teams

One extremely important aspect of preparing students for future work in teams involves building their confidence that group discussions are an effective way to accomplish intellectual work. In traditionally taught courses, instructors face a very difficult challenge in trying to sell students on the value of teams. In many cases, they are forced to try to overcome students' previous negative experiences with poorly functioning groups when their only selling point is secondhand evidence in the form of examples of successful teams. With team-based learning, however, instructors always have the opportunity to use students' own experience to drive that important lesson home, and, as with the New Truck Dilemma role play, the bigger the class, the better. All they have to do is report and discuss the cumulative scores on the individual and team RATs by using the following steps after students have taken several RATs (I usually wait until after RAT # 4):

1. Create an overhead transparency that shows, for each team, the cumulative RAT scores of the: (1) lowest team member, (2) average team member, (3) highest team member, (4) team, and (5) the difference between the team's highest member and the team score (see Figure 11.2 for an example from one of my recent courses).
2. Introduce the transparency by saying something like, "I've been looking at the data from your RATs, and I thought you'd be interested in seeing the big picture of how the teams are doing up to this point."
3. Show the transparency, briefly explaining what the numbers mean by following one line all the way across. For example, "In team #1 the lowest cumulative individual score is 142, the average score is 169, the highest individual score is 188, and the team score is 206—16 points higher than their own *best* member." (Historically, over 99 percent of the teams' scores will be higher than their own best member—see Michaelsen, Watson, & Black, 1989—and, as in the previous case, the lowest team in the entire class will often score above the highest individual in the class.
4. After giving students a few minutes to digest the data, I can always generate a rich discussion about the value of teams by simply asking something like, "What do you see here that you think is important?"

Most students will know that their own team has a higher score than any team member, but few, if any, will be aware of the pervasiveness of the outcome or will have

FIGURE 11.2
Readiness Assessment Test Scores

(Cumulative scores after 4 RATs)

Team #	Individual Member Scores: Low	Average	High	Team Score	Team Gain over BEST Member
1	142	169	188	204	16
2	126	154	168	201	33
3	135	164	183	210	27
4	149	165	184	197	13
5	149	173	192	213	21
6	107	166	187	207	20
7	135	162	181	213	32
8	140	163	186	203	17
Average	135.4	164.5	183.6	206.0	22.4

12% higher than the **BEST** team member

thought through the powerful message about the value of the teams that these score comparisons represents. Further, the impact of this activity directly increases with the size of the class because every team represents a concrete and meaningful example to support the value of teamwork in accomplishing intellectual tasks.

IMPLEMENTATION CATALYST #1:
SCHEDULING LONGER CLASS PERIODS

In traditional classes, a lecturer can simply end class when the time runs out and start again at the beginning of the next. On the other hand, using team-based learning in fifty-minute class periods usually makes it more difficult to develop a positive team and class chemistry for two reasons. One is that the short and rigid time blocks tend to create the impression that the instructor is not very efficient in his or her use of class time. For example, one option for giving RATs in a fifty-minute class period is making them short. However, even short RATs leave little time to do anything else if teams finish quickly and there is little need for corrective instruction. The other is that being limited to short blocks of time often forces the instructor to adjust in-class team assignments in ways that reduce their effectiveness. For example, the other viable option for giving RATs in a fifty-minute class period is spreading the different parts of the process across more than one class period (i.e., the individual test on the first day and the team test, appeals and instructor input on the next one). The disadvantage of this strategy is that the impact of comparing the individual and team RAT scores is significantly reduced by the fact that students have the opportunity to study between the two tests.

Efficient Use of Class Time

Most students have very low expectations about large classes, but are willing to give the "group thing" a try. Unfortunately, their patience tends to be limited because of two factors. One is the normal inefficiencies of newly formed groups. The other is that, because they are used to an instructor-controlled environment, twenty or more teams working at the same time tends to create what seems like a chaotic classroom environment. Consequently, quickly building a positive team and class chemistry has the potential to turn their skepticism into enthusiasm.

Unfortunately, short class periods tend to delay the team-development process because of real inefficiencies at both ends of most classes. The inefficiency at the beginning stems from the fact that each time a team meets, it takes a few minutes for members to warm up to each other and to their work. With fifty-minute class periods, by the time students get comfortable with each other and focused on their assignment, the class is almost over. The inefficiency at the end comes from the fact that instructors are forced to plan their assignments to end with some class time remaining because if they fail to allow enough time to talk at the end, they typically lose most of the value of an entire class period. Longer class periods reduce both problems simply because there are fewer opportunities for the problems to occur.

Flexibility for Designing and Managing
In-Class Team Assignments

Longer class periods provide flexibility in designing and managing in-class team assignments in two important ways. First, it is easier to take advantage of "teaching moments" that inevitably occur during the team work or subsequent class discussions. When I teach in longer class periods, I often go to class with materials for several different activities and use the outcomes of each to determine which one(s) I use and the order in which I use them. Second, longer class periods that provide the opportunity to use difficult and complex assignments capitalize on the fact that team-based learning builds teams into effective self-managed learning teams. Thus, for example, in teaching about organizations, I often use novels as cases and find that many of students' most remembered learning experiences come from team exams that focus on integrating concepts and that took two or more hours to complete.

IMPLEMENTATION CATALYST #2:
GETTING TO KNOW STUDENTS' NAMES

The other catalyst for implementing team-based learning in large classes is learning students' names. I have found that when I am able to call students by name, it helps in two ways. One is that students respond to me quite differently. For example, they are much more willing to approach me with questions and suggestions and are far more forgiving when I make mistakes. The other is that I have found that when I pay close enough attention to get to know students by name, I am able to do a much better job of reading their reactions and using them to improve my teaching.

Fortunately, compared to large lecture classes, the task of learning students' names is helped by two aspects that are inherent in the team-based learning process. One is that both the teams and their locations within the class provide cues that aid in the initial memorization process. The other is that, unlike giving a lecture to a vast sea of faces, the instructor has the opportunity to get to know students during class as he or she listens in on the teams at work. Most of my colleagues who use team-based learning in large classes capitalize on both factors by making an initial attempt to memorize students' names from team pictures taped on index cards, and reviewing the names as they circulate from team to team while students work on their team assignments. Although I am not particularly good at remembering names, I have found that, in a class of just over 100 students, it takes me about an hour to memorize the names from the team pictures. Then, I have to spend several class periods reviewing the names as I circulate among the teams as they work to get to the point that I can call everyone by name.

SOME CONCLUDING THOUGHTS

Team-based learning can be a very effective way to offset the disadvantages of large classes. However, successfully implementing team-based learning in any setting requires adherence to the basic key elements of the process. These include:

1. using permanent and purposefully heterogeneous learning teams;
2. grading based on a combination of individual performance, team performance, and peer evaluation;
3. devoting the vast majority of the class time to team activities;
4. employing the six-step instructional activity sequence.

Successfully implementing team-based learning in large classes requires particularly careful attention to adapting to the physical environment (space, noise, etc.), and creating procedures and props to handle the mechanics of running the class (handing out and collecting materials, pacing the teams, providing feedback, etc.). In addition, scheduling the classes in longer class periods and getting to know students' name will further facilitate the implementation process.

When properly implemented, the team-based learning approach produces a learning environment that very closely resembles that of small classes. Students are neither anonymous nor passive. The fact that the majority of class time is spent on team work ensures that students are accountable for, and receive, immediate feedback on their work. As a result, the vast majority of students naturally become actively involved in both the social and intellectual aspects of the class.

In addition, team-based learning changes the role of the instructor in two very positive ways by changing the way we interact with both the content we teach and the students in our classes. Because the process motivates students to prepare in advance and to attend class, lecturing (what little we do) is far more interesting because we can largely bypass simpler and more basic concepts. In addition, because we spend a lot more time listening and observing, the classroom is a much more social place for us as well. The sea of faces gradually resolves into individual students with real personalities who are willing and able to assist in the teaching and learning process.

REFERENCES

Maier, N. R. F., Solem, A. R., & Maier, A. A. (1975). *The role-play technique: A handbook for management and leadership practice.* La Jolla, CA: University Associates.

Michaelsen, L. K. (2002). Team-based learning in large classes. In *Engaging large classes: Strategies and techniques for college faculty.* Ed. C. Stanley & E. Porter. New York: Anker.

Michaelsen, L. K., Black, R. H., & Fink, L. D. (1996). What every faculty developer needs to know about learning groups. In *To improve the academy: Resources for faculty, instructional and organizational development.* Ed. L. Richlin. Vol. 15. Stillwater, OK: New Forums Press.

Michaelsen, L. K., Watson, W. E., & Black, R. H. (1989). A realistic test of individual versus group consensus decision making. *Journal of Applied Psychology 74*(5): 834–839.

CHAPTER 12

Using Team-Based Learning in a Very Traditional, Cultural, and Institutional Context

Jiři Popovský

Can team-based learning work in a culture and institution in which students are used to a very hierarchical relationship? The author tested this question in his own teaching at Charles University in the Czech Republic. He found that students were not only able to adjust effectively but did so with enthusiasm. He also noticed that the focused, give-and-take discussions that occur in team-based learning also prepare students well for the oral exams that come at the end of their diploma work.

I am a member of the faculty of Natural Science at Charles University in Prague, Czech Republic. My courses are in the area of technical hydrobiology and ecology, especially the ecology of cyanobacteria and algae (the "lower" plants). Although I am nearly 65 years old, I have only been teaching at the university for the past ten years. Before the end of the Council for Mutual Economic Assistance (Comecon) and the removal of Soviet influence in 1989, I was not allowed to teach the "new Communist generation" for political reasons.

Before that time, I had completed my studies in hydrobiology and phycology (the study of algae), and worked first in Prague's Wastewater Treatment Plant, then in the hydrobiological laboratory of the Academy of Sciences, and later in the Department of Hygienic Drinking Water for the State Public Health Institute. I have published over 100 scientific papers in hydrobiology and phycology and have been active in national and international scientific organizations.

A few years after I began teaching at Charles University, I visited Oklahoma and learned about the idea of teaching with small groups from a conversation with Dr. L. Dee Fink. The idea was intriguing, because it seemed to have the potential not only to generate more significant learning but also to make classes more interesting for both teachers and students.

The question remained, however, how would the use of small groups be received by students in our country? Charles University is like most other universities in Central Europe (East Germany, Austria, Hungary, and Poland), but these universities are quite different from those in the West. The Soviet system of education and science was dominant in all countries behind the Iron Curtain from 1948 to 1989. In that context, the relationship between the teacher and the students is similar to that between a lord and peasant in feudal societies. The educational process is strictly a one-way stream of knowledge and information. Would students who were used to this system accept and respond to a more active process of learning?

I decided to try the idea even though I did not know for sure how it would work. The idea seemed simple, relatively easy to use, and likely to lead to important kinds of learning.

MY EXPERIENCE WITH TEAM-BASED LEARNING

I have been using the idea of team-based learning in two classes: ecology, which emphasizes theoretical science, and technical hydrobiology, which is more applied science. Both classes meet two hours each week and conclude with a major examination at the end of the semester. Generally the classes are small, with four to twenty fourth- and fifth-year students, along with an occasional postgraduate fellow attending as well.

The students come from a variety of special studies: hydrobiology, hydrogeology, phycology, and environmental studies. They choose my courses from a set of approximately ten optional courses. Most probably choose to take mine because its subject matter is close to their own areas of special studies in terms of the subject matter.

GETTING STARTED WITH TEAM-BASED LEARNING

Because the students come from two different areas (biology and geology) and from working with three or four different chairs, and because I am partly retired, we do not all know each other well. Therefore, at the beginning we introduce ourselves and make a list of who is in the class, including each of our individual areas of study. This last piece of information helps all of us, especially me, when we get into discussions.

COVERING THE COURSE CONTENT

After the introductions, I explain the system of tests and questions that we will be using. The sequence of events is as follows:

1. I assign a section of material to read from the textbook.
2. Students are instructed to read this material closely and thoroughly.

3. I prepare several questions, usually four to six, that are on important or difficult themes.
4. When students come to the next class meeting, we do two things:
    a. They write on the test questions individually.
    b. Then they answer the same questions as a group.
5. Finally we evaluate their answers, and I comment or elaborate on answers that they got wrong or had difficulty with.

The whole testing process itself takes about forty minutes. This leaves about fifteen minutes or so to make additional comments on the subject, based on my own study of the topics.

Sometimes we talk about how the students study the textbook, looking for ways they could study this material more effectively. The questions on the test are short-answer essay, not multiple choice. Generally they call for answers of two or more sentences. This form of thinking seems to be appropriate for students working on a Bachelor of Science degree, and the follow-up discussion is good preparation for their eventual oral examination at the end of their diploma work.

BUILDING DEEPER UNDERSTANDING

After students have studied and learned some of the basic concepts and relationships, we then spend one or two class periods in which students practice using this knowledge by working on some application problems. I will describe one typical problem from each of my two classes.

In the technical hydrobiology course, one of the major topics is drinking water. Therefore, at some point, I pose the following question to the teams to work on: "What are the functions and properties of a good drinking-water supply for a city and region?"

Good answers on the "functions" portion of the question will include references to several possible functions: retention of a sufficient quantity of water, leveling function of water supplies (providing water during droughts and retaining water during floods), and ability to provide raw drinking water to a treatment or processing facility. The answer should not include recreation (fishing, sailing), water for irrigation, generating electric power, and so on. When addressing the optimal properties of a water supply, students should comment on: the average depth of the reservoir, the narrow body of the lake near the dam, the orientation of the lake, the level above sea level, having a catchment area without heavy settlement or agriculture (or better, with a coniferous forest), and protection from pollution.

In the ecology class, one of my fun questions each year is the following: "Can the Loch Ness monster exist?" Although the question seems somewhat frivolous, it prompts students to use some important principles and calculations to systematically think through a complex question like this. In order to answer such a question, students must answer certain questions in a particular order:

1. What is a "monster"?
   a. Is it a mammal or reptile?
   b. How big is it?
2. How does/might it operate biologically?
   a. What is the system of reproduction and growth? How many eggs or young ones does it have?
   b. What is the size of a family or group?
3. What is the food supply available here?
   a. What is the potential for primary production (phytoplankton) in Loch Ness? Secondary production (zooplankton)? Tertiary production (fish)?
   b. Are the monsters likely to be autochthonous or allochthonous?
4. Given the gross production in the lake, how many individuals can the lake support, if one assumes a size of the individuals, or monsters, as being at least two meters in length?
5. How many individuals are necessary to sustain continuous reproduction?
6. Given all the preceding, what is your conclusion of whether Loch Ness can support a Loch Ness monster?

THE EFFECTS OF USING TEAM-BASED LEARNING

Although such a style of education is very unusual in our country (my colleagues are still confounded by what I am doing), I have seen two important changes take place. The first is the students' acceptance of the process itself. At first, they are a little embarrassed because they are not used to doing what this style of teaching calls on them to do. However, as time goes on, they get used to it and accept it very well. Gradually their answers to the applied problems become richer and more detailed than at the beginning. The second important change is that the students gradually become more courageous in their discussions with each other and even with me. They learn to challenge the dominant personalities when they discover that those who dominate are not always right.

Both of these changes are very satisfying to me. I am convinced these students are achieving much more important kinds of learning than they would if I were lecturing all the time.

A FINAL COMMENT

When I visited with Dr. Fink in Oklahoma back in 1993, he made a side comment that struck me as valid and very important. "You are a 'bad teacher' if your knowledge is not greater at the end of the class than at the beginning." My conclusion is that both my students and I have greater knowledge as the result of using a more active and interactive mode of teaching and learning. As a result, I am enjoying my teaching very much, even though it is coming late in my professional career. I look forward to using this approach to teaching as long as I am able to continue at the university.

CHAPTER 13

Team-Based Learning in International Situations

Jon Cragin

Cragin has had an opportunity to test the limits of team-based learning, in both educational and corporate settings in Asia, the Middle East, and Europe. He learned some important lessons, both about the viability of team-based learning in different cultural settings and about why team-based learning can be successful in any cultural setting.

I had one of those direction-altering "aha!" experiences in 1979 when I was introduced to team-based learning as a doctoral candidate at the University of Oklahoma. I had spent the previous four years in Asia working in fourteen countries as a consultant, trying to develop training methods and materials that would cross cultural boundaries. During that time of trial and error, I experimented with several techniques that worked well, but I never could explain why these methods worked until I was a graduate assistant in the first large-class implementation of team-based learning at the University of Oklahoma Price School of Business. I decided to learn everything I could about how to apply the team-based learning theory and methods, and to contribute where I could to that growing body of knowledge.

Since completing my Ph.D., I have used team-based learning in three very different contexts: (1) teaching graduate and undergraduate students, (2) training career executives, and (3) developing employees in companies I built and led. The common denominator for all three contexts was that, unlike many college and university courses, the objective of imparting information was the starting point, not the primary objective of students' learning. In each case, there was a strong market-driven imperative for the recipients to master concepts and develop skills at a level that would enable them to immediately and significantly impact organization performance. As a result, my success was measured by what my students could do—not just what they knew.

I have also used team-based learning in thirty different foreign countries on three continents. Although the geographical locations and cultures (Hong Kong, China, Russia, Korea, Indonesia, Malaysia, Singapore, the Philippines, Brazil, and others) have varied greatly, the classroom settings were quite similar. For the most part, I taught using English, although in some cases, I had developed sufficient language skills that I was able to teach in Chinese. My observations include approximately 2,750 students and executives in class sizes ranging from 25 to 100. All the team-based learning applications focused on increasing learners' knowledge and skills in business.

QUESTIONS ABOUT USING TEAM-BASED LEARNING IN INTERNATIONAL SETTINGS

This chapter summarizes what I have found in the two decades since my first exposure to team-based learning, and addresses the following questions.

- Do team-based learning methods work in cultures where they are so much at odds with the mainstream of educational practice that students invariably start out being uncomfortable with the approach? In many parts of the world where I have worked, there is an extremely strong tradition of authoritative lecture and memorization methods of instruction.
- Will team-based learning be effective when English is a second language for learners but the majority of the teaching materials and the native language of the instructor is English? In many international higher education settings, learning is constrained when the training lectures and materials are in English. Even when my students had a good grasp of English, the words and ideas I used were necessarily based on experiences with which many students could not accurately identify. I wanted to know whether team-based learning was a practical way to minimize language problems by engaging students, who have a common experience set, in tasks that required working together to understand concepts from both the teaching materials and the instructor.
- Is team-based learning an effective way to develop interpersonal skills in cultures where the ability to work well in teams is even more important than it is in the United States? In many countries where group processes dominate, one percent or less of the population has the opportunity for a college education. As a result, a very high percentage of young college graduates are quickly promoted to positions of significant leadership. In these societies, organizations can ill afford to have these young leaders learn by trial and error on the job.
- To what extent would I have to adapt team-based learning to use it effectively in settings outside North America? Given the social–psychological foundation of

team-based learning, I might need to make adjustments when working with learners from other cultural traditions.

Because of the numbers involved and the extensive time period of the observations, I have had ample opportunity to examine these questions by making two types of comparisons. One was to compare results with other, more traditional teaching methods being used in the same settings. The other was to assess the extent to which the team-based learning approach, developed largely in U.S. university classrooms, needed to be modified to be effective in other cultural contexts.

IS TEAM-BASED LEARNING AS EFFECTIVE AS TRADITIONAL TEACHING METHODS?

A preliminary answer to the question of whether or not team-based learning could answer all four of my questions was not long in coming. My first postgraduate teaching position was in the early 1980s at the Chinese University of Hong Kong, where I taught M.B.A. courses to ambitious young Chinese executives who expected the program to help them master immediately marketable skills. Our graduate program was set up under the Harvard model, and my director was a Harvard D.B.A. Traditional case study methods dominated and team-based learning techniques were unknown. Feeling the pressure from students and administration for quick successes, I resorted to using team-based learning with virtually no modifications from what I had learned at the University of Oklahoma. There were a few raised eyebrows, but three important outcomes paved the way for further development of team-based learning. One was an obvious improvement in students' scores on rigorous, comprehensive qualifying exams. Another was that the demanding young executives who were students in five different courses gave such positive student ratings that they could not be ignored. Finally, starting before the end of the first semester and continuing well beyond graduation, students were writing and calling the director and me, saying that they were using what they learned with good success.

While in Hong Kong, I also found a significant demand for my services as a consultant, and many of my assignments involved designing and implementing training programs. My clients included Sheraton Hotels, Exxon Asia, Cable & Wireless, Hong Kong Telephone, Astec Electronics, Hong Kong Shanghai Bank, the Hong Kong government, and many others. Soon, these assignments led to requests from various organizations in the People's Republic of China, and I conducted training for many hundreds of communist cadres in various industries and locations in China. Team-based learning was the core of all of these consulting assignments, and eventually, I used team-based learning principles to develop extensive multimedia materials (in the Chinese language) that were used by many organizations within China.

During the period from 1980 to 1999, I added more countries and cultures to my experience, and my initial impressions about the potential effectiveness of team-based learning in international settings were confirmed by each new teaching experience.

Although students' initial resistance occasionally reached a level that I considered at least a temporary retreat to the comfort of a more traditional style, I am glad that I did not yield to the temptation because to have done so would have been taking the easy way out at the students' expense. Without question, compared to traditional methods, team-based learning enables students to understand concepts more deeply and retain them longer. In addition, students quickly develop the attitudes and skills they need to effectively work with, and learn from, their peers, and once the strangeness is overcome, they are also highly enthusiastic about the learning process. Most important, when faced with the common organizational challenges toward which their course work was directed, students report a sense of deja vu, "been there, done that" confidence with respect to both course concepts and teamwork skills.

DOES TEAM-BASED LEARNING REQUIRE CHANGES TO BE EFFECTIVE IN INTERNATIONAL SETTINGS?

In each new teaching situation, I started out using team-based learning exactly as I had learned it as a graduate student at the University of Oklahoma (see Table 13.1). In general, the answer to this question of how much team-based learning has to be modified for international settings is: not very much and not very often. Over the years, however, I have had a number of surprises in relation to various components of the approach that have both increased my appreciation for the value of team-based learning and helped me to understand why it works so well in so many different settings. Some of the more interesting are as follows.

Forming Groups

Assigning participants to learning teams can be a delicate and challenging process in some cultures. The goal in team-based learning is to have the groups balanced, composed of people with various backgrounds and experience and, if possible, with different types of personalities, so that all participants feel a sense of equal accountability and value, and so that resources across teams are more or less equal. However, in some cultures, the social pecking order students bring with them is so well established that they feel very uncomfortable operating outside those guidelines. Randomness is not seen as desirable by students who believe their careers will develop only in highly structured, organizational cultures with tightly proscribed protocols.

In the U.S. classroom, it is amazing how quickly a randomly formed group can, almost amoebae-like, reconstitute both roles and structure. This is not nearly so evident in cultures in which the social–psychological distance between individuals is both greater and more rigid. In these situations, when groups are formed according to team-based learning guidelines, I have observed confusion, uncertainty, silence, and occasionally rebellion (e.g., students try to re-form groups by switching with those in other groups).

TABLE 13.1
Elements of a Typical Team-Based Learning Course

<u>Teams</u>
- Permanent and purposefully heterogeneous.
- Formed by the instructor.

<u>Grading</u>
- Based on a combination of Individual Performance, Team Performance, and Team Maintenance (based on peer evaluations).
- Category weights set by use of "Grade Weight Setting Exercise."

<u>Content Coverage</u> (20-25 % of class time)
- Initial exposure achieved through students' pre-class individual study.
- Readiness Assurance Process used to assess and extend student understanding and build groups into teams.

<u>Concept Applications</u> (75-80% of Class time)
- Use of 8-15 topic-specific team activities and assignments (e.g., application problems, case studies, role plays, experiential exercises, etc.).
- Use of 2-3 integrative team assignments (e.g., business simulations, team projects, analysis of organizations portrayed in novels or full-length feature films, etc.).

<u>Graded Assessments</u>
- For Teams—1-2 topic-specific and 2-3 integrative application exams or projects.
- For Individual students—Exams can include both content questions and application problems (In many of my courses, the latter are frequently based on a full-length feature film "case".).

While the team-development process can take longer, a combination of unrelenting forces eventually enable groups to find a way to work together. Ironically, one important force is students' deference to the instructor's authority. Out of respect, students will cooperate long enough for the dynamics produced by the feedback-rich environment of team-based learning to come into play. Starting with the first RAT, students realize that they are in competition with other teams and are confronted with individual and group performance feedback that promotes the idea that, given the rules of this setting, they all have the same status; and frees them to respond to their cultural norm by cooperating as supporting each other as peers.

Grade-Setting Exercise

Involving students in establishing grading standards for the class is the first test of the new group cohesion. Because the groups are generally still in the process of trying to work out internal relationships, this is a difficult exercise. In American classrooms, students are often shocked when they first learn of the opportunity to set the grade weights. They consider the process weird but quickly jump at the opportunity to optimize their individual and group outcomes.

In countries where teachers are traditionally in positions of great authority, instead of being viewed as delightfully unusual, the idea of allowing students to set grade weights is sometimes viewed as grossly unfair and even wrong. It is inconceivable that the Master would require the novice to decide what is and what is not important. Believing that a teacher will honor the grade weight-setting contract is quite a leap of faith. Therefore, groups will sometimes invest their energies in trying to figure out how the teacher would want the grades to be structured (because they believe this will be the ultimate outcome anyway).

This guessing game does not happen in all situations. But when it does, I have learned to recognize the clues that group formation dynamics are being short-circuited by cultural norms. It is helpful to be aware of the results of the Hofstede (1991) comparative-management study for the country in which I am operating. His "Power Distance" measure can be a useful clue to the likelihood of this problem occurring. I can also test the waters using a simple but carefully selected case study and listening to the class discussion. When nearly everyone takes the same view, there is little disagreement about roles, and cultural norms are cited as support for positions, I have learned that I need to change the way I use the grade-weight exercise.

One solution is to allow the class to repeat the grade-setting process after the first RAT. By then the groups are more cohesive and have begun to believe that the exercise is a real opportunity rather than a teacher's trick. The dynamics the second time around are usually quite similar to what I observe in American classrooms and the stage is better set for the remainder of the course. As might be expected, being able to set the weights eliminates virtually all complaints of arbitrariness in the final grading process.

Readiness Assessment Tests (RATs)

The RAT technique is a multipurpose learning device; however, it seems that students in all cultures tend to look at it as a test. Students everywhere have trouble at first grasping why they take the same test twice, once as an individual and once as a group. As sometimes occurs in the American classroom, a few students have trouble freeing themselves from the idea that their individual score means more than the group score (although almost all groups put significantly more weight on the group test).

In many foreign cultures, there are often two opposing forces at play in the early RATs that I think of in terms of extracting juice from oranges. On the positive side, a strong social norm that individuals are strictly accountable to their group ensures that members are rarely unprepared for group work. As a result, many groups "ripen" (the oranges are full of juice) even earlier than those in the United States. On the other hand, groups in these cultures often have difficulty learning how to squeeze their orange. In the early going, much of the benefit of members' preparation can be lost because those without status (e.g., women and younger group members) are often totally ignored. However, once students grasp the importance of having everyone participate in the process, they fully expect to achieve perfect scores on all group tests. Then the juice really flows. The juice (i.e., potential ability to contribute) is there all along but only becomes available when the groups learn how to extract it from all members of the group.

RATs as Context for Process Learning

Part of the RAT process is the time limit placed on the combined individual and group test (groups cannot begin the group test until all individuals in the group have completed the individual test—thus giving an advantage to the group whose individuals come to class on time and complete the individual test promptly). This feature seems to work the same in all the cultures in which I have used it. Groups put pressure on individual members to perform quickly and to be more efficient in contributing to group discussions. In some cultures, however, I have found an added advantage to the time restrictions: helping students understand what happens when they have to operate under pressure. Most individuals behave differently under pressure, and group dynamics can change dramatically when time is running out. I have found that increasing the pressure in carefully selected situations and then discussing the changes and resulting behaviors and performance can help students gain significant insight into how to manage themselves and their groups under marketplace pressures.

The Readiness Assurance Process (RAP) also calls for the students to be able to challenge the approved answers to any question. The idea, of course, is stimulate restudy of difficult or complex concepts by encouraging students to think in depth about the ideas contained in the test questions by providing opportunities and incentives to challenge the instructor's answer or even the questions themselves.

Immediate Feedback

A key to the success of the RAP in any setting is being able to provide immediate feedback on individual and team tests. In the classes I worked with at the University of Oklahoma, we provided immediate feedback by bringing a test-correction machine into the classroom. In using RATs in international settings, I have seldom had the luxury of being able to machine-grade the individual and team tests. In trying to solve that problem, I discovered an alternative procedure for handling both the instant feedback and the appeals that also provides a unique advantage in cultures in which a concern about saving face is a barrier to openly challenging each others' ideas.

As soon as teams finish their test, I moderate a discussion in which students "discover" the correct answers so that they can correct the individual and group tests immediately in class. This involves building an answer key by having teams alternate in giving their answer to the questions, and when teams disagree, moderating the discussion in the same way I would handle a discussion involving differences of opinion on the application-focused assignments. Because the teams are challenging each other (and not me) I am also able to use the discussion to grant credit for an alternative answer in the same way I would with normal written appeals. Further, this process is particularly valuable in situations in which an open challenge is not acceptable because it is considered impolite to publicly embarrass another. Apparently, although finding fault with an individual is sometimes inappropriate, it is usually entirely acceptable to strongly challenge the views of another group. As a result, not only this test-correction procedure but also the team-based learning process in general provide an excellent antidote for this problem because both processes call for team (not individual) answers to be presented and discussed.

Performance Data Availability

Team-based learning generally encourages the groups to keep an ongoing record of individual and group scores on the RATs and other assignments. In the United States, I am sometimes asked whether or not students are concerned about this type of semi-public availability of student performance, based on the notion that it might be a violation of their privacy rights. In none of the foreign settings from which my observations have been taken have there been such sensitivities. I have observed that students in cultures that are group-oriented make excellent use of these performance records to encourage and discipline one another to do their best.

Applications Versus Content Coverage

One of the fears of many teachers is that the team-based learning focus on activities aimed at increasing students' ability to use concepts absorbs so much class time that all the required content cannot be covered. Based on my experience in international settings, just the opposite is true. Using team-based learning (i.e., RATs and carefully designed, application-focused activities) increases both the breadth and depth of students' learning. Even in situations in which students' learning needs have forced me to develop and use integrative content applications that require up to ten hours to complete (i.e., nearly 25 percent of course contact hours), I have never been forced to skimp on content coverage. In fact, the activities have worked so well overseas that I now use them in my courses in the United States.

LEARNING ABOUT TEAM-BASED LEARNING

The reasons team-based learning is so effective in international settings may shed some light on why it is so valuable in American classrooms. The fundamental challenge of language is to use spoken words to communicate new ideas. Language is a problem for the one-way communication of traditional lectures, even when an English-speaking teacher lectures to English-speaking students. Understanding the meaning of what is being said requires much more than understanding the individual words that are being spoken.

Communicating in the Same Language

An English-speaking teacher lecturing to Chinese-speaking students certainly intensifies the problem. The use of an interpreter to solve the problem is notoriously inefficient and can be hilariously ineffective. Thus, out of necessity, often what starts out as a lecture inadvertently becomes a simple version of team-based learning when the presenter is forced to reduce the content of the lecture and replace it with a concise explanation of a problem followed by a small group discussion. This enables the audience to become teachers as well as listeners. And this simplest form of team-based learning reduces the language problem by forcing an intensive exchange of ideas between learners using the same language, the same vernacular, and drawing from common experiences.

The Blind Leading the Blind?

How can people who know so much less than the teacher be expected to advance their knowledge and skills simply by getting a little guidance and then working on a problem as a group? Is this not like the proverb of the blind men all trying to explain the anatomy of an elephant? Yes it is. But in that proverb, the problem is not that the individuals are blind. The problem is the lack of team-based learning techniques. Allow those blind men to get together and turn the problem (elephant) around and around, each drawing on his own experience, all speaking the same language, and I assure you they will gain a far better insight into the anatomy of the elephant than ever could be communicated by a single sighted and even erudite lecturer.

Making Sure My Sky Does Not Become Their Limit

When I teach in another country, no matter how hard I prepare, no matter how much background research I do, I simply cannot obtain enough understanding of the situation to provide the breadth and depth of marketable skills my students need. If their learning is limited by what I know, students inevitably will be shortchanged. There is no way to keep up with the changing, complex commercial and technological changes in the United States, much less with the intricate developments in all the international markets I serve. Team-based learning allows me to help my students go far beyond my specific knowledge and experience. It allows the students and me to focus on the learning process rather than exclusively on the content. With a modest amount of guidance, students in the team-based learning context can use their knowledge of the learning process to go well beyond the limits of their teacher.

SOME CONCLUDING THOUGHTS

I would like to revisit the questions I posed at the outset of this essay. The first three questions were:

- Do team-based learning methods work in cultures where they are so much at odds with the mainstream of educational practice that students invariably start out being uncomfortable with the approach?
- Will team-based learning be effective when English is a second language for learners, but the majority of the teaching materials and the native language of the instructor is English?
- Is team-based learning an effective way to develop interpersonal skills in cultures in which the ability to work well in teams is more important than it is in the United States?

In my mind, the answer to all three questions is an unequivocal YES. I have been able to use team-based learning in multiple international situations in which all three of these conditions applied, and it was quite successful. Team-based learning succeeds because it allows the instructor to do more than provide instruction. Teaching with team-based learning is like coaching a winning basketball team. Once students master the fundamentals, the key to success is learning how to play effectively as a team. Although the coach runs the plays and scrimmages, and evaluates, corrects, and offers suggestions, the greatest advantage of team-based learning in international settings is that it allows team members, who have a common language and culture, to learn from each other as the game progresses. In team-based learning, we also focus on what really matters—the way it will be when students will have to use their knowledge and skills to make a difference in their workplace and in the society in which they live.

The final question I posed at the outset of this chapter was: To what extent does one have to modify team-based learning to use it effectively in settings outside North America? The answer to this question is, Not very much. The key to the success of team-based learning is creating effective teams, and although cultural differences do present groups with a different set of developmental challenges, the dynamics created by the model are robust enough to enable the development of effective teams in a wide variety of settings. Because they are free to decide how they do their work, team members' early interactions are heavily influenced by the dominant cultural norms. But because of the immediate and ongoing performance feedback, they cannot escape the consequences of poor choices about their decision-making processes. Thus, regardless of the cultural norms they bring to the classroom, students learn from both their mistakes and their successes and rapidly develop an understanding of, and confidence in, their ability to work together and learn from each other.

As a teacher, my performance must be measured not only by test scores and well-crafted theses of my students (i.e., by their performance during their educational years), but ultimately by their ability to go on to perform early and well in their lives and in the careers they choose. Whether in Kansas or in Kuala Lumpur, team-based learning gives our students a clear competitive advantage in today's highly demanding marketplace.

REFERENCE

Hofstede, G. (1991). *Cultures and organizations: Software of the mind.* London: McGraw-Hill.

CHAPTER 14

Team-Based Learning in a Course Combining In-Class and Online Interaction

Mark Freeman

Many changes have rocked the tertiary education landscape over the last decade, including larger class sizes and more diverse student populations. Competition between providers has become more intense as technology improvements have dissolved the traditional barrier between face-to-face and distance education. Employers are increasingly focusing on graduate outcomes beyond disciplinary knowledge to attributes like being an effective team worker or communicator. The primary objective of this chapter is to illustrate how a technology-supported teaching and learning environment, combined with team-based learning strategies, can provide huge opportunities for developing teamwork capabilities and learning generally.

BACKGROUND CONTEXT

Change, particularly in Australia, has been one of few constants in higher education over the last decade. In fact, technology changes have left few aspects of academic work unaffected. For example, students expect that they can e-mail individual queries to faculty even though class sizes have doubled. Student populations are increasingly diverse, with many students studying in a nonnative language because travel to, or enrolling in, an Australian university becomes relatively cheaper. Technology has also impacted research, causing academics to struggle to keep abreast of a rapidly expanding disciplinary knowledge base.

The University of Technology Sydney (UTS) subject[1] involved in this experiment with team-based learning, Securities Markets Regulation (SMR), has had to adapt to many changes over the last decade:

- Academia is rapidly moving to a technology-supported learning context. That change is supported by the fact that 80 percent of the students have Web-enabled computers at home or at work. As a result, few of them choose to contact faculty or staff by going to the on-campus office or even by using the telephone. Students have no hesitation in e-mailing their teachers, peers, or university personnel. (The costs and benefits of technology-supported innovation are documented in Freeman, 1996, and Freeman, 1997).
- There is an increasingly diverse student population on our campus. Nearly 80 percent (up from 5 percent) study in a language other than their native tongue.
- Students are more focused on quality and value for their money.
- Many undergraduate subjects are being moved to the postgraduate level. Postgraduate students should have more general knowledge, more business knowledge, and more generic capabilities (e.g., communication skills, teamwork skills). They should also be able to think in a more critical and creative manner.

To keep abreast of these changes in higher education, the faculty at UTS embraced the role of technology in both teaching and learning. We discovered that when technology is combined with team-based learning, the two become a powerful teaching strategy that can provide huge opportunities for both developing teamwork capabilities and enhancing learning.

WHY TEAMWORK AND TEAM-BASED LEARNING?

A decade ago, the faculty who were teaching SMR at UTS were already encouraging informal group work. For example, students were encouraged to help one another master the key concepts. Group work (at that time) consisted of two or more students working together in various activities such as ad hoc brainstorming or solving problems in class or out of class. While these activities were important and could count as credit toward assessment, they typically did not.

Although we were experiencing reasonable success with our version of group work, we were in for a major overhaul. At that particular time, a colleague attending a team-based learning workshop overseas triggered an entirely new focus on the use of groups in the classroom. This new focus called for the creation of situations in which students intentionally worked together in teams. As a result, the curriculum for SMR was totally rewritten to include learning teams as outlined by Michaelsen and his colleagues (e.g., Michaelsen & Black, 1994; Michaelsen, Watson, Cragin, & Fink, 1982; Michaelsen, Watson, & Schraeder, 1985).

MOTIVATION FOR USING LEARNING TEAMS

The first move into teamwork in 1991 was primarily to improve student learning. In fact, the subject objectives focused on improved student understanding of subject objectives. Equally important was our belief that the ability to work with others was a positive byproduct of team-based learning.

The second motive for requiring students to work in teams was a desire to achieve various graduate attributes, of which teamwork was one. At that time, we were aware that teamwork was an attribute that business employers recognized as being extremely valuable. We were also aware that, because the external environment had changed, other attributes, such as skill in the use of technology, and a culturally sensitive attitude, had also been added to the list of requirements for graduates. These expanded attributes went beyond disciplinary knowledge to reflect current priorities that a consultative process with employers rates as relevant for graduates on completion of a program of study.

In retrospect, the skills that were being developed implicitly in the SMR curriculum before (i.e., communication, interpersonal skills, and teamwork) have now been explicitly recognized as subject objectives. In fact, the accreditation process now requires that these attributes be required of graduates.

POSITIVE OUTCOMES FROM USING TEAMS

There were many positive outcomes from early experiments with team-based learning. For example, students did appear to know more, have a rounder understanding, and a deeper approach to learning. They also indicated they had fun, and felt it was a fair assessment system. The teachers enjoyed the positive student reactions and their new role as facilitator.

Although much greater planning was required in the re-engineering process (to redesign the subject for team-based learning) before the subject began, there were dividends during the very first semester. The dividends continued into the next semester in both this subject and others. Institutional benefits of the changes included exposure of the new approach (i.e., the use of learning teams) to other faculties and other institutions, as well as the development of new research avenues (e.g., business ethics, cross-disciplinary focus on securities markets regulatory issues, and educational innovation).

MOVING TO THE ELECTRONIC CLASSROOM

Based on the changes in academia previously described, our goal is to meet the needs of our students in the electronic age. We are aware that we live in an increasingly busy environment, and as a result, many students have significant competing work and domestic priorities. Therefore, making class attendance almost mandatory (as in a traditional classroom) can be unattractive to them. As a result, we redesigned our delivery by requiring students to enroll in either of two subjects (SMR offered by the business school, or Securities Markets Law offered by the law school), limiting the number of in-class meetings, and moving much of the interaction online. Instead of thirty-nine hours (thirteen weeks multiplied by three hours), we now require students to meet face-to-face for only 4.5 intensive Saturdays (for a total of thirty-two hours) over a fifteen-week period. It is still team-taught with faculty from law and finance present for the face-to-face hours, but has a greatly increased emphasis on using electronic learning space.

USING LEARNING TEAMS ONLINE

Once the first major decision, that is, to move our course online, had been made, the second was to select the most effective approach for the online dimensions of our subjects. Because of our great success with learning teams in the traditional classroom, we felt confident in trying teams in the electronic classroom. We believed that a technology-supported teaching and learning environment, combined with team-based learning, could provide huge opportunities for developing both their teamwork graduate attribute and their learning in general.

In the electronic classroom, both synchronous and asynchronous learning activities can be easily accomplished. For, example, team projects, which used to require students to arrange a convenient meeting time, can now be handled off-campus, at least in part. That is, students can now use technology to share files, search libraries and the World Wide Web, and interact both synchronously and asynchronously with other students, team members or faculty. An institutionally supported course management tool (originally TopClass and now Blackboard) is available to support many aspects of teaching and learning.

Students can also live or travel some distance from UTS during the duration of the term but, by electronically communicating with us and their class mates, can still meet the attendance requirements of an on-campus subject. Previously this was not possible. It also means that the teachers can travel during the duration of the course because they can continue to manage learning activities while they are not on campus.

Students in SMR work in teams on various types of in-class and out-of-class learning tasks (see Table 14.1). The in-class team assessment activities are interspersed with learning activities. The in-class assessable activities include four team tests (one is a practice, and an average of the remaining three count toward a student's subject mark, i.e., grade), a team presentation (which also counts), and a number of nonassessed team assignments. Teams also engage in three of the online team activities (team debate, role-play, and team topic-tracking). To the best of our knowledge, two of the three had never been used in anything other than synchronous, face-to-face settings. However, both team debates and role-plays have worked very effectively in a virtual situation.

TEAM ACTIVITIES FOR ONLINE CLASSES

Team Debate on the Web

In general, debates are a useful learning task, because students must think critically as they prepare arguments and counterarguments. Online debates work very well, because the dialog must be written to be sent electronically. The exercise of writing reduces the

TABLE 14.1
SMR Course Face-to-Face and Online Team Activities

Face-to-face meeting #1 (week 1: full day)
- Introduction of team learning method and electronic course management tools
- Formation of teams
- Administration of a practice team test
- Initiation of topic tracking*

Online learning period #1 (week 1)
- Continue topic tracking*
- Preparation for team test #1*

Face-to-face meeting #2 (week 2: full day)
- Administration of team test #1*
- In-class team activities

Online learning period #2 (weeks 2-5)
- Continue topic tracking*
- Preparation for team test #2*
- Asynchronous debate*
- Work on team presentations*

Face-to-face meeting #3 (week 6: full day)
- Administration of team test #2*
- Team presentations*
- In-class team activities

Online learning period #3 (weeks 6-10)
- Continue topic tracking*
- Preparation for team test #3*
- Asynchronous debate*
- Work on team presentations*

Face-to-face meeting #4 (week 11: full day)
- Administration of team test #3*
- Team presentations*
- Introduction to anonymous asynchronous role play
- In-class team activities

Online learning period #4 (weeks 11-14)
- Anonymous asynchronous role play acting
- Preparation for personal reflections report or for final exam based on role play*

Face-to-face meeting #4 (week 11: half day)
- Role play debrief
- Personal reflections report or final exam based on role play*

* These team activities count in computing student's subject mark [grade].

stress of thinking on one's feet, especially when the content is not in one's first language or has a substantial amount of jargon or evidence with which one is not familiar. An asynchronous debate held over one week has an added benefit in that the arguments can be more reflective and better researched because students have had twenty-four hours to prepare their submission. Because the debates are done in teams, the arguments are typically better than if they have been prepared and presented by a single individual. In addition, team members have an opportunity to learn from one another. For example, informal learning from peers occurs when students respond to other students' questions online. Learning is enhanced because students have the benefit of reading (with time to reflect on) other students' questions and answers before they submit their own response.

There are two other advantages that on-the-Web team debates have over face-to-face debates. First, students can use hyperlinks and provide references to extend their arguments or provide evidence. Second, other teams can access the debate in public space and benefit from the research. It is also very easy for future students (in this class) to understand what is expected of them, because a perpetual record can be made into exemplars and placed on the subject website for future cohorts. Students have commented very positively about these aspects.

Role-Play on the Web

With the role-play exercise, students have three distinct tasks. First, they are given the role of a "real player" in the Australian securities markets regulation scene (e.g., treasurer, prime minister, judge, chief regulator, major investor, stockbroker, banker). They are to research the character and interpret that person's concerns, ambitions, and strategies and post their findings to the website for all to see (worth 5%). To encourage deep immersion in the peer learning task, all roles are anonymous for the duration of the ten-day role-play.

The second task requires acting out that role online in response to various events and crises released daily by the instructors. Students can communicate privately by e-mail with other roles or publicly in one of the daily discussion forums. The quality and quantity of the role-playing is valued at 10 percent of the team component of the subject mark. The third and final task in the role-play involves a reflective report in which students analyze their learning against each subject assessment objective. This is worth 20 percent.

Although the role-play is quite intense and involving, the student feedback is extremely positive (Freeman & Capper, 1999). Students are able to be actively involved in the learning process. Anonymity provides deeper approaches to learning because students can immerse themselves in their roles without prior relationships clouding their interactions with other students. It is worthy to note that, without technology, an anonymous peer learning task like this role-play would not be possible.

Team Topic Tracking on the Web

This innovative task has evolved over several years into a very powerful learning and assessment tool. To begin the activity, each team is assigned a theoretical topic.

The activity proceeds with each team member searching the Web to locate articles and stories from the business press that relate to their theoretical topic. Once these are found, the team members post links to relevant websites, with a short commentary about the articles and stories. For example, Team 5 in 1999 had five members who were part-time students working in government, banking or accounting. Their assignment was to track takeovers that occurred over the semester. (It was also the topic of their subsequent in-class presentation.) On Monday, for instance, one member may find a useful article in the press. Later, on Monday night, someone else may find a Web address and post it with a short comment on its relevance to takeover regulation. On Tuesday and Wednesday team members react to these postings and possibly post another link from the business press. Over time, an initial comment may have from one to twelve comments in the related thread.

This task aims to get students to relate theory to practice, and to motivate broader research for the in-class presentation. Our experience has been that, as teams progress through the subject, their comments became increasingly sophisticated. Because the information is posted to the course website, other students focusing on other major topics can also benefit from their research and vice versa.

In 1999, Team 5 (the team that was covering takeover regulation) received a mark of 10 (this activity represents 10% of the course mark) because of the quality of their postings. The depth of analysis in each of the postings, combined with the quantity, was superb. In all, there were 262 postings over the thirteen weeks of the course. In addition, the in-class presentation of Team 5 was superb. Of course not all teams work at this standard. We believe, however, that the date-stamping function of the Web provides a great incentive for students to work more continuously. In addition, instructors can (and we do) facilitate the discussion or keep it on track.

In grading these assessments, we have found that each year students complete the task better, partly because a written record can be converted into an exemplar and placed on the course website for future students. The only disadvantage to the topic-tracking activity is that the teams produce so much information that the burden of monitoring their work has become nearly overwhelming. As a result, we have decided to reduce the emphasis on team assessment; in future offerings, students will be marked entirely on a short, 1000-word individual report which reflects their changed understanding. In this report students will also have to summarize the quantity and quality of their contributions to their team's discussion.

ASSESSING ATTAINMENT OF "EFFECTIVE TEAM WORKER" ATTRIBUTE

The final aspect needing elaboration (in regard to our use of learning teams) is the process of assessing each student's attainment of the course objective of being an effective team worker. The assessment is based solely on student feedback collected from students' responses to a carefully worded set of statements contained in our online SPARK (Self & Peer Assessment Resource Kit). The assessment procedure itself follows that put forward by Goldfinch (1993), in which each student's total team assessment mark (i.e., 50% of the subject mark) is adjusted for perceived contributions.

Students are exposed to SPARK at the beginning of the course and repeatedly reminded throughout the course that free-riding will have a negative consequence on their mark. An illustrative spreadsheet is available for students to evaluate different contribution levels. Students are advised to maintain a diary of the activities and reflections for each team task to help their subsequent evaluation for self- and peer-assessment purposes. A list of activities for each assessment task has been derived from focus groups, with each graduating class having a chance to modify it. At the end of the subject, students must then rate their own and their peer team members on each listed item for each activity. These prompting questions then form the basis for a series of six items relating to team maintenance. These latter questions are used in calculating the adjustment factor.

In 1999 there were sixteen prompting questions for the team tasks. For example, students evaluated themselves and their peers on two aspects for the topic-tracking task (quality and quantity of postings), five aspects of the debate, six for the presentation, and three for the tests. This evaluation was followed by six final statements relating to an effective team. Of course, a different context would motivate different statements and even a different rating scale.

Students can confidentially complete the form online as many times as they wish over a one-week period prior to the final date. Such an online system overcomes a number of problems of a paper-based system that is being completed under exam conditions. For example, the online system means students can take more time in their reflections. And having more time to reflect should make the results fairer and easier to substantiate in the event of a dispute. In addition, the self- and peer-assessment (SPA) adjustment calculations are much simpler and more accurate than a paper form, because the data are already in electronic form and the calculation is built into the program.

EFFECTIVENESS OF TEAMWORK AND THE TEAM-BASED LEARNING APPROACH

In this section I will review the effectiveness of team-based learning using a multistakeholder approach. I will begin with a focus on students, move to faculty and the organization, and conclude with the rest of the academic community.

STUDENTS' PERCEPTION OF TEAM-BASED LEARNING

Kirkpatrick (1994) suggests that educational innovations should consider the effect on students at four levels, namely reactions, learning, behavioral, and organizational. Student reactions to the changes in SMR have been sought at every stage of evolution via surveys, focus groups, and online feedback forums. As a result of student feedback, various team aspects have been eliminated, some have been expanded, while new ones have been introduced. For example, in response to student requests for synchronous online, anonymous interactions, a future refinement of the role play involves allowing students to interact via Internet relay chat in an environment specifically designed for these roles and their contexts. In addition, we have developed caricatures of each role and a number of stylized contexts (e.g., Parliament House and the bar of Parliament House).

As in normal situations, some teams thrived and worked extremely well while others simply coped. Evidence of the former includes faculty observing such teams having fun together completing team tasks on weekends or on campus: laughing while they made videos for their presentations, openly negotiating among the membership about what refreshments they would bring to class for everyone during the full-day sessions.

In the 1999 generic student feedback survey for the course, 92 percent of students agreed that the course had helped them to develop their ability to work as a team member. Given that it is a postgraduate course, where students have already worked and have begun to develop skills as a team member in their workplace, this is a great result.

A confidential, structured phone interview of students was also conducted in relation to the self- and peer-assessment system. Students overwhelmingly agreed that the rating items were appropriate for assessing teamwork and that it was a fair and honest solution for encouraging teamwork overall. Only some 10–14 percent disagreed with each of these statements. While most students thought a self- and peer-assessment system should be implemented wherever group work is used, two specific observations are worth highlighting. First, some 40 percent of the students said that they did not contribute a greater effort just because of the self- and peer-assessment system. Combined with the previous data, this is a positive outcome because it means social loafing was discouraged without pressuring students to do too much work at the expense of other courses. Second, some students said that the type of group work at university was quite different from that at work. In the workplace more hierarchical power-sharing arrangements and greater commitment levels are usually evident.

In some circumstances, the feedback has shown that students take their skills back to their workplace. In 1999, two examples became evident through the focus groups. One student had taken a concept-mapping task from SMR and asked his new team at work to brainstorm how they could better understand their core business. Other students commented on how the use of icebreakers, including the online ones, had been a great idea, one they would want to replicate in team development at work. In addition, team tests also had a positive effect because they apparently reduced stress for the individual student and encouraged learning from peers.

Students have responded favorably to the team-teaching approach and appear to appreciate being exposed to the conflicting views that are evidenced in the real world. As faculty, we have served as role models to indicate that it is okay to strongly disagree when that disagreement is expressed in a constructive and respectful manner. Students appear less likely to take a surface approach to learning by rote learning what they think the instructor wants to hear or see written. It becomes plain that a deeper understanding of the complex issues is required, because either instructor, complete with his or her own disciplinary biases, could be marking their exam papers.

Finally, it appears that the ability to learn from each other in teams has been greatly facilitated through technology. That is, students of diverse geographical locations can much more easily communicate and share their work in a Web-based learning environment. Students of a non-English-speaking background have particularly appreciated the use of written responses rather than total reliance on verbal communication, which can be easily misunderstood. In addition, students have appreciated the ability in the Web-based learning environment to access feedback, suggestions, and learning resources from peer colleagues, including those not in their team. For example, in a recent focus group, a student commented on how the experience of communicating online had been very valuable because he had learned how important, yet how difficult, it was to sound "chatty" in an e-mail. These are extremely important aspects of teamwork development for graduates in the 21st century.

Faculty Perceptions of Team-Based Learning

Although the outcomes have been satisfying, undertaking constant realignment in response to changes in the teaching environment has been costly to faculty in development time. On the other hand, dealing with teams in an online environment has been much less stressful, because it is so much easier to communicate with teams (be it one or many) rather than with individual students. We must note, however, that although more sharing of learning is possible in a Web-based learning environment, e-mail can be one major possible disadvantage if not correctly managed. That is, although faculty can be quickly made aware of team problems needing addressing, e-mail etiquette (or "netiquette") needs to be implemented to avoid misunderstandings arising from novice users.

Team-based learning has also made the subject more interesting to teach. Because students cover much of the basic content through their own study and coaching from their peers, there is very little need to lecture on basic concepts. Many of the team-based learning tasks have also helped the instructors avoid feeling overloaded. For example, the team tests and the online self- and peer-assessment systems have been a win–win for faculty and students.

The provision of exemplars of teamwork (on video, Web, and/or print) has proved useful in reducing faculty stress levels in several ways. For example, it has been easier to explain to students what is expected in terms of product (e.g., team topic tracking or debates on the Web), and also in terms of quality (e.g., videos of past team presentations). Each year the teamwork tasks appear a little better on average than those in previous years. In addition, the fact that face-to-face team presentations are videotaped has reduced the risk of accusations of bias in marking. If there were ever such a charge, we could easily ask for an independent marker to view the team presentations on tape.

Another issue that needs to be carefully managed is the formation and maintenance of teams in a multicultural environment. There are various opportunities for developing international respect of cultures when teams are configured from classes with high diversity as in SMR. But there is also the possibility of inadvertently bringing together people who traditionally clash. In 1999 this was magnified because there were a number of students from a country with which Australia, among other countries, was experiencing considerable tension at a national level.

The final faculty effect relates to planning the time for team tasks. Too often we appear to underestimate the amount of time it takes to complete a team task. The danger of this is that it leads to surface learning and even team tension. We have learned to err on the side of generosity in managing the time on team tasks, depending on how we observe the completion of the task. For example, if we see students locked in worthwhile persuasive debate in a team test, we would ask if they wished a few extra minutes to complete the tasks. Students not only appreciate the extra time but quickly get the perception that we are interested much more in their learning than completing our assessor role.

Perceptions of Team-Based Learning at the Departmental Level

Reactions have been mixed at the departmental level. Some colleagues have sought to replicate some aspects of the teamwork and team-based learning in their classes (e.g., team tests). But other colleagues have commented that the cost of reengineering their course is too great, irrespective of the reengineering, because of competing priorities such as research. In fact, in some cases teamwork has been reduced because "it is too hard to get the students with such diverse backgrounds to work together." In other cases, faculty have viewed teamwork simply as a solution to the extra marking of larger classes. However, when this happens, students can recognize, and will criticize, such poorly motivated reasons for using teamwork.

At the societal level, we need to be doing something to develop the graduate attribute of teamwork. The development of the online confidential self- and peer-assessment system is producing positive signs in Europe and Australia. It can be used for both summative assessment as in SMR, for settling up after teamwork, or for formative feedback to team members.

CONCLUSION

Peer learning is explicitly used in many aspects of the online SMR course. In an asynchronous Web-based learning context, students compete in debates, challenge each other in role-play exercises, and undertake to track various theoretical topics in the press. They also interact with one another in various group-learning tasks that are asynchronous (online) or synchronous (in-class) but aimed at formative learning. Some of these, such as an anonymous online role-play, are simply not possible in a face-to-face context. Finally, the confidential online self- and peer-assessment system offers considerable promise as a tool for reducing the likelihood of social loafing.

NOTE

1. This is the Australian term for a course.

REFERENCES

Freeman, M. A. (1997). Flexibility in access, interaction and assessment: The case for web based conferencing and teaching programs. *Australian Journal of Educational Technology 13*(1): 23–29. Available: http://cleo.murdoch.edu.au/gen/aset/ajet/ajet13/wi97p23.html.

Freeman, M. A. (1992). Motivating student learning in large classes. *Quality of Teaching Matters at UTS.* UTS Centre for Learning and Teaching: 11–19.

Freeman, M. A. (1995). Peer assessment by groups of group work. *Assessment & Evaluation in Higher Education 20*(3): 295–306.

Freeman, M. A. (1996). The role of the internet in teaching large undergraduate classes. *Flexible Online Learning Journal 1*(1). Available: http://www.lib.uts.edu.au/folp/journal/index.html.

Freeman, M. A., & Adams, M. A. (1999). Australian views on insider trading. *Australian Journal of Corporate Law 10*(2): 148–161.

Freeman, M. A., & Adams, M. A. (1992). Experimenting with new teaching and assessment methods in a business degree subject. *Quality of Teaching Matters at UTS.* UTS Centre for Learning and Teaching: 27–39.

Freeman, M. A., & Capper, J. M. (1999). Exploiting the Web for education: An anonymous asynchronous role simulation. *Australian Journal of Educational Technology 15*(1): 95–116. Available: http://cleo.murdoch.edu.au/ajet/ajet15/freeman.html.

Goldfinch, J. (1993). Further developments in peer assessment of group projects. *Assessment and Evaluation in Higher Education 19*(1): 29–35.

Kirkpatrick, D. (1994). *Evaluating training programs: The four levels.* San Francisco: Berrett-Koehler.

Michaelsen, L. K., & Black, R. H. (1994). Building learning teams: The key to harnessing the power of small groups in higher education. In *Collaborative learning: A sourcebook for higher education.* Vol. 2. Ed. S. Kadel & J. Keehner. State College, PA: National Center for Teaching, Learning and Assessment.

Michaelsen, L. K., Watson, W. E., Cragin, J. P., & Fink, L. D. (1982). Team learning: A potential solution to the problems of large classes. *Exchange: The Organizational Behavior Teaching Journal 7*(1): 13–22.

Michaelsen, L. K., Watson, W. E., & Schraeder, C. B. (1985). Informative testing: A practical approach for tutoring with groups. *Exchange: The Organizational Behaviour Teaching Journal 9*(4): 18–33.

CHAPTER 15

Team-Based Learning

A Strategy for Transforming the Quality of Teaching and Learning

Arletta Bauman Knight

The purpose of this book has been twofold: to explain the idea of team-based learning and to present a case for its value as a sophisticated, yet practical, instructional strategy. We (the editors) believe that team-based learning, while obviously not a panacea for all the ills of college teaching, is certainly capable of curing many of the problems that teachers face today.

The major reason for our convictions about the "power" of teams is the impact it has on student learning. When we shift our attention from "What am I going to teach?" to "What do I want my students to learn?" incredibly good things can happen. As Larry Spence (2001) quipped in a recent article arguing for a learning-centered approach to teaching: "It's not the teaching, stupid, it's the learning!" If one accepts the view that the quality of student learning is what should matter most when deciding how to teach, then team-based learning is an extraordinarily powerful option for teachers to consider.

For those readers who are wondering whether to use team-based learning or are trying to identify its specific values, the collection of real-life experiences reported in part II provide perhaps the most persuasive argument that can be made for this unique approach to teaching. These chapters provide multiple examples that clearly illustrate the successful use of teams. It has been our experience that when the principles set forth in part I are followed, success is almost guaranteed.

In addition, the collective experience of the teachers reporting in part II shows that learning teams can literally be used in any discipline, in almost any class size, with students from almost any culture in the world. This approach to teaching is definitely not limited to small classes in the humanities. Therefore, this concluding chapter includes a review of the major themes that are heard in the voices of experience that comprise part II.

Although we are obviously hopeful that readers will be convinced to try team-based learning, we also recognize that various factors may impact one's willingness to embrace a new teaching strategy, especially if one happens to be experiencing success with current methods. With this thought in mind, I have identified three major themes recurring in part II that may help readers make the transition to team-based learning. The first section of this chapter focuses on issues involved in the decision to adopt a new teaching strategy, such as overcoming initial skepticism and dealing with concerns about covering the content. The second section illustrates the use of teams in a wide range of class situations, and the final section discusses the many benefits that accrue as a result of using team-based learning.

MAKING THE DECISION TO TRY TEAM-BASED LEARNING

It comes as no surprise that all of the teachers contributing to part II of this book are individuals who are dedicated to their profession. In addition, almost all of them have experienced a great deal of success with their teaching. Documentation of their success has come in the form of teaching awards and positive student evaluations. It is interesting that many of the teachers were recognized for their success while using the lecture as their primary teaching strategy. The irony of the situation is that, even though these teachers were being rewarded for their apparent good use of the lecture method, they were also experiencing frustration with the same. For example, Dinan writes that although he worked harder on the lectures trying to clarify the material, students were still doing poorly on the exams. Goodson reports that her students had difficulty engaging in the lecture. Streuling comments that "students were only passive participants in the learning process." And, Herreid writes that even though the students thought they understood the lecture, they were still failing. In addition, many of the teachers in our sample report that student withdrawal and failure rates in their lecture classes were high (e.g., Dinan).

Although there was much evidence (e.g., teaching awards and good student evaluations) to support the continuation of their current methods, these particular teachers elected to take the risk involved with making changes in their teaching. It would certainly have been much safer for them to maintain the status quo. In fact, numerous teaching awards and positive student evaluations call to mind the old adage "If it ain't broke, don't fix it." However, concern for improving the quality of student learning apparently gave these individuals the courage to turn their backs on their own success to try a new, exciting, and innovative teaching strategy. From the perspective of teaching awards and student evaluations, their teaching "wasn't broke." But when they looked at the situation from the perspective of student learning, it wasn't working as well as it needed to.

Even more intriguing is the fact that many of these teachers, in addition to taking the chance of compromising their own previous success, were actually quite skeptical about the use of learning teams. Examples of their various skepticisms are included in the following paragraphs.

Overcoming Initial Skepticism

Although we believe that anyone who implements team-based learning can be successful, we can also understand a newcomer's skepticism. And we have discovered that skepticism can come in many packages. For example, there are teachers who

- have had an unpleasant experience with groups as students themselves;
- have tried groups and failed because they did not know to incorporate essential elements necessary to build groups into teams;
- are concerned that course material cannot possibly be covered adequately and, as a result, student learning will be compromised;
- are in the position of having to answer to colleagues or administrators who have doubts about team-based learning.

The list of reasons employed by skeptics goes on and on. However, what we have witnessed over and over again, and what our sample of teachers has reported in the preceding chapters, is that team-based learning can be successful when proper procedures are followed. Professor Streuling (Chapter 9), for example, had a devastating first-time experience with team-based learning. In his first attempt at using groups he made the critical mistake of assigning a group term paper. Unfortunately, he also violated a number of other principles as well; for example, he allowed the students in his groups to self-select and he made no provision for peer review. As a result, his students were so dissatisfied with the process that they gave him the lowest student evaluations he had ever received. The low evaluations were such a blow to Professor Streuling's ego that he decided he was simply someone who could not use groups and went back to lecturing. As luck would have it, he attended a workshop on learning teams conducted by Larry Michaelsen and decided to try again. This time he corrected the previous problems. That is, he followed the guidelines set forth by Michaelsen:

1. Groups must be properly formed, that is, diverse groups selected by the teacher.
2. Procedures must be in place to insure student accountability—both individually and to the group.
3. Group assignments must require input from all group members.
4. Students must receive immediate and frequent feedback.
5. Students must have the opportunity to evaluate their peers.

Now Professor Streuling reports that there is no more apathy in his classes because the students are truly engaged in the learning process. In fact, the teams in his class have, on occasion, become so engaged with the assignment that he has had a hard time restraining them when it is time to move on to other assignments. And to make the situation even better, his student evaluations are now higher than they were when he was lecturing.

Professor Goodson (Chapter 7) is another example of a professor who was somewhat skeptical about trying team-based learning. She had had an unpleasant experience with small groups when she was a student. However, Goodson found herself motivated to try teams because she was experiencing a great deal of difficulty with the lecture-and-group-discussion format that was currently in use. She was especially distressed with the lecture–discussion format because her students routinely came to class unprepared and, as a result, class discussion was a failure. However, the scene changed dramatically when she began incorporating group quizzes. The students who had been so disengaged before were now debating and defending their own points of view. Goodson reports that she was "stunned" by how quickly success came.

While skepticism about team-based learning can be well founded, as evidenced by the experiences of both Streuling and Goodson, it has been our experience in scores of examples that lack of success with learning teams is typically the result of improper implementation. Fortunately, that problem can be remedied.

Concerns about Covering the Content

Perhaps one of the most frequently expressed concerns regarding team-based learning is that one cannot possibly cover the content when using this method. In fact, Professor Lucas (Chapter 10), along with her colleagues, was quite concerned that student learning would be compromised if team-based learning was adopted. Both Lucas and her colleagues were alluding to what so many teachers fear regarding this issue: "If the teacher doesn't say it, it cannot possibly be learned." While this belief is unfortunately quite pervasive, we have strong evidence to support the contrary. For example:

- Lucas, after using teams, reports that students learn the material with the team-based learning approach as well as they would in a traditional lecture environment. In fact, the complexity of one group activity allowed for the incorporation of at least fourteen course concepts.
- Dinan writes that when two versions of a course are taught simultaneously, the lecture method has difficulty keeping up with the team-based learning classes. The team-based learning class can cover 10–15 percent more course material.
- Goodson tells us that, because she can cover more content with team-based learning, she is able to go beyond the textbook.
- Herreid reports that, with team-based learning, he can cover all of the content that he wants.

- Cragin discovered that even in international settings, covering the content was not an issue. In fact, he believes that team-based learning "increases both the breadth and depth of students' learning."
- Nakaji tells us that "the process of explaining concepts to each other clearly enabled team members to understand core concepts on a deeper, more meaningful level." Before team-based learning she had only been able to cover two chapters by midterm. However, after switching to team-based learning, she was able to cover the remaining six chapters in what was left of the semester.

Because of our collective experience, as well the evidence reported here, we are convinced that any teacher who properly implements team-based learning can overcome any doubts about covering the content.

So far, in this chapter we have been examining areas of possible concern regarding the use of team-based learning. Now it is time to focus on those myriad situations in which this teaching strategy works exceptionally well.

TEAM-BASED LEARNING IN A BROAD RANGE OF CLASSES

Using Team-Based Learning Across Disciplines

Intuitively, one would probably believe that small groups are most effective when used in classes that typically involve discussion, such as courses in the humanities and the social sciences. Quite the contrary is true, however. One has only to refer to the experiences reported by our sample of teachers to see that learning teams have been used successfully in a variety of disciplines. For example:

- Professor Dinan has used team-based learning very successfully in "high content" subjects such as organic chemistry and general chemistry;
- Professor Streuling's learning teams have proven to be exceptionally effective in accounting, one of the highly detailed subjects;
- Professor Popovský has successfully used teams in his natural science classes in botany and microbiology;
- Professor Herreid reports great success in his classes in evolutionary biology;
- Professor Goodson has used teams very effectively in her classes in the social and behavioral sciences;
- Professor Lucas was successful in the use of learning teams in her legal studies classes;
- Professor Nakaji was exceptionally successful in her class in the humanities;
- Professors, Cragin, Freeman, and Michaelsen have used teams very effectively in their various classes in business.

Although the disciplines of our professors are disparate, all report similar outcomes. These positive outcomes include improved attendance, lower attrition rates, increased student preparation, and a high incidence of individual members of groups working together, as a team, to solve diverse, real-world kinds of problems.

In addition to being remarkably effective in a broad range of disciplines, the chapters in part II also support the successful use of learning teams in (1) diverse kinds of classes, including on-line classes and large classes, (2) classes with a wide variety of student types, and (3) a wide range of cultural settings.

Online Classes

Who would have ever believed that team-based learning could be implemented in classes that involve a great deal of time online? Any previous thoughts we had about learning teams needing a traditional classroom setting were thoroughly dispelled by Mark Freeman at the University of Technology in Sydney, Australia (Chapter 14). He has taken "landlocked" activities such as role-play and debate and applied them quite successfully to learning teams in courses in which students spend much of their time in an electronic environment.

In fact, Freeman has discovered that there are several benefits from using role-play and debate on the Web that are not possible when the same exercises are used in a traditional setting. For example, when students debate on the Web, they have the luxury of time to adequately compose a response and, as a result, are spared the stress of thinking on their feet. This is extremely helpful for those students who are not native speakers. In addition, with the extra time to reflect, students produce better-quality responses. They can also use hyperlinks to pull in additional data to substantiate an argument.

As with debate, role-play exercises on the Web are also blessed with benefits not available to their traditional counterparts. For example, one of the greatest strengths of the exercise in the electronic classroom is the veil of anonymity. Because no one knows who is role-playing a particular character, students can totally involve themselves in their roles without concerns about offending any of their classmates. In addition, doors to learning are opened to an entirely different perspective when students have to struggle with solving problems and respond to crises as his or her character would do in a real situation.

Large Classes

Once again, when it comes to the use of learning teams, class size is apparently of little consequence. In Chapter 11, Larry Michaelsen relates his successful experience with learning teams in a class of over 100 students. He reports that, even in a class that large, the outcomes of team-based learning are virtually the same as in a much smaller class. That is, students become actively engaged in the learning process and newly formed groups bond into learning teams. In addition, individual students, as well as teams, are given immediate feedback, have the opportunity to engage in whole-class discussion and, amazingly, also have the opportunity to interact with the instructor—just as they would have in a much smaller class.

Michaelsen writes that, to accommodate large classes, the single major modification that must be made is one of logistics. That is, special care must be taken to address problems of the physical environment of the classroom, with seating configuration being one of the primary concerns. Once those modifications have been made, however, the size of the class is no longer an issue, and both the teacher and the students can begin to experience the benefits of learning from one another in teams.

Students with Disabilities

Perhaps the most amazing and fascinating example of the incredible versatility of learning teams is this strategy's effectiveness with students who are disabled. We (the editors) were thrilled when we learned how successfully Melanie Nakaji has used learning teams in classes that are totally composed of deaf students (Chapter 8). We were delighted to discover that students with such a disability can benefit from the structure of learning teams as well as their hearing counterparts. Each of the specific elements required for the successful use of teams (e.g., the Readiness Assurance Process, group assignments, peer assessment, etc.) are wonderfully adaptable to groups of nonhearing students.

Before the implementation of team-based learning, Nakaji reports that her students attended class "grudgingly," were apathetic during the lecture, failed to participate in class activities, and either failed to turn in homework or turned it in late. After the implementation of team-based learning, Nakaji writes that one of the most noteworthy changes in the class was the great improvement in classroom climate. Because the team assignments truly challenged the students, apathy was no longer a problem. In its place was a newfound student motivation to learn, and a desire to cooperate with fellow teammates. Nakaji summarizes her success with the following comment: "The team-based approach provided a challenge and gave the deaf students an incentive to learn and synthesize core concepts."

The successful marriage of learning teams and disabled students does not end with the story of the deaf students taught by Melanie Nakaji. In Chapter 7, Goodson reports that the team process has "worked every time" for students who are diagnosed with attention deficit disorder (ADD), as well as with students who have test anxiety.

Goodson discovered that both groups of disabled students (ADD and test anxiety) can be successfully integrated into learning teams if she can first persuade them to remain in the class. And she has the following strategy for convincing these students not to drop the class. While both groups of students are typically very anxious at the beginning of the course, she tries to calm their fears by patiently listening to all of their concerns about working in teams. After hearing them out, she requests that they at least try a few Readiness Assessment Tests. She believes that the key to success (for disabled students) is ensuring that they have the opportunity to experience working together as a group with a common goal. The students are instructed to report back to her after they have had such an experience.

Goodson writes that after working with their individual teams, no student has ever made further complaints and none have dropped out of the class. What is most remarkable is that one student with ADD said she "loved" the new method because she did not have to sit through a seventy-five minute lecture, a time that in the past was a "torturous" experience.

Minority Students and Nonnative Speakers

Goodson (Chapter 7) also reports great success with learning teams in classes with minority students. Her classes typically include many Hispanic students for whom English is a second language. Because these students were nonnative speakers, Goodson and her colleagues always worried that the basic course content would never get covered when using a teaching method that relied on reading (such as the Readiness Assurance Process used in team-based learning). They were also quite concerned that nonnative speakers would have difficulty interacting with members of their group who were fluent English speakers.

However, Goodson found quite the contrary to be true in both instances. She reports that student difficulty with reading and understanding the text was never a problem that could not be handled by the students themselves. In fact, team-based learning offers two advantages in relation to this issue. Students for whom English is a problem have a better chance of truly comprehending the content if they can read and reread the text than they have with a lecture in which their major opportunity to understand the material is one quickly passing opportunity.

In addition, her nonnative-speaking students developed another method to overcome difficulties with the readings by simply asking for help from their English-speaking group members. Goodson reports that she frequently observes the nonnative speakers coming to class early to be helped by one of their team members. In the true spirit of team-based learning, they were helping each other learn.

Students in Various Cultures Around the World

Although we have documented success with learning teams in various disciplines, with large classes, and with exceptional students, we believe we also have excellent data to support the effectiveness of teams in multiple cultures around the world.

In Chapters 12, 13, and 14, we have excellent documentation of the successful implementation of learning teams in multiple cultures. Freeman was quite successful in Australia, and Popovský experienced success in the Czech Republic. We also have a remarkable account from Cragin, who has been incredibly successful with learning teams in China as well as thirty additional countries around the world.

Amazingly, regardless of the culture, these teachers all discovered that the opportunity to bond with one's peers as members of a learning team transcended inbred cultural norms for their students. One result of their bonding was the enthusiasm with which students participated in their groups. As one might surmise, "engaged" and "interactive" are not typical descriptors for academic classes in China or in former Communist Block countries such as the Czech Republic. However, two of our professors report exactly those characteristics when they tried team-based learning.

Popovský writes that his students in the Czech Republic became "courageous" in their discussion. And Cragin reports that once the strangeness of interacting in teams was overcome, his Chinese students were "highly enthusiastic about the learning process." Even more important are the teachers' comments about the quality of their students' learning. Popovský writes that students' answers to applied problems became "richer and more detailed" when they were working in their groups.

Cragin does an excellent job of summing up the effectiveness of team-based learning (with students of another culture) with his statement that, "Without question, compared to traditional methods, team-based learning enables students to understand concepts more deeply and retain them longer."

BENEFITS OF LEARNING TEAMS

Students Working Together to Learn

Our sample of teachers in Part II reports that with team-based learning, in contrast to the typical lecture format, students are no longer passive recipients in the classroom. Passivity is reduced because the nature of the assignments in team-based learning provides an environment in which students become actively engaged in the learning process. As was mentioned earlier, Streuling comments that his students often become so engrossed with the project that it is hard to get them to move on to something else. It is the process of working together to solve a common problem that builds a sense of connection between the students. There is a genuine sense of belonging to the group that prompts students to attend class regularly and, even more important, to come to class prepared. Dinan writes that over the course of the semester, he could observe the strengthening of support between students within the groups. Herreid sums it up with his comment that "once groups have bonded, the students realize their absence hurts their new friends."

Improved Student Learning

Without exception, all of the teachers in the preceding chapters reported improved student learning after team-based learning was implemented. In fact, the general consensus among our sample is that working in teams truly promotes the development of critical thinking. Students move from merely hearing and reading about abstract concepts, to working with their teammates to apply those concepts to solve real-world kinds of problems. In addition, through the reinforcement of concepts, issues, ideas, and so on (provided by the Readiness Assurance Process), students also achieve a higher level of retention. Cragin writes that he is absolutely convinced that—compared to traditional methods—team-based learning empowers students to understand concepts more thoroughly and retain them for extended periods of time. In fact, his students have gone out of their way to phone or write, many times long after graduation, to say that they remembered what they had learned in his class and were using it successfully.

Abundant Rewards

When learning teams are properly implemented rewards are abundant, for both the teacher and the students. Streuling points out that one of the greatest benefits of team-based learning is that the teacher's stress level is lower because the responsibility of learning has "shifted from the professor to the students." In other words, with team-based learning, students are more actively engaged in the learning process. As a result, the teacher can relax and enjoy teaching again.

One significant benefit of team-based learning is detailed in Herreid's observation that students cannot remain hidden for the duration of the semester (as they can in many lecture classes) because no one can be anonymous in a small group. That is, it is quite obvious to their fellow team members when students do not keep up with their work and, as a result, are unable to contribute to quizzes or assignments. This kind of exposure creates a genuine sense of accountability, and students quickly learn to come to class prepared. Also, over time, students' confidence in their teams grows to the point that they are willing and able to tackle difficult assignments with little or no external help. Herreid remarks that "it is no wonder the grades are better."

In addition, gone forever is the relentless pursuit to cover the content. The teachers in our sample report that team-based learning allows them to cover more course material than in a typical lecture class. Perhaps Lucas says it best when she comments that, after almost ten years of teaching, she has stopped worrying about having to cover "every concept." She believes that her students have developed the critical thinking skills to seek out and acquire information on their own.

Another reason that the teacher who uses team-based learning can relax and enjoy teaching is that he or she no longer has to worry about being the focus of attention in the class. That is, the teacher can relinquish the role of "entertainer" because he or she no longer has to work at making the class interesting. When group assignments are properly designed, students are drawn into the activity and no longer need to be entertained. Teachers also commented that being freed from the lecture allowed them to become more closely involved with their students during the learning process. Several professors reported that with team-based learning they had the opportunity to get to know their students as individuals, something that was never possible when they were lecturing.

As teachers learn to know their students better, students are also bonding as a group. In fact, many times students develop relationships that last over time. For example, seniors have reported friendships with classmates that began when they were freshmen working on the same team. In addition, many times after having been exposed to the team-based learning experience, students form their own ad hoc groups in subsequent semesters.

CONCLUDING REMARKS

Perhaps the most compelling argument for adopting team-based learning as a teaching method is the ultimate effect it has on teachers themselves. We are somewhat amazed and always delighted to see how many times the teachers in our sample use the word "joy" in reference to their experience with learning teams. In chapter after chapter they speak of the joy involved with seeing students mature into young adults who are responsible for their own learning. Several of the teachers report that they are actually having fun in the classroom again. Professor Streuling, who is close to retirement, writes that he is enjoying using teams so much that he may teach "forever." And Goodson rates her experience with teams as "invaluable and extremely motivating," so much so that she never wants to teach any other way. In fact, Goodson sums it up quite eloquently: "To hear students say that they are able to learn better and faster while retaining their knowledge for longer periods of time, coupled with making new friends and learning how to work in groups, is a precious reward for any professor."

When one has the opportunity to use a teaching strategy that cannot only greatly enhance student learning, but can also energize and enthrall the teacher, why not give it a try?

REFERENCE

Spence, L. (2001). The case against teaching. *Change Magazine 23* (6): 10–19.

Frequently Asked Questions about Team-Based Learning

Larry K. Michaelsen

In the 20-plus years since I first saw the tremendous potential of team-based learning, I have tried to share my experiences and insights in a variety of ways. These include writing more than twenty-five journal articles and conducting over 200 workshops for thousands of higher-education faculty at professional meetings and at schools in thirty-five U.S. states, nine Canadian provinces, and countries on five continents.

Thus, over the years I have had the opportunity to work with a wide variety of faculty peers who have attempted to use team-based learning in their own classes. For some, the transition to team-based learning was a relatively smooth one. Others, however, have encountered situations that prompted them to contact me for advice. Over time their questions have helped me to understand many of the potential pitfalls of team-based learning as well as how to avoid the majority of them.

I have compiled the most frequently asked questions and, in the pages that follow, have answered them as well as I could. In my responses here, I have tried to do three things. First, in most cases, I have tried to offer an explanation of the cause of the problem that prompted the question. Second, I have provided as direct an answer as I can. Finally, in many cases, I suggest other places in this book that may provide additional insights on how to proceed.

THE QUESTIONS

I have grouped these questions into three parts, based on the nature of the concerns that instructors need to resolve before deciding to adopt team-based learning. First, they must be convinced that team-based learning is appropriate for their specific situation. In other words, is team-based learning appropriate for instructors with their particular set of personal strengths and weaknesses, the subject matter that they teach, and the physical setting in which they will be teaching (e.g., class size, classroom configuration, class length, etc).

Second, largely because of previous negative experiences with poorly designed group work, they must resolve questions related to what they anticipate will be the risks and costs of using team-based learning. Questions of this type include such things as:

- Can I cover enough course content?
- Will costs related to free-riders outweigh the benefits of group work?
- Will students be motivated to prepare for in-class group work?
- Can I resolve interpersonal conflicts that will inevitably arise among group members?

Finally, once the decision to use team-based learning has been made, instructors must answer a set of questions that deal with "how to" issues.

The purpose of this chapter is to succinctly and directly address these three kinds of questions about team-based learning. This will be done in two ways. One is by referring to specific examples that have been given earlier in this book. The other is to offer advice based on two different types of experience: my experience in using team-based learning in my own classes, and the experience of colleagues who have used team-based learning and have shared their experiences with me.

WILL TEAM-BASED LEARNING WORK FOR ME?

Are There Any Instructors for Whom Team-Based Learning Will Not Work?

Based on our experience, there are four groups of instructors who should not try to use team-based learning. These are instructors who: (1) are not yet certain what they want students to do beyond the goals of "learn and remember," (2) feel threatened by frequent student challenges, especially when the challenges come from students who are united in groups, (3) really enjoy the "performing" aspect of the teaching role, or (4) are unable to invest the time needed to redesign their approach to teaching.

Going Beyond Knowing

One of the greatest advantages of team-based learning is also a limitation. The advantage is that it shifts the focus of instruction from learning about concepts and ideas to learning how to use them in meaningful ways. The limitation is that it will not work unless the instructor is ready and willing to reward students for pre-class study by providing the opportunity to learn how to use the basic content in a meaningful way. Thus, if the instructor's primary focus is on covering content and he or she fails to use application-focused assignments, students are likely to rebel at having to invest time and energy learning what seems to them to be an endless string of meaningless details.

Comfort with Being Challenged by Students

This is another situation in which an advantage of team-based learning turns out to be a problem for some instructors. Team-based learning promotes a climate in which students feel free to challenge the instructor. In most cases, this is an advantage because it promotes both learning and instructor satisfaction. For some instructors, however, being challenged can be an anxiety-provoking experience. Thus, we would not recommend using team-based learning until you have a firm grasp on the material you will be teaching and are intellectually and emotionally up to being challenged by your students.

Satisfaction from the "Performing" Aspect of Teaching

Although the majority of instructors who adopt team-based learning will not even consider going back to their old way of teaching, it can be very unrewarding for others. Due to the decreased role of lectures, faculty members who really enjoy preparing and delivering lectures end up feeling as though team-based learning robs them of the aspect of their teaching that they enjoy most.

Time Needed to Redesign Your Course

Shifting from a traditional approach to team-based learning does require a significant time investment for the developing of Readiness Assessment Tests (RATs) and application-focused activities. Although the time required for the redesign process can be kept to a minimum, you are much more likely to have a positive experience if you delay your first team-based learning start up until you have time to plan out what you are going to do.

Should I Try to Use Team-Based Learning with My Subject Matter?

This question is most frequently asked by instructors with exactly opposite concerns. On one end of the spectrum, some instructors worry that team-based learning will not work in courses that have a great deal of factual material to cover and that lend themselves to right or wrong answers such as chemistry, physics and many of the natural sciences. On the other end of the spectrum, some instructors, mainly in the humanities, worry that team-based learning will not work because there are no right or wrong answers.

In both cases, the answer to whether or not team-based learning is appropriate for the subject matter is an unequivocal "yes," and the key for both groups is having a clear picture of what you want students to do with the material. In both cases, their concerns surface as they try to implement the Readiness Assurance Process. However, the nature of their concerns is quite different for courses with lots of factual material than for courses with no right or wrong answers.

Courses Emphasizing Factual Material

In this kind of course, the key is focusing the RATs on key concepts, not on details or computations. That is, the questions should focus on making sure that students understand the material in the table of contents and not on the material that is only in the index. If students get a clear "big picture" from the Readiness Assurance Process, they will add (and retain) the details as they complete application-focused assignments (see Chapter 1, Figure 1.2). If the RATs focus on details or computations, students are likely to feel that they are being punished for not memorizing everything. In addition, if the RATs focus on details, the potential value of the group RATs will be lessened by the fact that the discussion will be brief and will focus on what the reading says as opposed to what it means. Further, if the RATs emphasize doing computations rather than setting them up, there is seldom very much discussion because one member will simply act on behalf of the group.

Courses with No Right or Wrong Answers

The key in this situation is focusing the Readiness Assessment Process on ensuring that students understand the criteria that you will apply in grading their assignments, that is, the RAT questions should assess their understanding of the models that you want students to use to complete their assignments. For example, a sociology instructor could use a RAT to ensure that students understand concepts related to socioeconomic status, then test their ability to use the concepts by assigning them to use the concepts to discriminate between effective and ineffective campaign strategies in a presidential election, interactions among characters in a movie clip, the focus of television ads during different prime-time television programs, and so on.

Should I Try to Use Team-Based Learning with My Class Size?

This question is most frequently asked by instructors with either very large or very small classes. In both cases, the answer to whether or not team-based learning is appropriate is an unequivocal "yes." In both cases, the key is using decision-based assignments and procedures that enable immediate comparisons with other teams. In large classes, this means the teacher needs to ensure that all the teams work on the same problem and then provide a way for teams to simultaneously reveal the choices they have made (see Chapter 12).

In classes that are too small to divide into two teams (i.e., fewer than eight students), then the best option is using a single team and, whenever possible, providing them with ongoing comparisons to teams in similar classes, for instance, their RAT scores versus average RAT scores from previous classes.

Should I Try To Use Team-Based Learning If I Am in a Classroom with Inflexible Seating?

Faculty members often worry that team-based learning will not work unless they can get their class scheduled into a classroom with round tables or movable chairs. Based on our experience, this fear is largely unfounded. Although the physical layout of the classroom can be somewhat of a problem, team-based learning can be used effectively in virtually any classroom. The only essential condition is providing a space in which members have the possibility of having eye contact with each other (see Chapter 12). For example, in tiered classrooms with fixed individual seats, instructors should make seat assignments such that members on one row can turn around and be face-to-face with the rest of their team. As long as teams have the possibility of doing so, they will develop procedures for overcoming the physical barriers inherent in the space to which they have been assigned.

Should I Try to Use Team-Based Learning If I Teach in a Fifty-Minute Time Slot?

Although team-based learning can be used effectively in fifty-minute class periods, doing so usually requires making some adjustments. For example, RATs must be either very short or the Readiness Assurance Process has to be spread across more than one class period, that is, the individual test on the first day and the team test, appeals, and instructor input on the next one. Further, although a lecturer can simply end class when the time runs out, and start again at the beginning of the next with very little disruption of the flow of the class, using blocks of time for in-class group work makes timing issues much more important. As a result, longer class periods help in two ways. One is that they allow more efficient use of time. The other is that they provide more flexibility for designing and managing in-class group assignments (See Chapter 12).

Will Team-Based Learning Force Me to Invest a Lot More Time in My Teaching?

This question is not an easy one to answer. On one hand, successfully implementing team-based learning does require most instructors to invest a significant amount of time to restructure their courses and develop effective team assignments. On the other hand, this task is largely a one-time effort. Once the course is up and running, the time required for operating and maintaining a team-based learning course is not substantially different from the time required to effectively teach a course in any other format. In addition, most teachers are able to streamline the course-restructuring process by using a variety of resources (including Chapters 2 and 3 of this book, and the articles listed in the references), and by sharing ideas and assignments with other team-based learning users. Further, most team-based learning users find that their first course-restructuring effort is the most time consuming and that the conversion process is much easier with subsequent courses.

Given the significance of the start-up costs, we have three recommendations. One is starting with the basics and adding sophistication over time. At a minimum, this means starting off each unit with a RAT that prepares students for one or more appropriate, application-focused assignments. "Appropriate" here calls for all groups to be working on the same problem and making (and simultaneously reporting their) specific choices. Second, we recommend a strategy of implementing team-based learning in one course at a time. Finally, it is best to start with a course that has as many advantages as possible. These would include: familiar subject matter, a moderate number of students (20–40), at least a seventy-five-minute time slot and, a classroom in which students do not face significant physical barriers to working face-to-face with each other.

Do I Need Any Special Skills to Use Team-Based Learning Successfully?

The personal characteristics of any teacher have an impact regardless of the teaching approach that he or she uses. For example, being organized and having a flair for the dramatic are two keys to being an effective lecturer. However, although getting organized is something that anyone can learn to do—it simply takes a commitment to do it—learning how to make spellbinding presentations can be very difficult for a large percentage of would-be lecturers.

Based on our observations, the majority of experienced teachers already have most of the skills required to effectively implement team-based learning. Most of us have already learned how to organize material, create and give tests and assignments, and provide feedback on student performance. The major change, which can be a difficult one, involves thinking differently about what should be happening in our classrooms. Instead of thinking about how we should be teaching, we have to focus on what we can do to enhance student learning. Beyond that, the one new skill that appears to provide the greatest challenge to new team-based learning users is developing the ability to design effective group assignments.

ANTICIPATED PROBLEMS WITH GROUP WORK

Can I Cover the Required Course Content If I Use Class Time for Group Work?

The greatest fear of most instructors is that if they use class time for group work, they will not be able to cover enough content. For the most part, this fear is based on the observation that, even in the face of threats such as pop quizzes, only a small minority of students even try to prepare for class and even fewer come to class actually well prepared. The fact that students rarely appear to be prepared for lecture-based classes, I contend, results from a powerful combination of negative incentives for completing pre-class reading assignments, and a lack of positive incentives for students to reveal what they know when they are prepared.

Most students have learned that, as long as they attend and pay attention, they will either be able to do well on the tests based on the lectures alone or they will be adequately warned if additional reading is really necessary. As a result, such things as the costs of buying the text, using discretionary time to read it, and then being bored during the lectures, end up being powerful disincentives for pre-class preparation. Further, when students do prepare, they are often reluctant to speak up for two reasons. One is that, if they are wrong, they worry about looking bad. The other is that, even if they are right, many worry that they might be seen as one-upping their peers.

Team-based learning, however, provides multiple incentives for pre-class individual study and for students to speak up when they do have information to share. One strong incentive is that the individual RAT scores have an impact on their grade. In addition, because teams cannot do well unless their members are prepared, interaction during the team RATs provides several other powerful incentives for both pre-class preparation and for sharing information within teams. Students learn quickly that their peers will hold them accountable for pre-class reading because every time a disagreement occurs, members will be asked about the reasons for their choices. As a result, there is both immediate social pressure to study and the realization that failing to do so is likely to result in the negative consequence of receiving a low peer evaluation at the end of the term. In addition, over time, members are increasingly motivated to study to ensure the success of their team.

Given this combination of factors, the vast majority of team-based learning users have found that, because students are willing to take responsibility for completing pre-class work, they are actually able to cover more material (e.g., see Chapters 5, 6, 7, 8, 10, and 13). In addition, the efficiency of the Readiness Assurance Process allows them to shift the primary focus of in-class work from covering content to decision-based team assignments that focus on developing higher-level thinking skills.

Will Costs Related to Free-Riders Outweigh the Benefits of Group Work?

Faculty members who ask this question tend to have one of two situations in mind. By far the most troublesome is when one or two members end up being saddled with doing far more than their fair share of the group work. This type of free-rider problem is almost always the result of poorly designed group assignments that can be (and usually are) completed by individual members working alone. Because one member doing a poor job can sink the group, better students do not trust others to do the work to their satisfaction, and will do a disproportionate share and then resent (and complain about) having to do it.

Based on our experience, free-riding based on parceling out assignments to group members occurs when either of two conditions exists: (1) assignments involving tasks that can be completed by an individual member (i.e., group interaction is in fact not needed), or (2) assignments involving a great deal of writing. Because writing is inherently an individual activity, the only real group activity will be deciding how to divide up the work.

For a variety of reasons, this kind of free-riding is virtually never a problem with team-based learning. One is that the RATs so powerfully illustrate the value of give-and-take discussion in tackling intellectual problems (e.g., over 98% of the teams will outperform their own best member; see Michaelsen, Watson, & Black, 1989). Another is the multiple incentives for completing pre-class assignments. The most important reason, however, is that application-focused assignments provide both incentives and opportunities for face-to-face interaction because they are designed around reaching decisions (not producing a lengthy document), and are largely conducted during class time.

The other problem that many instructors view as free riding is when students get higher grades than their individual scores would seem to merit. In most cases, this results from using a traditional grading scale (i.e., 90% = A, 80% = B, etc.) when a significant part of the grade is based on teamwork. Because the teams do such good work (average team RAT scores are typically at least 15–20% above average individual scores), a low-scoring member of a high-performing team can end up with a relatively high grade. The best way to avert free-riders of this type is to make sure that the mechanics of the grading system take into account the fact that group scores will normally be higher than individual scores.

Will Students Be Motivated to Prepare for Group Work?

This concern typically results from a combination of instructors' lack of faith in students to complete pre-class assignments, and the frequency with which they have to deal with complaints about free-riders. What the teachers lack, however, is an understanding of how much their own failure to create conditions that foster individual and group accountability has contributed to the problem.

With team-based learning, a combination of factors, many of which are listed in the answers to the two previous questions, encourage members to be individually prepared for class. Further, because group performance is a major component of the course grade, students are motivated to prepare for, and participate fully in, the team assignments. They realize that team members will sink or swim together.

Can I Resolve Interpersonal Conflicts that Will Inevitably Arise among Group Members?

This concern also typically results from a lack of understanding of the tremendous negative impact of poorly designed group assignments. Most of the really troublesome cases of conflicts in learning groups are associated with assignments in which students are able to parcel out the subtasks of the assignment. In some instances, the conflict is either over which member gets to make the decisions of who does what, or who gets the easiest (or hardest) part. In other cases, the conflict arises when members are impatient with members' failure to agree on or meet deadlines. Occasionally, the conflicts are content-based and result from differences of opinion about the quality of each other's work.

With team-based learning, lots of disagreements occur, but neither process nor content issues are significant problems because of the frequent and immediate feedback on team work. For example, although each RAT provides multiple opportunities for both process and content conflicts to occur, disagreements of both types are quickly resolved by feedback resulting from the scoring of the exams. As a result, team-based learning instructors almost never have to spend front-end time coaching groups on to how to resolve conflicts or midcourse time adjudicating problems that arise from group meltdowns.

"HOW TO" IMPLEMENTATION QUESTIONS

How Should I Form the Teams?

In forming groups, we recommend trying to do three things. One is spreading assets and liabilities (i.e., background factors that are likely to make a difference in students' performance in this course) across the teams. Assets are often such things as attitudes toward, or performance in, previous course work, or course-related life experience; liabilities often include such factors as no (or poor) preparation in related courses, language barriers, and so on. Thus, the team-formation process should be criterion-based. A second objective of the team-formation process is to avoid preexisting, cohesive subgroups (e.g., a group of three students from the same fraternity and three students who did not previously know each other would probably struggle). For these two reasons, teams should not be self-selected. Third, the process you use for team formation should foster the perception that none of the teams was given a special advantage. Thus, we recommend using a very public team-formation process.

As a practical matter, I literally have students form a single line, in order of a set of categories with the most rare but important category first. For example, in undergraduate management principles courses, the rare and important category is usually full-time work experience, so that is the first category. (By contrast, I rarely use work experience as a category in graduate courses because most students have worked for at least a year or two.) The next category for undergraduates is typically "Those who were born and raised outside of Oklahoma and the immediately adjacent states." Students array themselves from most to least distant; this makes it possible to spread out English-as-a-second-language students without specifically singling them out. Next, I have accounting and finance students join the line (they tend to see things in "black or white"), followed by management and marketing students (who are more comfortable with various "shades of gray").

In graduate classes my most important but rare category is typically Ph.D. students and students from programs outside of business—for instance, I often have several law students and want them in separate groups. As a result, I start off by asking students to raise a hand if they are from outside the college of business. Then I have them line up alphabetically by discipline. Then I invite the "born and raised outside of Oklahoma and the immediately adjacent states" category to come next, and the final set of categories has to do with undergraduate majors.

When the entire class is standing in line, I then have them count off by the number of groups I want. When the counting-off process is finished, I have the groups assemble themselves in designated locations in the classroom.

How Big Should the Teams Be?

The size of the teams always represents a compromise between being large enough to have sufficient intellectual resources to complete the assignments, and small enough to develop into true teams. Historically, we have found that if teams have at least five members, they usually have the intellectual resources to complete the team assignments. On the other end of the spectrum, we have found that groups larger than seven tend to have difficulty in the team-development process. Hence the optimum size for team-based learning is five to seven students.

What Should I Do If Students Have Difficulty with the Required Pre-Class Reading?

In some cases, students' reading limitations are a very legitimate cause for concern. These include: difficult subject matter, poorly written reading materials, insufficient reading skills, limited [English] language skills, and physical or mental handicaps. Although the answer of what to do about it depends, to some extent, on the reason(s) that students are having difficulty, the severity of the problem can be greatly reduced by one or a combination of the following:

1. Prepare a reading guide containing questions that students should be able to answer after having read the text.
2. Allow a limited question-and-answer session (e.g., let each group pick one question immediately before each of the RATs).
3. Create short text supplements (often a single page or less) that clarify specific issues that create problems for students.
4. Create or locate Web-based tutorials (note: publishers are frequently making these available as part of a text-purchase package).
5. Create and make available an audio "walk-through" of the text. For example, a physics colleague largely resolved his students' reading concerns in less than two hours by talking into a tape recorder as he thumbed through the pages of his text.

He then allowed students to make their own copy of his tape to guide their individual study.

6. Provide tutorial help to individual students or teams.

7. Develop teams to the point that members voluntarily help each other prepare for the RATs (e.g., see Goodson's discussion in Chapter 8 of the volunteer help given to English-as-a-second-language students in her courses).

8. If all else fails, use class time (usually a small fraction of that required in a lecture course) to remediate misunderstandings that surface during the Readiness Assurance Process.

How Do I Set Up an Effective Grading System?

An effective grading system for team-based learning contains three essential components: individual performance, team performance, and peer evaluation. The individual performance component provides a basis for student accountability to the instructor and to each other. The group performance component provides incentives for the development of group cohesiveness and justifies putting effort into group work. The peer evaluation solves two important motivational problems. One is providing an incentive for individuals to participate in group discussions. The other is removing the students' fear that they will have to choose between getting a low grade on the group assignments and having to carry the group work if other group members fail to do their fair share.

The final weight of each of these three components should be a balance of three factors. First, each of the components should be given enough weight so it is clear to students that the instructor thinks it is important. Second, the instructor must be personally comfortable with the relative weights in the chosen grading system. Third, the grading system must be responsive to student concerns for fairness and equity.

In our classes, we involve students in the development of the grading system through an exercise called "Setting Grade Weights" (described in detail in Appendix C). This is an exercise in which we set maximum and minimum limits for each component of the course grade, and then representatives of the groups negotiate a mutually acceptable set of weights for each of the grade components. Over the years, it has proven to be a highly effective way to create a grading system that is both acceptable to all the parties involved, and supports the individual and team behaviors that are necessary for learning and team development.

How Can I Provide Grade-Based Incentives for Group Work and Still Avoid Giving Higher Grades Than the Weaker Students Deserve?

A relatively common problem with new team-based learning users is finding a way to count group work in their grading system without giving higher-than-deserved grades to some of their students. The apparent dilemma is created by the fact that most groups will score over 90 percent on most tests and other assignments. Further, even though team-based learning increases both attendance and pre-class preparation, users sometimes find that when a large percentage of the grade is based on group work, locking themselves into a 90 = A, and so on grade distribution forces them into "giving away" grades to students who really do not deserve them.

One way to at least partially avoid the problem is to not use percentages as the foundation for determining students' final course grades. Even though I carefully explain my rationale to the students, I still get some initial resistance. But it dissolves as students come to realize that you will be fair with them. (Note: Students are almost universally convinced that there is something magic about a 90. In my experience, however, it is really an arbitrary cutoff because most instructors try to peg the difficulty level of their tests to give the "appropriate" number of As. If the test turns out to be too difficult, they curve it up, give an easier test the next time, or both. If the test is too easy, they give a harder one next time around.)

As a practical matter, I generally work with an overall 1,000-point base and also 1000-point-within-category base. Thus, if group analysis of a movie or novel is worth 30 percent of the group part of the grade, I treat it as though a perfect score would be 300. I also have just over 100 questions on my total of six RATs, and the group RATs are 30 percent of the group grade. At three points per question, that adds up to about 300 points for the groups. As a result, I simply have my spreadsheet add up the total of the raw scores on the six RATs.

At the end of the semester, I multiply the subset totals by the weights determined by the class (e.g., if students have set the weight of the group part of the grade at 65%, I simply multiply the total of the raw group scores by .65). Then I sum the weighted points from the three major grading components (individual scores, group scores, and peer evaluations). This gives me an overall score for each student. I then have my computer sort the students into a distribution based on this weighted total score and look for "break points" for As, Bs, etc. at approximately the level that I think represents a fair overall grade distribution. I typically take three factors into account: (1) grade norms for similar courses [I use this as a base]; (2) my personal impressions about how well the students have performed relative to other classes that I have taught; and (3) extenuating circumstances (e.g., textbook problems, weather problems, etc.).

Should I Give a RAT Every Class Period, Or Every Week?

This answer is an unequivocal no. In fact, when someone says they tried team-based learning and they got a negative student reaction, my first question is: How many RATs did you give?" At least 80 percent of the time they will answer that they have given at least 12–15. If you give too many RATs, you are likely falling into a trap of pushing students into memorizing details that are not really significant to either you or the students.

The primary purpose of the RATs is to assess student readiness to engage in related application-focused activities, all of which are open-book. The RATs should focus on ensuring that students have an understanding of the basic concepts that is thorough enough to be allow them to tackle the application-focused assignments, and use their assigned readings as reference material to digest additional detail as they work. Thus, the test questions should focus on the concepts that would be found in a typical table of contents, not just in the index. In my judgment, focusing on details is counterproductive for a variety of reasons. First, it limits the amount of material that students are willing to be responsible for, because they feel like they have to memorize everything. Second, if your goal is long-term recall of the material, then you are better off reinforcing the fundamental concepts (the details are not all that important—partly because they are always changing—and students will never retain them anyway). Third, they can pick up—and are more likely to retain—the details when they are encountered in a meaningful context as they are working on the applications.

How Much Should the RATs Count?

A primary benefit of the individual RATs is that they make members accountable for their individual preparation. Students realize that, because of the give-and-take that occurs during the group test, they will not be able to hide a lack of individual preparation for the group RATs. Thus, regardless of how much the individual scores actually count toward the course grade, they make members accountable to their group. As a result, as long as the group RATs and the peer evaluation both have a significant impact on the course grade, it is not essential that individual RATs count very much at all. On the other hand, even though we typically develop a grading system using an exercise that gives students the option of not counting the individual RATs at all, they rarely choose that option. Instead, they typically set the weight for the entire set of individual RATs at about 10 percent, and the group RATs at about 15 percent of the overall course grade.

What Should I Do When Students Are Absent?

In general, I try to create a situation that is similar to what students will experience in the workplace. Thus, I say something like:

In the workplace, when someone is gone, the group has to pick up the slack but the absent member still benefits from the group work. If the absent person has a good reason for being gone, explains the reason to the group, and does their best to make amends, most groups will gladly extend the benefit. If, however, members have doubts about the reason for the absence, feel like the member is trying to freeload or both, then the absence is likely to be a black mark that may not be forgotten when the peer evaluations come around. So, if you have to be absent, let your peers know in advance and make sure that you do your best to make up for it. Otherwise, you are at risk.

Then, if they do need to miss a RAT or some other graded activity, I give them the team score and also allow them the opportunity to take the individual test using one of two options. One is to take the test early so that I can let their team have access to their individual answers during the team test. The other option is to take the test later.

Some professors are uncomfortable with the idea of giving makeup tests. They worry that allowing some students to take a late exam will give them an unfair advantage over other students, but see the task of creating comparable but different exams as extremely time consuming. It turns out that neither of these problems is as big as they seem.

In my case, I do not create an alternative exam. If a students misses a RAT when it is given in class (and few do), I leave a copy of the regular exam with the departmental secretary. Then, any student who needs to take a makeup RAT contacts her to make arrangements to take the exam in a nearby room. In the many years I have done this, the vast majority of students taking such makeup exams get scores that are lower than their average on the RATs they take at the normal time. This means I can simply use the same exam for the makeup exam, and doing so does not give students any significant, unfair advantage.

If allowing makeup RATs turns out to be too much of a problem, another option is to set up the grading system that allows students to drop one individual RAT score. When students calculate their overall score for the individual RATs, for example, they would only count the best five out of six. If they have no absences, they get to drop their lowest score. If they have one absence, they simply have a zero for that score and drop it. If they have more than one absence, they get to drop one of those but they have to calculate the other zeros into the total. The advantage of the approach is that it reduces the hassles associated with giving makeup exams. The disadvantage, and one that I personally feel is important, is that it eliminates the opportunity to reward students who are willing to put in the effort to be prepared on every test.

Should I Use Peer Evaluations on All Projects?

Although it is essential to have a peer evaluation that counts at the end of the course, we see arguments both ways with respect to every project or even midcourse peer evaluations. The strongest argument in favor of frequent peer evaluations is that they give members earlier feedback on their behavior and hence an earlier opportunity to change it. Some students are honestly unaware that some of their behavior is seen as counterproductive by their peers and are willing to try very hard to change when they learn that change is needed.

There are, however, two arguments against frequent peer evaluations as well. One is that having members evaluate each other tends to disrupt the development of group cohesiveness. The other is that we have seen a few instances in which an assertive member received high evaluations for taking charge on early assignments. This encouraged the person to dominate the group even more on later assignments but led to the person receiving the lowest peer evaluations in the group at the end of the course.

Thus, if you choose to do peer evaluations along the way, we recommend: (1) providing a mechanism for giving anonymous comments; (2) making sure that members give each other both positive and negative (i.e., room for improvement) feedback; and (3) counting the later feedback the most. (See Appendix B for more detail.)

How Should I Handle the Scoring of Appeals?

There are several issues in relation to handling score changes that result from appeals. However, in every case we think it is important to make sure that we are not reinforcing a behavior that we really do not want. For example, we make it clear that any team has the opportunity to submit appeals; but if they choose not to appeal, we hold them responsible for their choice (i.e., an appeal granted for one team will not improve the scores of other teams). In doing so, we also make it clear that it would be unethical to teach in a way that implied that it is fine for students to sit back and let others do their work for them. Similarly, we only accept appeals on the questions the teams have missed; allowing individual appeals would eliminate the incentive for members to stand up for their point of view during the team test. However, if we grant a team appeal, we also change the scores of each member who had the same answer as the team. Finally, we do not take away points from a member who had correctly answered the question in the first place.

How Should I Give Feedback on Multiple-Choice Questions?

There are two aspects to the feedback process. One is the actual scoring of the tests. The other, which is by far the most important, is providing students with information on how their overall performance compares to other teams and whether or not each of their answers was correct. The simplest way to score the individual tests is using a portable test-scoring machine. We use a Scantron 888P+ scoring machine that we actually take into the classroom. This allows us to score the individual tests while students are taking the team tests.

We provide immediate feedback on the team tests in one of two ways. The first method is using IF-AT answer sheets (Epstein, 2000) to provide both immediate feedback on a question-by-question basis and partial credit if students have partial, but incomplete, understanding of the concepts on which the questions are based. With IF-AT answer sheets, students scratch off the covering of one of four boxes in search of a mark that indicates that they have found the correct answer. If they find the mark on the first try, they receive full credit. If not, they scratch until they find the mark, but their score is reduced with each unsuccessful scratch. The other method is having a member score their answer sheet on the Scantron scoring machine as soon as the teams complete their test. We then have the team member post the score on the board or on an overhead transparency (to provide the inter-team comparisons) and pick up the team folder containing the individual (already-scored) answer sheets.

Having immediate access to both the individual and team answers provides immediate feedback on two key aspects of their work. One is their level of mastery of the assigned readings. The other is whether they effectively incorporated the input that was potentially available from each team member. Further, because the feedback is literally instantaneous, the IF-AT answer sheets have a particularly powerful and positive effect on the teams for two quite different reasons. One is that students very rapidly learn the value of voicing their own and listening to each others' ideas. As a result, they are able to develop and benefit from effective interaction patterns in a fraction of the time it would take in a less feedback-rich environment. The other is that, even if they do not find the correct answer until the second or third scratch, members experience, and are motivated by, a series of immediate successes from working together.

We have also discovered a way to promote team development by limiting the feedback we provide in machine scoring the answer sheets. If we give information on which answer was correct (which is one of the automatic scoring options), teams often fail to discover situations in which the team missed a question that was answered correctly by a team member. On the other hand, when we limit our feedback to simply identifying the incorrect answers, their first question to each other is, "Did anyone get this one right?" Thus, with no coaching at all, teams obtain the feedback that enables them to develop a decision-making process that is effective in obtaining input from even their most timid members.

How Can I Provide Immediate Feedback on the RATs If I Do Not Have Either IF-AT Answer Sheets or a Scoring Machine?

In reality, actually scoring the individual tests is not essential for either learning or team development. What is important is providing immediate feedback. Thus, in large classes, if we do not have either IF-AT answer sheets or a scoring machine, we do not actually score the individual tests until later. Instead, we have team representatives turn in their team folder containing the individual answer sheets before they start the team test. When the teams finish their tests, we provide an answer key that they use to "score" their team test as soon as they turn in their answer sheet. Further, as long as members record their answers on the test itself (which they have to retain to take the team test), providing feedback on the team tests also enables members to score their own individual tests.

You can also use class discussion to let students discover the correct answers (see Cragin, in Chapter 13). This involves having teams alternate in giving their answer to the individual questions, and when teams disagree, moderating the discussion between teams. Further, because the teams are challenging each other (and not the teacher), it is also possible to use the discussion to grant credit for an alternative answer in the same way as would normally be done with written appeals (i.e., declaring more than one "winner").

Another alternative is quickly hand-scoring the individual tests using an answer sheet with a companion answer key in the form of a transparency overlay (see Figure A.1) with clear windows (for correct answers) and shaded boxes (for incorrect answers). Then you can let the teams use the overlay to quickly score their own tests.

FIGURE A.1
Forms for Quick Hand-Scoring of Multiple-Choice Exams

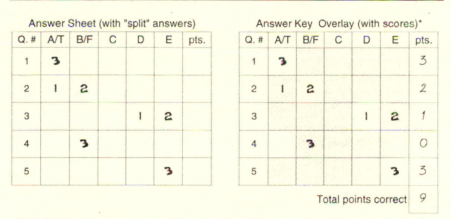

Answer Sheet (with "split" answers)

Q. #	A/T	B/F	C	D	E	pts.
1	3					
2	1	2				
3				1	2	
4		3				
5					3	

Answer Key Overlay (with scores)*

Q. #	A/T	B/F	C	D	E	pts.
1	3					3
2	1	2				2
3				1	2	1
4		3				0
5					3	3

Total points correct   9

*This depicts a transparency overlay answer key. The score for each question is simply the number that appears in the un-shaded "window" in the answer key transparency.

What Are the Benefits of Using a "Split-Answers" Format on the RATS?

Early on, most team members are somewhat timid about challenging each other out of fear of being perceived as overly aggressive. As a result, newly formed groups always look for ways to incorporate everyone's input without having to risk a confrontation between members with differing views. With normal true or false and multiple-choice questions, their natural inclination is to select answers by a majority vote after a very brief discussion. However, voting with minimal discussion tends to hamper both learning and team development because members tend to withhold information that would stimulate give-and-take discussion. Further, the fact that voting often produces the correct answer tends to obscure the importance of obtaining input from everyone in the group.

Once we understood the dynamics of the process, we were able to develop a procedure that largely solves the problem. Our solution is providing a way for teams to incorporate everyone's input without having to risk a confrontation between members with differing views. This procedure highlights, instead of obscures, the importance of getting input from every team member. With this system, we have each question count for three points. If we are using machine-scored forms, we have students answer each RAT question three times (i.e., as though it was three separate questions—and number the questions accordingly). Thus, the first question would be numbered 1–3, the second would be 3–6, and so on, and we enable them to "split" their answers by filling in up to three different answers to each question. For example, if they want to hedge their bets on the first question (which we would have numbered 1–3), they might want to answer A on answer spaces 1 and 2, and B on answer space 3. In this case, if the correct answer was A, they would get two of the three possible points. If the correct answer was B, they would get one point, and they would get no points at all for a C, D or E. If we are hand-scoring the questions, we have students distribute three points in the boxes on each row of the answer sheet (see Figure A.1).

Early on, most groups choose politeness over rightness by splitting answers to smooth over member differences. By allowing split answers, however, we focus their attention on the fact that they incur a cost (i.e., the loss of at a point) every time they reach a decision without exploring the reasons behind members' choices. This, in turn, provides a powerful incentive for members to start talking out differences instead of sweeping them under rug. As a result, teams quickly develop to the point that give-and-take discussions are the norm, and they are rewarded by increasing their ability to incorporate members' input into their decisions.

Are There Alternatives to Using Multiple-Choice Questions on the RATs?

The critical attribute of any RAT question is whether or not it can be used to provide immediate feedback on both individual and team performance. Although multiple-choice questions are particularly well suited for providing immediate feedback, other types of questions will work as well. For example, one faculty member hands out a sheet containing fill-in-the-blank, short-answer essay, and other questions that are designed to test concept understanding by completing simple computations. When students complete their individual RAT, they slip it into a photo album page so that it is visible on both sides but they will not be tempted to write on it during the team test (same questions but on colored paper). When they finish their team test, the teacher gives them a copy of the answer key that his graduate assistant will use to correct the test. After comparing their test to the answer key (which provides immediate feedback on both the individual and team tests), students have the opportunity to fill out an additional form on which they submit any appeals or comments that they would like to have considered in completing the grading process.

What Kinds of Questions Are Good Questions for the RATs?

In addition to providing the basis for immediate feedback on both individual and team performance, the test questions should also emphasize key concepts (i.e., avoid asking questions about inconsequential details) and enhance learning. With respect to enhancing learning, one characteristic is that at least some of the questions must be difficult enough to stimulate discussion. Otherwise, teams will simply defer to their best member. In addition, using related questions that require increasingly complex levels of understanding are particularly helpful for two reasons. First, if the questions are correctly chosen and sequenced, students can learn from the questions themselves while they are taking the RAT. For example, by asking one or two recognition-type questions followed by a question that requires synthesizing the concepts from the two earlier questions students are provided with the opportunity to develop a deeper understanding of the concepts themselves. Second, questions that require higher-level thinking skills are far more likely to stimulate the kind of discussion that promotes peer teaching.

Can I Use a Writing Assignment for the Application Phase of Team-Based Learning?

In many ways using "good" in relation to "writing assignments for groups" is an oxymoron. Writing is inherently an individual activity. As a result, group writing assignments typically set in motion a series of events that tend to inhibit learning, and often foster very negative attitudes toward group work (see Chapter 3). Learning suffers because when groups are assigned to create a lengthy document, the only rational way to accomplish this overall task is to divide up the work so that each member independently completes part of the assignment (usually the part that he or she already knows the most about). The negative attitudes are caused by the fact that if any member does not do a good job on his or her share of the writing, his or her peers will be forced to accept a lower grade, or engage in a last-minute attempt to salvage a disaster. In fact, high-achieving students often express the feeling that getting an acceptable grade on a group term paper feels like having crossed a freeway during rush hour without being run over.

Is It OK to Use Group Presentations?

Group presentations have both a positive and a negative side. The work leading up to a group presentation is usually more productive than writing a group paper. Because they realize they will all be in the public spotlight at the same time, members tend to spend more time working together to make sure they are at least somewhat familiar with the major content issues. As a result, the preparation phase of group presentations often enhances both learning and interpersonal relationships. Unfortunately, the actual presentations are often almost a waste of time. For listeners, it is just another lecture, except that they usually have serious doubts about whether or not their peers are expert enough to be taken seriously. As a result, the energy level so low that, in far too many cases, the only ones who benefit from the experience are the presenters.

If I Cannot Use Group Papers or Presentations, What Can I Use?

In general, the value of group assignments is largely a function of the extent to which they cause members to engage in give-and-take, content-related discussions. As a result, the best group assignments require groups to make decisions that involve complex applications of course concepts. The thinking required is simply too complex to be handed out to individual members working on their own (see Chapter 3, and Chapter 11 on large classes). Further, in addition to having the teams make a specific decision, having them all work with the same problem or case, and simultaneously report their decisions dramatically increases the value of the group assignments for two quite different reasons. One is that the resulting give-and-take discussions between teams produces timely, content-related feedback on students' concept understanding; the other is that it builds commitment to, and enhances the problem-solving capabilities within, the teams.

REFERENCES

Epstein, M. L. (2000). A testing/teaching multiple-choice answer form. Workshop presented at the Fourteenth Annual Conference, Teaching of Psychology: Ideas and Innovations, Ellenville, NY. http://enigma.rider.edu/~epstein/ifat/>

Michaelsen, L. K., Watson, W. E., & Black, R. H. (1989). A realistic test of individual versus group consensus decision making. *Journal of Applied Psychology 74*(5): 834–839.

Calculating Peer Evaluation Scores

Larry K. Michaelsen and L. Dee Fink

If group work is going to be a component of students' course grades, it is imperative that peer evaluations are included as part of the grade-calculation process. There are a number of ways this can be accomplished. In this appendix, we will describe two different peer evaluation approaches that, for over twenty years, have produced good results in a wide range of teaching situations. One was developed by Michaelsen, the other by Fink. Both were originally developed for a hard-copy environment but are now being used online.

Both peer evaluation procedures involve having each student formally participate in the grading process by assessing the overall contribution of the other members of their team, and both procedures result in a number that is used in calculating each student's course grade. The difference lies in the way that number is generated and how it is incorporated into the overall calculation of the course grade. In one approach, that number is an independent component of the course grade (Michaelsen's procedure), while in the other approach it is used as a percentage multiplier of the group's graded work before being added into the course grade (Fink's procedure).

OPTION #1: PEER EVALUATION AS AN
INDEPENDENT COMPONENT

In Michaelsen's approach, the overall course grade consists of the sum of a student's scores in three areas: individual performance, team performance, and team maintenance. The number for the team maintenance score is in essence the peer evaluation score and is created as follows.

Calculating the Peer Evaluation Score

As part of the final exam, each student fills out a form for evaluating the helpfulness of other members of his or her team (see Exhibit B.1). In a six-member team, and when team maintenance is worth ten points, each individual would be asked to: (1) assign a total of fifty points to the other five members in their team and, (2) differentiate some in their ratings (i.e., each rater would have to give at least one score of 11 or higher—with a maximum of 15—and at least one score of 9 or lower). Each member's peer evaluation score is the average of the points they receive from the members of their team (see Table B.1).

An example can show how this works. As shown in Table B.1, Amy and Felicia are both in Team #1. Their Team Performance scores (i.e., the sum of the scores received by

EXHIBIT B.1
Peer Evaluation Form (Michaelsen)

Peer Evaluation   Name_____   Team # _____

Please assign scores that reflect how you really feel about the extent to which the other members of your team contributed to your learning and/or your team's performance. This will be your only opportunity to reward the members of your team who worked hard on your behalf. (**Note: If you give everyone pretty much the same score you will be hurting those who did the most and helping those who did the least.**)

Instructions: In the space below please rate each of the **other** members of your team. Each member's peer evaluation score will be the average of the points they receive from the other members of the team. To complete the evaluation you should: 1) List the name of each member of your team in the alphabetical order of their last names and, 2) assign an average of ten points to the <u>other</u> members of your team (Thus, for example, you should assign a total of 50 points in a six-member team; 60 points in a seven-member team; etc.) and, 3) differentiate some in your ratings; for example, you must give at least one score of 11 or higher (maximum = 15) and one score of 9 or lower.

Team Members	Scores	Team Members	Scores
1)		5)	
2)		6)	
3)		7)	
4)		8)	

Additional Feedback: In the space below would you also briefly describe your reasons for your highest and lowest ratings. These comments -- but not information about who provided them -- will be used to provide feedback to students who would like to receive it.

Reason(s) for your highest rating(s). (Use back if necessary.)

Reason(s) for your lowest rating(s). (Use back if necessary.)

TABLE B.1
Calculation of Peer Evaluation Scores

Team #1

Member Evaluated	Evaluator						Average Score*	Points toward Grade**
	Amy	Bob	Carolyn	David	Eugene	Felicia		
Amy	X	13	12	11	11	11	11.6	174
Bob	12	X	11	11	10	10	10.8	162
Carolyn	11	11	X	11	10	10	10.6	159
David	10	10	10	X	9	10	9.8	147
Eugene	9	9	9	10	X	9	9.2	138
Felicia	8	7	8	7	10	X	8	120
Avg. rating	10	10	10	10	10	10	10	150

Team #2

Member Evaluated	Evaluator						Average Score*	Points toward Grade**
	Arnold	Betty	Calvin	DeeAnn	Everett			
Arnold	X	10	10	9	11		10	150
Betty	10	X	9	11	10		10	150
Calvin	9	11	X	10	10		10	150
DeeAnn	11	10	10	X	9		10	150
Everett	10	9	11	10	X		10	150
Avg. rating	10	10	10	10	10		10	10

* This number would be multiplied by the "weight" for "Team Maintenance and added to the Individual Performance and Team Performance scores to compute a total score for each student.

**This number = the average score multiplied by 15 (if "weight for Team Maintenance = 15% and total points = for Individual Performance + Team Performance + Team Maintenance = 1000

their team on the various team assignments and exams) will always be the same (525 out of 650 points). Let us also assume for the moment that their Individual Performance scores (i.e., the sum of the scores for the individual RATs and other individual assignments) were also the same (e.g., 125 out of 200 points). Their Team Maintenance scores, however, are different. Their course grades would thus be calculated as follows:

	Amy	Felicia
Individual Performance:	125	125
Team Performance	525	525
Peer Evaluation	174	120
TOTAL COURSE POINTS:	824	770

When a hard-copy version of the peer evaluation is used, students fill out this form privately and turn it in to the teacher. When they complete the evaluations online using a program we developed specifically for that purpose, students log in using their student identification numbers and submit their evaluations and comments via the Internet. In both cases, the average score for each team member is used as their peer evaluation score. In computing course grades, this score is then added to scores from individual and team performance to create an overall score for each student, as in the example above.

With the hard-copy version, the comments from the forms are retained and, upon request, provide students with feedback on what was said about them but not who said it. When students do the peer evaluations online, they can log in (using their student ID) to a website that provides access to comments but not to which of their peers provided them.

OPTION #2: PEER EVALUATION AS A PERCENTAGE MULTIPLIER

A second way of incorporating peer evaluation into the course grade is to use it as a percentage multiplier rather than as an added component. Here is how this approach works.

Calculating the Peer Evaluation Score

At the end of the semester, each student is given a form for evaluating the other members of his or her group. (see Exhibit B.2). The form offers some general criteria for evaluating the contributions of each person to the work of the group. However, the key part is where the student is asked to (1) distribute 100 points among the other members of the group, and (2) add some comments for each person, indicating the reasons for the evaluators' point assignments.

The students fill out the form privately and turn it in to the teacher. The numbers from the form are entered in a table for each group, as shown in Table B.2. (Note: The examples shown in Option #2 use the same teams and individual students as shown for Option #1.)

If all members of the group contributed equally (as in Team #2), students will give the same number to each person, and the Peer Evaluation Score for each person will 100. If there were differences, students will give some students more points and other students less, and the totals for the students will be more varied, as shown for Team #1 in Table B.2. The total of each student's scores from his or her team members then becomes that student's individual Peer Evaluation Score and is used to calculate each student's course grade.

Calculating the Course Grade

As with all team-based learning courses, part of the course grade is based on individual work and part on graded group work. In the example shown in Table B.3, 100 possible points are based on graded individual work (part 1) and 50 possible points

EXHIBIT B.2
Assessment of Contributions of Group Members (Fink)

At the end of the semester, it is necessary for all members of this class to assess the contributions that each member of the group made to the work of the group. This contribution should presumably reflect your judgment of such things as:

Preparation – Were they prepared when they came to class?
Contribution – Did they contribute productively to group discussion and work?
Respect for others' ideas – Did they encourage others to contribute their ideas?
Flexibility – Were they flexible when disagreements occurred?

It is important that you raise the evaluation of people who truly worked hard for the good of the group and lower the evaluation of those you perceived not to be working as hard on group tasks. Those who contributed should receive the full worth of the group's grades; those who did not contribute fully should only receive partial credit. Your assessment will be used mathematically to determine the proportion of the group's points that each member receives.

Evaluate the contributions of each person in your group <u>except yourself</u>, by distributing 100 points among them. <u>Include comments for each person.</u>

Group #: _____

Points
Awarded:

1. Name: _____   _____
   Reasons for your evaluation:

2. Name: _____   _____
   Reasons for your evaluation:

3. Name: _____   _____
   Reasons for your evaluation:

4. Name: _____   _____
   Reasons for your evaluation:

5. Name: _____   _____
   Reasons for your evaluation:

Your Name: _____   TOTAL: 100 Points

TABLE B.2
Calculation of Peer Evaluation Scores

Team #1

Member Evaluated	Evaluator						Sum of Ratings
	Amy	Bob	Carolyn	David	Eugene	Felicia	
Amy	X	20	20	20	20	20	100
Bob	21	X	22	21	19	22	105
Carolyn	22	23	X	22	23	20	110
David	17	20	18	X	19	21	95
Eugene	22	20	23	18	X	17	100
Felicia	18	17	17	19	19	X	90
Avg. rating	20	20	20	20	20	20	100

Team #2

Member Evaluated	Evaluator						Sum of Ratings
	Arnold	Betty	Calvin	DeeAnn	Everett		
Arnold	X	25	25	25	25		100
Betty	25	X	25	25	25		100
Calvin	25	25	X	25	25		100
DeeAnn	25	25	25	X	25		100
Everett	25	25	25	25	X		100
Avg. rating	25	25	25	25	25		100

on graded group work (part 2). The total course grade is based on the sum of these two components.

However, the points for the group work are adjusted before they are added into the course grade. The initial points for the graded group work is the same for everyone in each group (e.g., 45 for Group 1 in Table B.3). This number is then multiplied by a given student's peer evaluation score, taken from Table B.2. In the example shown, the student (Carolyn) received a peer evaluation score of 110, and her peer evaluation therefore increased the number of points she received for the group work, which is the Adjusted Group Score (see Table B.3). The Adjusted Group Score (e.g., in Carolyn's case, 49.5) is then added to her Individual Score (i.e., 86) and the sum of the two (i.e., 135.5) is her points toward the course grade. However, a student who had a peer evaluation of 100 percent (e.g., Amy in Team #1) would receive the full credit for the group work (45 in this case), no more and no less. On the other hand, a student who had a low peer evaluation score (e.g., Felicia in Team #1, with a 90%) would have an Adjusted Group Score that would be lower than the score for the group as a whole (40.5 in Felicia's case).

TABLE B.3
Form for Calculating the Course Grade: Peer Evaluation as a Percentage Multiplier

Student's Name: _____ Carolyn _____

	Points Earned	Total Points Available
I. Graded Work: Individual Items		
A. Individual activity, #1	13	15
B. Individual activity, #2	13	15
C. RATs: Individual Portion	21	25
D. Term Paper	13	15
E. Final Exam	26	30
SUB-TOTAL "Individual Score":	86	100
II. Graded Work: Group Items		
A. Readiness Assurance. Tests: Group Portion	13	15
B. Mid-Semester Application Project	8	10
C. Final Group Project	24	25
Initial "Group Score":	45	50

Adjustment for Peer Evaluation:

Initial Group Score	**45**
Carolyn's Peer Evaluation Score (from Table B.2)	**110%**
Adjusted Group Score (45 X 110%)	**49.5**

Calculation of Carolyn's Course Grade Points

I. Individual Score	**86.0**
II. Adjusted Group Score:	**49.5**
TOTAL	135.5

BENEFITS OF THESE TWO APPROACHES

One benefit of both approaches to calculating the peer evaluation score is that they work well, regardless of the number of students in a given group. Even with teams of different sizes, the peer evaluation scores will always vary around a score that is the same for each of the teams in the class. Because the scores will produce differences in grades only within teams, members cannot help everyone in their team get an "A" by giving them high peer evaluation scores. The only way for everyone in a group to earn an "A" is by doing an outstanding job in their individual work and on group exams and projects.

A second advantage of both approaches is that they work well, regardless of whether everyone in a group worked equally hard or whether some worked harder than others. With both approaches it is possible for each member of a team to receive approximately the same number of points when everyone works more or less equally hard. When there are variations in individual contributions to the group, both procedures will generate scores that reflect that variation.

A third benefit is that both approaches ensure that peer evaluations will have a significant impact on students' course grades. As a result, students take the evaluation process seriously and will rarely carry a member who has not been willing to do their fair share of the work.

Finally, in those rare but occasional situations in which two students in a group have a personality conflict and do not get along well, this procedure tends to dampen any revenge such students might want to inflict via the peer evaluation scores. If one student gives an unduly low score to another student, that gets averaged in with scores from other students who will be acting from other motives, so the impact is minimized.

OBSERVATIONS OF HOW THIS PROCEDURE
WORKS IN PRACTICE

After watching how these procedures work for several years, we have seen one major benefit, one frequent problem, and one potential problem that can turn into a major benefit. Both of the problems can be avoided by some simple preventive measures.

The major benefit is that both approaches generate a strong sense of fairness among the students. When everyone in a group works together well and the group achieves a certain score, everyone will receive very nearly the same credit for what the group earned. And that strikes most students as being fair. Similarly, if there are workhorses and social loafers in a group, both procedures will result in the workhorses receiving more points and the loafers receiving fewer. Most students find that to be fair.

One frequent problem with peer evaluations is that many students underestimate the impact of the peer evaluation scores until after the final course grades have been calculated and turned in. This is true even when this information is stated quite clearly in the course syllabus.

The potential problem that can be a benefit occurs when a student receives a peer evaluation from the other members of the group that is considerably lower than what he or she expected. Sometimes, for example, a given student thinks he or she is contributing a lot, maybe even more than anyone else in the group. But the other members of the group see that student as overly domineering and not able to listen to the ideas and contributions of other members of the group. In these situations, the domineering student is usually surprised by a low peer evaluation score when he or she expected to be the highest in the group. The positive side of this situation, however, is that the feedback almost always creates a "teaching moment" in which we have the opportunity to help students learn some very important lessons about themselves.

PREVENTING POSSIBLE PROBLEMS

To deal with these last two situations, we recommend one of two practices. One is having teams do an analysis and review of the team process about a third of the way through the course. This involves using a three-stage activity. First, students individually fill out three forms (Exhibit B.3). On Form 1 they identify: (1) the behaviors of team members who are contributing most to their team's success, and (2) things they think members could do to improve their team's performance. For Form 2 the students share their views with their team members and decide on the top two items in each category. For Form 3, each team develops a list of criteria that they think would make sense as a basis for their end-of-semester peer evaluations.

The second approach is doing a midsemester practice grade calculation using either of the above peer evaluation approaches based on members' contributions during the activities and assignments up to that point in the course. This works just like the regular peer evaluation, except that the scores are not entered into the course grade book.

Both approaches aid members in the development of their interpersonal and team interaction skills but each has advantages over the other. The midcourse team analysis and review process generally creates both a positive feeling within the teams and alerts members to the kinds of behavior that help and hinder their success. Further, because the feedback to individuals is less direct, there is little risk of creating a rift that is difficult for teams to overcome. On the other hand, because of the less direct feedback, a disadvantage is that a team member occasionally feels like he or she is a good contributor when, in fact, their behavior is more of a problem than a help.

The other approach, of having students practice peer evaluation, has two very positive features. One is that it provides a clear illustration of how much the end-of-semester peer evaluation scores will impact the overall course grade. As a result, if anyone was not previously taking the group interactions and their relationship with other members of their group seriously, they do so from that moment on. The other potentially positive impact is on the one or two students who are surprised by their low peer evaluation scores. They almost always make an appointment with the teacher to talk about this situation, and this often turns out to be a wonderful opportunity to do some personal counseling. The comments of the other students are a rich source of feedback on what the person was doing that bothered the other members of the team, that is, "what behavior is causing the problem?" Then we point out to the student: "If you can figure out how to change and improve your working relationship with other members of your group, this will be one of the most important lessons you will ever learn in life and certainly one of the more important lessons you will learn this semester in college." In the vast majority of cases, those students have succeeded—more or less on their own—in improving their relationship with their peers and, as a result, receive much more favorable peer evaluation scores at the end of the semester.

EXHIBIT B.3
Forms for Soliciting Feedback on the Team Maintenance Process

Form #1: <u>Feedback on Class and Group Process</u>

1. What could the instructor do that would help most to improve the class?

2. List several ways in which members have helped your group to be successful and identify the member(s) who are particularly good at each one so that you can share your perceptions with the group):

3. What could members of your group do that would help most to improve your group's performance?

Form #2: <u>Feedback on Class and Group Process</u>—Summary from Team #___

Instructions: Discuss the ideas from your individual sheets and decide:

1. What two things could the instructor do that would help most to improve the class?

2. What two or three "helping behaviors" have been most important in the success of your group thus far?

3. What two things could members of your group do that would help most to improve your group's performance?

Form #3: <u>Preliminary List of Peer Evaluation Criteria</u> for Team #____

Instructions: Develop a list of criteria that the members of your group would feel comfortable using for your peer evaluations for this course.

CONCLUDING COMMENTS

Peer evaluations are an essential component of team-based learning. The performance of each team as a whole needs to be assessed and included in the calculation of the course grade. However, the relative contribution of each member to the work of the team also needs to be reflected in the credit that each member receives for the course grade.

In this appendix, we have described two different approaches for calculating peer evaluation scores. There are undoubtedly many different procedures that would accomplish the same goal of providing fair peer input into students' final grades. Whatever procedure the instructor uses, it should be capable of:

- Accommodating teams of different sizes;
- Accurately reflecting the work of members in teams (i.e., whether everyone contributes equally or differently);
- Making a significant impact on the course grade.

When this is done, students will generally see the group grading process as being fair, thereby removing the biggest concern that students have about using small groups in a course.

The use of team-based learning by itself gives students an opportunity to use their own teamwork skills and to observe those of other students. These are both valuable learning opportunities, but when the teacher includes some kind of midcourse procedure for giving students feedback on the quality of their teamwork skills, the likelihood that students will be able to significantly improve their skills is greatly enhanced. This is simply an application of the "practice and feedback" principle to the goal of helping students learn how to be effective members of a team.

Setting Grade Weights
A Team-Building Exercise

Larry K. Michaelsen

As soon as students are assigned to groups, it is important to begin building them into teams. As a first step, we have students participate in an exercise that, in addition to jump-starting the team-building process, accomplishes two other important purposes. One is to emphasize that students are responsible for their own learning by giving them a say in how their grades will be determined. The other is to ensure that they are neither surprised nor uncomfortable when team performance, as often happens, ends up being the most heavily weighted component of the grading system for the class.

THE SETTING

The Grade-Weight-Setting Exercise[1] should be conducted very shortly after the teams are formed, which, depending on the length of the class periods, might be on the first, second or possibly even the third class meeting. Prior to actually setting grade weights, students need to understand the objectives of the course and how the team-based learning process works. As a result, in preparation for the Grade-Weight-Setting-Exercise, we typically hand out a course syllabus containing an explanation of the course requirements and grading procedures, and what the students might expect regarding in-class and out-of-class activities. We also orally review the objectives of the course and outline the key differences between traditionally taught courses and team-based learning by contrasting how our course objectives would be met with the two approaches (see Appendix D, Exhibit D–A1.1 and D–A1.2), and provide an opportunity for questions. Next, we form the class into permanent, heterogeneous, six- or seven-member teams, and give them ten minutes to read their course syllabus to prepare for a practice Readiness Assessment Test (RAT).

The practice RAT accomplishes several things. Just like any other RAT, it promotes team development and ensures that students have the prerequisite knowledge for accomplishing the tasks that we want them to perform, which, in this case, is setting their grade weights and locating and reading the material for their first real RAT. In addition, giving a practice RAT allows students to learn how the process works before having to do it for real. Once the practice RAT is completed, we begin the Grade-Weight-Setting Exercise.

CONTRIBUTIONS TO THE TEAM-BUILDING PROCESS

The Grade-Weight-Setting Exercise is highly effective in building teams because it accomplishes several functions simultaneously. It succeeds in:

- Providing a forum and an incentive for discussing factors that affect team performance and the level of commitment of team members (e.g., work schedules, course loads, and other individual constraints);
- Demonstrating that the individuals in their group can function as a team;
- Exposing students to the resources available to their teams;
- Providing a forum and incentive for team members to obtain commitments from each other early in the course;
- Building interdependence and mutual support in the newly formed teams;
- Allowing the student to see that he/she is able to perform reasonably well in the team;
- Ensuring that students understand the processes by which their grades will be determined;
- Increasing student acceptance of the grading process.

PROCEDURES

1. We inform students that the remainder of the class period will, within the limits we have set, be devoted to deciding on weights to be assigned to the performance criteria outlined in the course syllabus. (Note: We have two recommendations about setting the limits. One is that we think it is important for instructors to be open with students about their grading philosophy and concerns. The other is allowing students as much latitude as the instructor is comfortable with; see Table C.1 for an example from one of our classes.)
2. We instruct the teams to meet briefly (about 10 minutes) and decide:
   a. the percentage of the grade they would like to allocate for each of the major performance areas (i.e., Individual Performance, Team Performance, Team Maintenance);
   b. the grade percentage they would like to allocate within the individual performance area (i.e., individual RATs vs. the final exam);

TABLE C.1
Example of Grade Weights in an Organizational Behavior Course

<u>**Exams and Projects:**</u>

There will be six short, true-false, multiple choice Readiness Assessment Tests (RATs) given during the course—one at the *beginning* of each unit. (The same RATs will be given to individuals and to teams.) All other exams will be open book, open-note exams over novels or full-length feature films. On team exams and projects all team members will receive the same score.

<u>**Grading Criteria:**</u>

Scores in three major performance areas will determine the grades in this class: **Individual Performance**, **Team Performance** and **Team Maintenance**.

	Grade Wts. & Percentages	
Grade Weights:	**within Area**	**of Total**
1. Individual performance		____% *
Individual Readiness Assessment Tests (0-50%)	____% *	
The Sting Final Exam (50-100%)	____% *	
2. Team Performance		____% *
Team Readiness Assessment.	30%	
Organizational Structure Critique/Exam.	10%	
Great Escape Application Exam.	30%	
Serpico Application Exam.	30%	
3. Team Maintenance (Evaluated by Peers)		____% *
		100%

    c. which member of their team will represent them in the temporary task force in which the final grade-weight decisions will be made. (The task force is made up of one member from each team.)

3. We assemble the task force, made up of one representative from each team, in a "fish-bowl" setting (i.e., in a location such as the center of the room so that their deliberations can be observed by the class as a whole) and explain the ground rules for their discussion. The rules we use for the exercise are as follows:

    a. Decisions about the grade weights must be *within the limits we have set* and must be by consensus, that is, every representative must agree with any proposed decision before it becomes final. In the example shown in Table C.1, a minimum of 10% must be assigned to each of the three major performance areas and a maximum of 50% of the Individual Performance grade can be determined by the individual RATs.

    b. We will not intervene in the discussion unless there is either a misunderstanding about a specific aspect of the grading process (how scores will be computed, what is expected in regard to a specific assignment, etc.) or to honor a request for a brief team strategy conference.

    c. Teams and/or representatives should indicate their desire to confer within their individual teams by raising their hands. When two hands are raised, we will interrupt the fishbowl discussion and release the representatives for a brief team-strategy conference with their team members.

    d. When the representatives reach a consensus, the grading system will be estab-
       lished.

4. Once the ground rules are in place, the instructor should step out of the picture
   and allow the team representatives to negotiate with each other either until two
   hands are raised (indicating the need for team-strategy conferences) or until a consensus on one of the aspects has been reached.

5. Each time two hands are raised, the instructor should stop the fishbowl discussion
   and send the representatives back to their teams for a brief (about 2-minute) strategy
   conference, and call the representatives back to the fishbowl when their time is up.

6. Each time the representatives appear to have reached a consensus on one of the
   grade-weight components, the instructor should confirm that all representatives
   agree with the decision and then allow the discussion to continue.

7. When representatives reach a consensus on the final grade-weight component, the
   exercise is completed, and class is dismissed.

THE DECISION-MAKING PROCESS

The Initial Ten-Minute Team Meeting

The purpose of this meeting is for individual groups to determine their choice of
grade weight for each performance activity. The Grade-Weight-Setting Exercise involves
an outcome in which the stakes are high. Faced with determining grade weights for the
class—a decision which is very clearly associated with each student's academic well-
being—an intense discussion develops within each group. High achievers often push for
heavy emphasis on individual performance, whereas others marshal arguments for emphasizing team performance. They usually reason that there is safety in number,s or that
it will help fulfill the purpose of the class, that is, helping them learning interpersonal
and team skills. In many groups, the question of how much individuals can rely on
other members is openly discussed. This leads to a discussion of the constraints that individual members face (job interviews, work schedules, family responsibilities, etc.) and
provides a rich source of information about the team's resources. Teams usually reach a
tentative decision in less than ten minutes. With most groups, the dominant personality
is frequently selected to represent the team in the task force deliberations. At this point
a hint of we–they feelings emerge as the teams send forth their champions to do battle.

"Fish-Bowl" Discussions

This phase of the decision-making process generally begins with each representative making a hard-line statement of his or her team's positions. With these statements
out in the open, the members of the task force turn to the representatives holding the
most extreme positions, forcing them to defend themselves against considerable pressure from the majority. The pressure on the deviants steadily increases as others display a willingness to compromise. This pressure often results in representatives

seeking support from their teams by calling for a strategy conference. After strategy meetings within individual groups, representatives rejoin the task force to continue to negotiate toward some sort of agreeable conclusion.

Team-Strategy Conferences

In most situations, the primary topic of discussion in the first one or two of these strategy conferences is identifying the most effective argument for convincing other teams to accept their position. Later it is more a matter of "how much are we willing to give in?" By this stage, two things have happened. First, intragroup competition has generally declined to the point at which individual members are motivated to reevaluate and increase their own willingness to commit time and effort to the team work. Second, most teams gain confidence in their ability to compete with other teams and, as a result, are more comfortable with accepting a compromise decision.

Reaching a Decision

As the number of deviant teams decreases, the pressure on those who refuse to co-operate increases dramatically. During the final stages of the discussion (within the task force), each compromise is accompanied by cheers from members of the task force as well as from individual groups. The loudest of these cheers occurs when a consensus is reached, and tensions between teams are relieved—at least temporarily.

TIME REQUIRED

The exercise requires from thirty minutes to an hour, depending on the number of teams in the class. The exercise has been used with as few as three teams and as many as ten. With classes of more than sixty students, it is desirable to move half the teams to a separate room. By splitting the class in this way, two separate grade-weight systems are developed for the same class. As far as time is concerned, even the larger classes seldom take longer than an hour. As the scheduled end of the class approaches, peer pressure to resolve the remaining, and usually minor, differences becomes intense.

RESULTS

Typical Decisions

Both graduate and undergraduate classes assign 20–30 percent of the total grade to Individual Performance, 60–65 percent to Team Performance, and 10–15 percent to Team Maintenance (peer evaluation). In twenty-five years of experience with this ex-ercise, the ranges have been from 15–50 percent for Individual Performance, 40–80 percent for Team Performance, and 10–30 percent for Team Maintenance.

Understanding of, and Commitment to, Grading Processes

This process is extremely effective. In fact, we cannot recall a single example in which a student later raised a question about how the grading system was supposed to work. In addition, we rarely receive complaints about grades in general. Those we do receive are directed at a team for failing to perform well or at the results of their peer evaluations rather than the grading system itself.

Group Cohesiveness

We feel that this exercise makes its greatest contribution in the area of building group cohesiveness. By the conclusion of the first class period, most groups are well on their way to achieving a level of cohesiveness that will allow them to become a team that can effectively deal with the assignments they will receive later in the course.

One reason for the extremely rapid development of team cohesiveness is the high level of intergroup competition that is an integral part of the exercise—the brief team conferences look more and more like football huddles as the exercise progresses. Another reason is that dealing with the problem of shaping the reward system for the class dramatically speeds up the process of discovering and adapting to individual constraints as commitments are obtained from individual team members. Finally, the exercise results in an incentive system that places a great value on working together as a team.

Student Reaction

Although some students are somewhat frustrated with the initial inability of the task force to reach a decision, most are extremely enthusiastic about having the opportunity to be involved in the process of deciding how their grades will be determined. One measure of the success of the exercise is that only about one percent of the students transfer to more conventional sections or drop the course. They choose to remain in the class despite the fact that over 50 percent of the grade will be determined by criteria with which students have had little experience. Perhaps even more important, attendance at the next class session is usually 100 percent.

POTENTIAL PROBLEMS

Although we are completely convinced of the effectiveness of the Grade-Weight-Setting Exercise, we are not unaware of problematic areas. For example, we have observed several situations in which caution should be exercised:

1. It is extremely important that the instructor resist the temptation to influence the decision; otherwise it will be the teacher's grading system and not the students'. At

times it may seem as though the students will never be able to come to a decision, but peer pressure will eventually force an acceptable compromise.

2. This exercise works best when the course makes major use of learning teams. If working in teams is only a minor aspect of the course, the exercise is probably not worth the investment of time, and in fact, may establish expectations that are counterproductive.

3. The discussion process can be somewhat disconcerting when students do not clearly understand the rationale for the exercise. Consequently, we introduce the exercise with a statement such as, "We recognize that we are asking you to work intensively with your new group members, but we want you to shape the grading system into something with which you can feel comfortable."

4. The effectiveness of the exercise in building team cohesiveness is so great that it can be difficult to integrate students who did not attend the first day of class. As a result, latecomers, for whatever reason, are much more likely to become isolates and to receive low evaluations from their peers.

MODIFICATIONS FOR SPECIAL CIRCUMSTANCES

After twenty-five years of using this exercise in a wide variety of teaching situations, we have only three additional pieces of advice or caution, as follow:

1. The most difficult aspect of managing the process is keeping the nonrepresentatives quiet during the task force discussions. We have not found a good cure for the problem beyond stopping the action to remind students that: (1) they need to hear the discussion so they will be able to give instructions to their own representative; and (2) if they really need to talk, they should raise their hand and we will have the representatives come back to the teams for consultation or to change representatives.

2. If the fishbowl discussion gets really bogged down because the only remaining issue is saving face, an effective way to break the deadlock is having all of the teams change representatives.

3. In large classes (over 15 teams), an effective alternative procedure is to modify Step #3 in the description of "Procedures" by:
   a. announcing that the final decision for the class will be the average of the team preferences at the conclusion of a negotiation period;
   b. beginning the negotiation period (usually 15 minutes) by projecting a spreadsheet containing the set of team grade-weight preferences (from step 2) and the resulting averages, and allowing a spokesperson to state the rationale for the most extreme positions in each grading category;
   c. encouraging teams to attempt to change the overall distribution by forming alliances with other teams or changing their own scores to a more extreme position;
   d. immediately changing teams' entries on the spreadsheet so that students have real-time feedback on the progress of the negotiations.

CONCLUSION

The Grade-Weight-Setting Exercise is a dramatic demonstration that the class will be conducted differently from those to which students have previously been exposed. This knowledge, acquired on the first day of class, allows students to make a decision about whether to stay enrolled or not. As a result, we seldom have the problem of the students feeling trapped in a class that offers a curriculum they did not expect.

The exercise is also highly effective in reducing anxiety because the students have the opportunity to understand and accept the grading process. In addition, having teams make and defend decisions about how much of the grade they are willing to assign to the products of their collective effort helps to insure the rapid development of interpersonal support and team cohesiveness.

Over the years, we have discovered that the Grade-Weight-Setting Exercise has a self-correcting feature. For example, anxiety about working as a team dissipates when pressure from other classmates (outside one's own team) causes individual members (within the team) to become more and more cohesive. In fact, almost without exception, teams that are attacked the most vigorously in the Grade-Weight-Setting Exercise turn out to be the most cohesive teams in the class.

Finally, we are convinced the exercise is successful because students learn a great deal about us, the teachers, in the process. During this first class period, we demonstrate that we:

1. have needs of our own that must be satisfied and are willing to openly discuss them;
2. have strong feelings about the importance of the concepts we teach;
3. expect students to work hard developing interpersonal and team skills;
4. care about students as individuals;
5. intend to conduct the class in a way that, to the extent possible, will allow their needs to be met;
6. are confident that the course will be a rewarding experience for students and the instructor alike.

NOTE

1. This version of the Grade-Weight-Setting Exercise was adapted from Michaelsen, Cragin, & Watson (1981).

Miscellaneous Materials Related to Team-Based Learning

This appendix contains a collection of charts, diagrams, and tables that teachers may find useful in a variety of situations. We have grouped these materials into two sets of exhibits:

A. *Explaining Team-Based Learning to Others.* From time to time, you may feel a need to explain team learning, either to students who are experiencing it for the first time, or to colleagues who need to understand the ideas behind a significantly different way of teaching. These materials present some ideas on how team-based learning works and why it operates the way it does.

B. *Helpful Forms.* This set contains four forms that may be useful as you are getting started with team-based learning.

Below is a full list of the exhibits. Each numbered exhibit is a separate illustration. The actual exhibits have been numbered sequentially: Exhibit D–A1.1 or Exhibit D–B1.2, and so on.

A. *Explaining Team-Based Learning to Others*
  1. Comparisons of Traditional Teaching and Team-Based Learning
    1. Course Objectives and Instructional Strategies
    2. Course Objectives and Use of Class Time
    3. The Means by which Students Gain Their Initial Exposure to Content and Learn to Apply Concepts.
  2. How Team-Based Learning Promotes the Learning of Complex Concepts
    1. What Are the Sources of Learning?
    2. Impact of Team-Based Learning on Driving a More Powerful Process

Learning Objectives and Instructional Strategies

Learning Objectives	How Objectives Accomplished with:	
	Traditional Teaching	Team-Based Learning
Ensure students' mastery of course subject matter	• Lecture • Class discussion • Individual study (post-class?)	• Pre-class individual study • Readiness Assurance Process
Develop students' ability to use course concepts in thinking & problem-solving	• Class discussion • Individual exams/projects • Group presentations and/or papers, etc. (outside-class)	• In-class group/team work (problem-based discussion within, then between groups) • Individual exams/projects
Enhance students' interpersonal and team interaction skills	• "Sink or swim" (Since group work is outside class, instructors CAN'T help students learn from their experience working in a group.)	• In-class group/team work (Tasks require cooperation; provide feedback on and rewards for both individual and group performance)
Prepare students to be lifelong learners	• Little or nothing (Mostly counteproductive because passive role reinforces student dependency.)	• Active learning (Exposes students to multiple learning strategies; learners become confident & resourceful.)
Enjoy course	• Content well organized • Instructor delivers content with enthusiasm and "style" • Lectures supported by high-quality visuals, etc.	• Team assignments that are interesting, relevant and challenging • Immediate feedback • Friendship/social support

Learning Objectives and Instructional Strategies: Relative Time Spent on Different Activities

Note: The type size reflects the amount of class time used for each activity–the larger the type, the greater the class time used.

Learning Objectives	How Objectives Accomplished with:	
	Traditional Teaching	**Team-Based Learning**
Ensure students' mastery of course subject matter	**· Lecture** · **Class discussion** · Individual study	· Individual study (pre-class) · **Readiness Assurance Process**
Develop students' ability to use course concepts in thinking & problem-solving	· **Class discussion** · Individual exams/projects · Group work on presentations, papers, etc. (outside-class)	· **In-class group/team work** (problem-based discussion within, then between groups) · Individual exams/projects
Enhance students' interpersonal and team interaction skills	· "Sink or swim"	· **In-class group/team work** (Tasks require cooperation; provide feedback on & rewards for both individual & group performance)
Prepare students to be lifelong learners	· [Counterproductive]	· **Active learning** (Exposes students to multiple learning strategies; learners become confident & competent.)

256

Means for Accomplishing the Key Educational Tasks Required for Higher-Level Learning

Basic Learning Tasks to be Accomplished
1. INITIAL EXPOSURE (develop familiarity with & language to discuss concepts)
2. APPLICATIONS (develop students' ability to USE concepts)

Primary Opportunities
- Students working alone
- Instructor and students in class
- Students working in groups

Additional Modes*
- Assistant and students in "lab"
- Students 1-on-1 with instructor
- Students working with mentor

*These "additional modes" usually increase instructional costs (time and/or $).

Traditional Teaching

1. Initial Exposure to Content
- Instructor and students in class

2. Applications
- Students working alone
- Group assignments outside class (Students working in groups?)
- Assistant and students in "lab"
- Students 1-on-1 with instructor

Team-Based Learning

1. Initial Exposure to Content
- Students working alone (pre-class)
- Students working in groups (in-class, i.e., Readiness Assurance Process)

2. Applications
- Students working in groups (in-class)
- Instructor and students in class

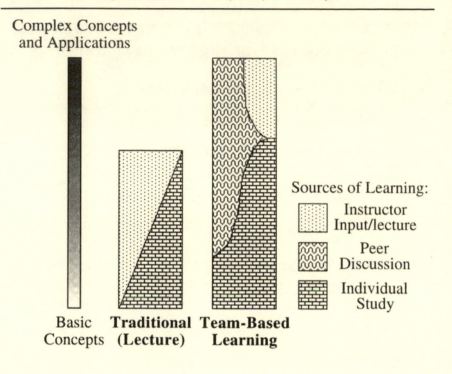

Impact of Team-Based Learning on Driving a More Powerful Learning Process

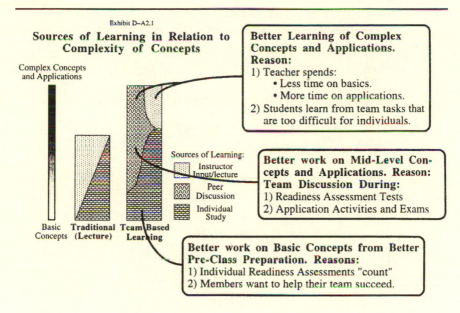

Exhibit D–A2.1

Sources of Learning in Relation to Complexity of Concepts

Complex Concepts and Applications

Basic Concepts

Traditional (Lecture)

Team Based Learning

Sources of Learning:
- Instructor Input/lecture
- Peer Discussion
- Individual Study

Better Learning of Complex Concepts and Applications. Reason:
1) Teacher spends:
   - Less time on basics.
   - More time on applications.
2) Students learn from team tasks that are too difficult for individuals.

Better work on Mid-Level Concepts and Applications. Reason: Team Discussion During:
1) Readiness Assessment Tests
2) Application Activities and Exams

Better work on Basic Concepts from Better Pre-Class Preparation. Reasons:
1) Individual Readiness Assessments "count"
2) Members want to help their team succeed.

1. **What do I want students to be able to DO when they have completed this unit of instruction (or course, program, etc.)?**

   • This defines the desired outcomes in <u>behavioral</u> terms.

2. **What will students have to KNOW to do #1?**

   • This defines the content that must be covered in assigned readings or in other ways.

3. **How can I ASSESS whether or not students have successfully mastered key course concepts?**

   • This guides the selection of questions for the Readiness Assessment Tests (which enable instructors to pinpoint their input/lectures on <u>only</u> the specific points that need further clarification).

4. **How can I tell if students will be able to USE their knowledge of key course concepts?**

   • This guides the development of projects and exams that require students to <u>use</u> the concepts to solve the same kinds of problems they will face in subsequent course work and/or future jobs.

EXHIBIT D–A4
Team-Based Learning Instructional Activity Sequence

(Repeated for each major instructional unit, i.e., 5-7 per course)

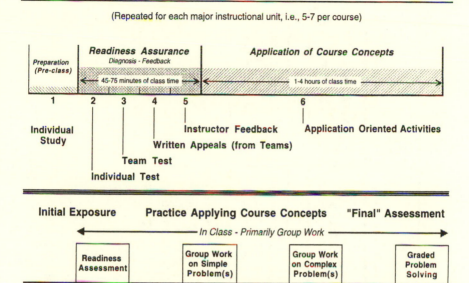

EXHIBIT D-A5
Readiness Assessment Test Procedures

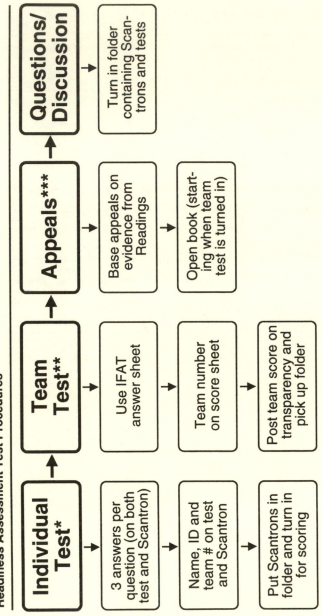

Individual Test*
- 3 answers per question (on both test and Scantron)
- Name, ID and team # on test and Scantron
- Put Scantrons in folder and turn in for scoring

Team Test**
- Use IFAT answer sheet
- Team number on score sheet
- Post team score on transparency and pick up folder

Appeals***
- Base appeals on evidence from Readings
- Open book (starting when team test is turned in)

Questions/Discussion
- Turn in folder containing Scantrons and tests

* Teams can begin as soon as they turn in their Scantrons and pick up the team test.
** A 5-minute warning will be given when one third of the teams finish the team test.
*** Teams can begin working on appeals as soon as their score has been posted.

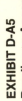

EXHIBIT D–A6
Criteria for Effective Group Assignments

Prior to Group Discussions:

❑ *Are group members required to use newly acquired concepts to make a specific choice, individually and in writing?* (Note: This individual accountability is especially important in newly formed groups.)

During Discussions within Groups:

❑ *Are groups required to share members' individual choices and agree (i.e., reach a group consensus) on a specific choice?*

❑ *Will the discussion focus on "Why?"* (and/or "How?")

❑ *Will the groups' choice(s) be represented in a form that enables immediate and direct comparisons with other groups?**

During Discussions between Groups:

❑ *Are group decisions reported simultaneously?**

❑ *Do group "reports" focus attention on the absolutely key issues?**

❑ *Are groups given the opportunity to digest and reflect on the entire set of "reports"* before total class discussion begins?*

❑ *Will the discussion focus on "Why?"* (and/or "How?")

The more "Yes" answers, the better. If the answer to all eight questions is "Yes", the assignment will effectively promote both learning and group development.

---

* The form in which individual and group choices are represented largely determines the dynamics of the discussions that follow. Both individual reports to groups and group reports to the class should be as absolutely succinct as possible. One-word reports are the very best (e.g., yes/no, best/worst, up/down/no change, etc.) because they invariably stimulate a discussion of why one choice is better than another.

EXHIBIT D–A7
Frequency of RATs and Application Exercises in a Specific Example Course: Organizational Behavior

Week(s)	Topic/Class Activity(ies)	Topic(s) Involved
1	Introduction; Form groups; Set grade "weights"	–
2	RAT #1 ("Effectiveness"); Application Activity	1
3	RAT #2 ("Org. Design"); Application Activity	2
4	Application Exam; Instructor & group/peer feedback	2
5-6	RAT #3 ("Motivation"); Application activities (2)	3
6	RAT #4 ("Communication/Decision Making");	4
7-8	Application Activities (3)	4
9	Integrative Application Exam (e.g., "Star Trek")	1-4
10	RAT #5 ("Groups"); Application Activity	5
11	RAT #6 ("Org. Climate/Development");	6
11	Application Activities (2)	6
12-13	Integrative Project & Oral (e.g., *Final Diagnosis*)	1-6
14	Application Activity (Course Review)	1-6
15	Preparation for Final	1-6
16	Application Final (e.g., "The Sting")	1-6

Totals:
 6 Readiness Assessment Tests–early in the course
12 Topic-Specific Application Activities & Exams
 4 Integrative Application Activities & Exams

EXHIBIT D–A8.1
Impact of Time Working in Groups on Effectiveness of Using Members' Knowledge

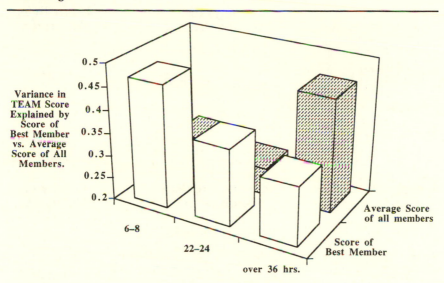

Variance in TEAM Score Explained by Score of Best Member vs. Average Score of All Members.

Comments:

1 This illustration indicates that, as groups spend more time working together, their group performance scores correlate less and less with the score of their best group member, and more and more with the average score of all members of the group. This reflects the growing tendency of the groups to discuss issues fully and reach consensus on the best answer, rather than simply going with the answer of the perceived smartest member.

2. The time that it takes for groups to mature to the point that they have truly effective decision-making processes can be considerably shortened IF:
   - The groups are given really effective assignments and clear and immediate performance feedback, and
   - The teacher uses a "split-answer" format for Readiness Assessment Test questions to increase student awareness of the benefit of deliberating fully before deciding on a group answer.

Source: Watson, W. E., Michaelsen, L. K., & Sharp, W. Member Competence, Group Interaction and Group Decision-Making: A Longitudinal Study. *Journal of Applied Psychology*, 1991, 76(6), 801–809.

EXHIBIT D–A8.2
Impact of Cultural Diversity on Group Process and Group Performance over Time

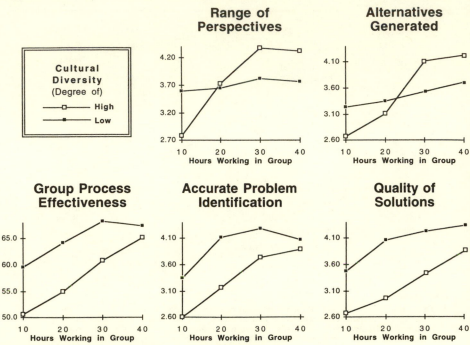

Source: Watson, Kumar, & Michaelsen. *Academy of Management Journal*, 1993, *36*(3), 590–602.

(Cumulative scores after 4 RATs)

Team #	Individual Member Scores:			Team Score	Team Gain over BEST Member
	Low	Average	High		
1	142	169	188	204	16
2	126	154	168	201	33
3	135	164	183	210	27
4	149	165	184	197	13
5	149	173	192	213	21
6	107	166	187	207	20
7	135	162	181	213	32
8	140	163	186	203	17
Average	135.4	164.5	183.6	206.0	22.4

12% higher than the **BEST** team member

Team
Performance & Attendance Record

Note: This column containing tudents' names should be folded under when mounted on folders.

Name	ID#	Readiness Assessment Tests/Totals*							Absences**			
		1	2	3	4	5	6	Date	Known	???	Total
								1/18			
	cum->							1/20			
								1/23			
	cum->							1/25			
								1/30			
	cum->							2/1			
								2/6			
	cum->							2/8			
								2/13			
	cum->							2/15			
								2/20			
	cum->							2/22			
								2/27			
	cum->							3/1			
	Group RATs							3/6			
	cum->							3/8			

Structure Test	
Star Trek	
Serpico	

* Please record the number correct as soon as you have the results on each test and the <u>cumulative</u> scores below the dotted line. (Please use a pencil so that we can change your scores when we grant appeals.)

** Please record the number of absences for your group each time the class meets. (Note: it is always helpful to the group to know when a member is unable to attend class. If you have a problem and can't reach someone in your group, call the managment office - 325-2651 - and we will pass the word on to your group.

Notes: 1) The names should be folded under when the chart is attached to the team folders.
2) We use the last 4 digits of student's ID numbers and/or have them provide an ID number we can use.

Purposes of the appeals process:

1. Clarify uncertainty about your understanding of the concepts.
2. Give additional recognition and credit when "missing" a question was caused by:
   - Ambiguity in the reading material.
   - Disagreement between the reading material and our choice of the "correct" answer.
   - Ambiguity in the wording of the question.

Guidelines for preparing successful appeals:

Appeals are granted when they demonstrate that you understood the concept(s) but missed the question anyway or that your confusion was due to ambiguity in the reading material. As a result:
- If the appeal is based on ambiguity in the question, you should:
  1. Identify the source of ambiguity in the question and,
  2. Offer an alternative wording that would have helped you to avoid the problem.
- If the appeal is based on either inadequacies in the reading material or disagreement with our answer, you should:
  1. State the reason(s) for disagreeing with our answer and,
  2. Provide specific references from the reading material to support your point of view.

Impact of appeals on test scores:

When an appeal is accepted on a question that a <u>group</u> has missed (no <u>individual</u> appeals will be accepted):
1. It "counts" i.e., the points missed will be added to:
   - their group score.
   - the score of any individual in the group who answered the same way the group did.
   - only those groups that appeal.
2. Group member(s) who had the original correct answer will continue to receive credit on the question.

EXHIBIT D–B2.1
Peer Evaluation Form (Michaelsen)

Peer Evaluation   Name_____   Team # _____

Please assign scores that reflect how you really feel about the extent to which the other members of your team contributed to your learning and/or your team's performance. This will be your only opportunity to reward the members of your team who worked hard on your behalf. (**Note: If you give everyone pretty much the same score you will be hurting those who did the most and helping those who did the least.**)

Instructions: In the space below please rate each of the **other** members of your team. Each member's peer evaluation score will be the average of the points they receive from the other members of the team. To complete the evaluation you should: 1) List the name of each member of your team in the alphabetical order of their last names and, 2) assign an average of ten points to the <u>other</u> members of your team (Thus, for example, you should assign a total of 50 points in a six-member team; 60 points in a seven-member team; etc.) and, 3) differentiate some in your ratings; for example, you must give at least one score of 11 or higher (maximum = 15) and one score of 9 or lower.

Team Members	Scores	Team Members	Scores
1)		5)	
2)		6)	
3)		7)	
4)		8)	

Additional Feedback: In the space below would you also briefly describe your reasons for your highest and lowest ratings. These comments -- but not information about who provided them -- will be used to provide feedback to students who would like to receive it.

Reason(s) for your highest rating(s). (Use back if necessary.)

Reason(s) for your lowest rating(s). (Use back if necessary.)

270

EXHIBIT D–B2.2
Assessment of Contributions of Group Members (Fink)

At the end of the semester, it is necessary for all members of this class to assess the contributions that each member of the group made to the work of the group. This contribution should presumably reflect your judgment of such things as:

> Preparation – Were they prepared when they came to class?
> Contribution – Did they contribute productively to group discussion and work?
> Respect for others' ideas – Did they encourage others to contribute their ideas?
> Flexibility – Were they flexible when disagreements occurred?

It is important that you raise the evaluation of people who truly worked hard for the good of the group and lower the evaluation of those you perceived not to be working as hard on group tasks. Those who contributed should receive the full worth of the group's grades; those who did not contribute fully should only receive partial credit. Your assessment will be used mathematically to determine the proportion of the group's points that each member receives.

Evaluate the contributions of each person in your group except yourself, by distributing 100 points among them. Include comments for each person.

Group #: _____

Points Awarded:

1. Name: _____ _____
   Reasons for your evaluation:

2. Name: _____ _____
   Reasons for your evaluation:

3. Name: _____ _____
   Reasons for your evaluation:

4. Name: _____ _____
   Reasons for your evaluation:

5. Name: _____ _____
   Reasons for your evaluation:

Your Name: _____   TOTAL: 100 Points

Bibliography

Amason, A. C. (1996). Distinguishing the effects of functional and dysfunctional conflict on strategic decision making: Resolving a paradox for top management teams. *Academy of Management Journal 39*(1): 123–149.

Amason, A. C., & Schweiger, D. M. (1994). Resolving the paradox of conflict, strategic decision making and organiztional performance. *International Journal of Conflict Management 5:* 239–253.

Ancona, D. G., & Caldwell, D. F. (1992). Demography and design: Predictors of new product team performance. *Organization Science 3:* 321–341.

Anderson, J. R. (1993). Problem solving and learning. *American Psychologist 48:* 35–44.

Argote, L., & McGrath, J. E. (1993). Group processes in organizations: Continuity and change. In *International Review of Industrial and Organization Psychology.* Ed. C. L. Cooper & I. T. Robertson. Vol. 8: 333–389. Chichester, UK: Wiley.

Arrow, H., & McGrath, J. E. (1993). Membership matters: How member change and continuity affect small group structure, process and performance. *Small Group Research 24:* 334–361.

Bales, R. F. (1950). *Interaction process analysis: A method for the study of small groups.* Cambridge, MA: Addison-Wesley.

Bargh J. A., & Schul, Y. (1980). On the cognitive benefits of teaching. *Journal of Educational Psychology 74*(5): 593–604.

Bies, R. J., & Shapiro, D. L. (1988). Voice and justification: Their influence on procedural fairness judgments. *Academy of Management Journal 31*(3): 676–685.

Birk, J. P., & Foster, J. (1993). The importance of lecture in general chemistry course performance. *Journal of Chemical Education 70:* 180–182.

Birmingham, C., & Michaelsen, L. K. (1999). Conflict resolution in decision making teams: A longitudinal study. *Proceedings Midwest Academy of Management,* Chicago.

Bloom, B. S. (1956). *Taxonomy of educational objectives: The classification of educational goals.* New York: David McKay.

Bouton, C., & Garth, R. Y., eds. (1983). *Learning in groups: New directions for teaching and learning series,* Vol. 14. San Francisco: Jossey–Bass.

Brandon, D., & Pratt, M. G. (1999). Managing the formation of virtual team categories and prototypes by managing information: A SIT/SCT perspective. *Academy of Management Proceedings,* D1–D6.

Bray, R. M., Kerr, N. L., & Atkin, R. S. (1978). Effects of group size, problem difficulty, and sex on group performance and member reactions. *Journal of Personality and Social Psychology 36:* 1224–1240.

Brickner, M. A., Harkins, S. G., & Ostrom, T. M. (1986). Effects of personal involvement: Thought provoking implications for social loafing. *Journal of Personality and Social Psychology 51*(4): 763–770.

Bruffee, K. A. (1999) Collaborative learning: Higher education, interdependence, and the authority of knowledge. 2d ed. Baltimore: Johns Hopkins University Press.

Bruning, R. H., Schraw, G. J., & Ronning, R. R. (1994). *Cognitive psychology and instruction.* 2d ed. Englewood Cliffs, NJ: Prentice-Hall.

Chatman, J. A., & Flynn, F. J. (2001). The influence of heterogeneity on the emergence and consequences of norms in work teams. *The Academy of Management Journal 44*(5): 956–974.

Craik, F. L. M., & Lockhart, R. S. (1986). CHARM is not enough: Comments on Eich's model of cued recall. *Psychological Review 93:* 360–364.

Davis, J. H., Kerr, N. L., Atkin, R. S., Holt, R., & Meek, D. (1975). The decision processes of 6- and 12-person mock juries assigned unanimous and two-thirds majority rules. *Journal of Personality and Social Psychology 32:* 1–14.

Deppe, L. A., Sonderegger, E. O., Stice, J. D., Clark, D. C., & Streuling, G. F. (1991). Emerging competencies for the practice of accounting. *Journal of Accounting Education 9:* 257–290.

Dinan, F., & Frydrychowski, V. A. (1995). A team-based learning method for organic chemistry. *Journal of Chemistry Education 72:* 429–431.

Duch, B. J., Groh, S. E., & Allen, D. E., eds. (2001). *The power of problem-based learning.* Sterling, VA: Stylus.

Eisenstat, R. A., & Cohen, S. G. (1990). Summary: Top management groups. *Groups that work (and those that don't): Creating conditions for effective teamwork.* Ed. J. R. Hackman. San Francisco: Jossey-Bass.

Ellis, D. G., & Fisher, B. A. (1975). Phases of conflict in small group development: A Markov analysis. *Human Communication Research 1:* 195–212.

Epstein, M.L. 2000. A testing/teaching multiple-choice answer form. Workshop presented at the Fourteenth Annual Conference, Teaching of Psychology: Ideas and Innovations, Ellenville, NY. Available: http://enigma.rider.edu/~epstein/ifat/.

Evans, C. R., & Dion, K. L. (1991). Group cohesion and performance: A meta analysis. *Small Group Research 22*(2): 175–186.

Evans, J. R. (1988). Team selection. *Social Science Journal 25:* 93–104.

Feldman, D. (1984). The development and enforcement of group norms. *Academy of Management Review 9:* 47–53.

Fiechtner, S. B., & Davis, E. A. (1985). Why some groups fail: A survey of students' experiences with learning groups. *The Organizational Behavior Teaching Review 9*(4): 58–71.

Frank, F., & Anderson, L. R. (1971). Effects of task and group size upon group productivity and member satisfaction. *Sociometry 34:* 135–149.

Freeman, M. A. (1997). Flexibility in access, interaction and assessment: The case for Web-based conferencing and teaching programs. *Australian Journal of Educational Technology 13*(1): 23–29. Available: http://cleo.murdoch.edu.au/gen/aset/ajet/ajet13/wi97p23.html.

————. (1992). Motivating student learning in large classes. *Quality of Teaching Matters at UTS.* UTS Center for Learning and Teaching: 11–19.

————. (1995). Peer assessment by groups of group work. *Assessment & Evaluation in Higher Education 20*(3): 295–306.

————. (1996). The role of the Internet in teaching large undergraduate classes. *Flexible Online Learning Journal 1*(1). Available: http://www.lib.uts.edu.au/folp/journal/index.html.

Freeman, M. A., & Adams, M. A. (1999). Australian views on insider trading. *Australian Journal of Corporate Law 10*(2): 148–161.

————. (1992). Experimenting with new teaching and assessment methods in a business degree subject. *Quality of Teaching Matters at UTS.* UTS Centre for Learning and Teaching: 27–39.

Freeman, M. A., & Capper, J. M. (1999). Exploiting the Web for education: An anonymous asynchronous role simulation. *Australian Journal of Educational Technology 15*(1): 95–116. Available: http://cleo.murdoch.edu.au/ajet/ajet15/freeman.html.

Gagné, R. M. (1970). *The conditions for learning.* 2d ed. New York: Holt, Rinehart & Winston.

Gersick, C. J. G. (1989). Making time: Predictable transitions in task groups. *Academy of Management Journal 32*(2): 274–310.

————. (1988). Time and transition in work teams: Toward a new model of group development. *Academy of Management Journal 31:* 9–14.

Gersick, C. J. G., & Hackman, J. R. (1990). Habitual routines in task-performing groups. *Organizational Behavior and Human Decision Processes 47*(1): 65–98.

Goldfinch, J. (1993). Further developments in peer assessment of group projects. *Assessment and Evaluation in Higher Education* 19(1): 29–35.

Greenburg, J., & Baron, R. A. (2000). *Behavior in organizations.* 7th ed. Upper Saddle River, NJ: Prentice-Hall.

Griffin, J. (1985). Some problems of fairness. *Ethics 96:* 100–118.

Gruenfeld, D. H., & Hollingshead, A. B. (1993). Sociocognition in work groups: The evolution of group integrative complexity and its relation to task performance. *Small Group Research 24*(3): 383–405.

Gruenfeld, D., Mannix, E. A., Williams, K. Y., & Neale, M. A. (1996). Group composition and decision making: How member familiarity and information distribution affect process and performance. *Organizational Behavior and Human Decision Processes 67:* 1–15.

Gulati, R. (1995). Does familiarity breed trust? The implications of repeated ties for contractual choice in alliances. *Academy of Management Journal 38*(1): 85–112.

Hackman, J. R., ed. (1990). *Groups that work (and those that don't).* San Francisco: Jossey-Bass.

Hackman, J. R., & Oldham, G. R. (1976). Motivation through the design of work: Test of a theory. *Organizational Behavior and Human Performance 16:* 250–279.

————. (1980). *Work redesign.* Reading, MA: Addison-Wesley.

Hambrick, D. C., Davison, S. C., Snell, S. A., & Snow, C. C. (1998). When groups consist of multiple nationalities: Towards a new understanding of the implications. *Organization Studies 19*(2): 181–205.

Hamilton, S. J. (1997). *Collaborative learning: Teaching and learning in the arts, sciences, and professional schools.* 2d ed. Indianapolis, IN: IUPUI Center for Teaching and Learning.

Harkins S. G., & Jackson, J. M. (1985). The role of evaluation in eliminating social loafing. *Personality and Social Psychology Bulletin 11*(4): 457–465.

Harkins, S. G., & Petty, M. M. (1982). Effects of task difficulty and task uniqueness on social loafing. *Journal of Personality and Social Psychology 52*(2): 1214–1229.

Harrison, D. A., Price, K. H., & Bell, M. (1998). Beyond relational demography: Time and effects of surface- and deep-level diversity on work group cohesion. *Academy of Management Journal 41*(1): 96–107.

Hernandez, S. A. (2002). Team-based learning in a marketing principles course: Cooperative structures that facilitate active learning and higher-level thinking. *Journal of Marketing Education 24*(1): 45-75.

Herreid, C. F. (1999). The bee and the groundhog: Lessons in cooperative learning—Troubles with groups. *Journal of College Science Teaching 28*(4): 226-228.

———. (1998). Why isn't cooperative learning used to teach science? *Bioscience 48:* 553–559.

Hofstede, G. (1991). *Cultures and organizations: Software of the mind.* London: McGraw-Hill.

Innami, Ichiro. (1994). The quality of group decisions, group verbal behavior, and intervention. *Organizational Behavior and Human Decision Processes 60*(3): 409–431.

Jarvenpaa, S. L., Knoll, K., & Leidner, D. E. (1998). Is anybody out there? Antecedents of trust in global virtual teams. *Journal of Management Information Systems 14*(4): 229–264.

Jehn, K. (1994). Enhancing effectiveness: An investigation of advantages and disadvantages of value-based intragroup conflict. *International Journal of Conflict Management 5:* 223–238.

———. (1995). A multimethod examination of the benefits and detriments of intragroup conflict. *Administrative Science Quarterly 40:* 256–282.

———. (1997). A qualitative analysis of conflict types and dimensions in organizational groups. *Administrative Science Quarterly 42:* 530–557.

Jehn, K. A. (2000). The influence of proportional and perceptual conflict composition on team performance. *International Journal of Conflict Management 11*(1): 56–74.

Jehn, K. A., Chadwick, C., & Thatcher, S. (1997). To agree or not to agree: Diversity, conflict, and group outcomes. *International Journal of Conflict Management 8:* 287–306.

Jehn, K. A., & Mannix, E. A. (2001). The dynamic nature of conflict: A longitudinal study of intragroup conflict and group performance. *Academy of Management Journal 44*(2): 238.

Johnson, D. W., & Johnson, R. T. (1983). The socialization and achievement crisis: Are cooperative learning experiences the solution? *Applied Social Psychology Annual,* Vol. 4. Ed. L. Bickman. Beverly Hills: Sage.

Johnson, D. W., Johnson, R. T., Johnson, J., & Anderson, D. (1976). Effects of cooperative versus individualized instruction on student prosocial behavior, attitudes toward learning and achievement. *Journal of Educational Psychology 68*(4): 446–452.

Johnson, D. W., Johnson, R. T., & Maruyama, G. (1983). Interdependence and interpersonal attraction among heterogeneous and homogeneous individuals: A theoretical formulation and a meta-analysis of research. *Review of Educational Research 53*(1): 5–54.

Johnson, D. W., Johnson R. T., & Scott L., (1978). The effects of cooperation and individualized instruction on student attitudes and achievement. *Journal of Social Psychology 104:* 207–216.

Johnson, D. W., Johnson, R. T., & Smith, K. A. (1991). *Cooperative learning: Increasing college faculty instructional productivity.* ASHE–ERIC Higher Education Report, No. 4. Washington, DC: George Washington University.

Kagan, S. (1995) Group grades miss the mark. *Educational Leadership 52*(8): 68–71.

Kerr, N. L., & Bruun, S. E. (1983). The dispensability of member effort and group motivation losses: Free-rider effects. *Journal of Personality and Social Psychology 44:* 78–94.

———. (1981). Ringlemann revisited: Alternative explanations for the social loafing effects. *Personality and Social Psychology Bulletin 7*(2): 224–231.

Kirkpatrick, D. (1994). *Evaluating training programs: The four levels.* San Francisco: Berrett-Koehler.

Knoll, K., & Jarvenpaa, S. L. (1995). Learning virtual team collaboration. *Hawaii International Conference on System Sciences Conference Proceedings*, 92–101.

Kowitz, A.C., & Knutson, T. J. (1980). *Decision making in small groups: The search for alternatives.* Boston: Allyn and Bacon.

Kravitz, D. A., & Waller, J. E. (1980). Effects of task interest and competition on social loafing. Paper presented at meeting of Academy of Management, Anaheim, CA.

Kurfiss, J. G. (1988). *Critical thinking: Theory, research, practice, and possibilities.* Washington, DC: George Washington University, School of Education and Human Development.

Langfred, M. S. C. (1998). The importance of organizational context, II: An empirical test of work group cohesiveness and effectiveness in two governmental bureaucracies. *Public Administration Quarterly 21*(4): 465–486.

Latane, B., Williams, K. D., & Harkins, S. G. (1979). Many hands make light the work: The causes and consequences of social loafing. *Journal of Personality and Social Psychology 37:* 822–832.

Lawler, E. E. (1988). Substitutes for hierarchy. *Organizational Dynamics 17:* 4–15.

Lazarowitz, R. (1991). Learning biology cooperatively: An Israeli junior high school study. *Cooperative Learning 11*(3): 19–21.

Lazarowitz, R., & Karsenty, G. (1990). Cooperative learning and students' self-esteem in tenth grade biology classrooms. In *Cooperative learning theory and research.* Ed. S. Sharon. New York: Praeger.

Lazarowitz, R., Sjaram, S., & Steinberg, R. (1980). Classroom learning style and cooperative behavior of elementary school children. *Journal of Educational Psychology 72:* 97–104.

Leana, C. R. (1985). A partial test of Janis' Groupthink model: Effects of group cohesiveness and leader behavior on defective decision making. *Journal of Management 11*(1): 5–18

Levine, J. M., & Moreland, R. L. (1990). Progress in small group research. In *Annual Review of Psychology.* Ed. M. R. Rosenzweig & L. W. Porter. Vol. 41:585–634. Palo Alta: Highwire Press.

Light, R. J. (1990). *The Harvard assessment seminars: Explorations with students and faculty about teaching, learning, and student life.* Cambridge, MA: Harvard University.

Likert, R. (1961). *New patterns of management.* New York: McGraw-Hill.

Locke, E. A., Shaw, K., Saar, L. M., & Latham, G. P. (1981). Goal setting and task performance: 1969–1980. *Psychological Bulletin 90:* 125–152.

Maier, N. R. F., Solem, A. R., & Maier, A. A. (1975). *The role-play technique: A handbook for management and leadership practice.* La Jolla, Ca: University Associates.

Mandler, J. M. (1984). *Stories, scripts, and scenes: Aspects of schema theory.* Hillsdale, NJ: Lawrence Erlbaum.

McAllister, D. J. (1995). Affect- and cognition-based trust as foundations for interpersonal cooperation in organizations. *Academy of Management Journal 9:* 494–504.

McGrath, J. E. (1984). *Groups: Interaction and performance.* Englewood Cliffs, NJ: Prentice-Hall.

McGrath, J. E. (1991). Time, interaction and performance (TIP): A theory of groups. *Small Group Research 22:* 147–174.

McGrath, J. E., Arrow, H., Gruenfeld, D. H., Hollingshead, A. B., & O'Connor, K. M. (1993). Groups, task and technology: The effects of experience and change. *Small Group Research 24:* 406–420.

McGrath, J. E., & Gruenfeld, D. H. (1993). Toward a dynamic and systemic theory of groups: An integration of six temporally enriched perspectives. *The future of leadership research: Promise and perspective.* Ed. M. M. Chemers & R. Ayman. Orlando, FL: Academic Press.

Michaelsen, L. K. (1999). Integrating the core business curriculum: An experience-based solution. *Selections 15*(2): 9–17

———. (1999). Myths and methods in successful small group work. *National Teaching and Learning Forum 8*(6): 1–5.

———. (1983). Team learning in large classes. In *Learning in groups.* Ed. C. Bouton & R. Y. Garth. *New Directions for Teaching and Learning Series,* Vol. 14. San Francisco: Jossey-Bass.

———. (2002). Team-based learning in large classes. In *Engaging large clases: Strategies and techniques for college faculty.* Ed. C. Stanley & E. Porter. New York: Anker.

———. (1992). *To improve the academy: Resources for faculty, instrucional and organizational development.* Ed. R. H. Wulff & J. D. Nyquist. Vol. 11. Stillwater, OK: New Forums Press.

Michaelsen, L. K., & Black, R. H. (1994). Building learning teams: The key to harnessing the power of small groups in higher education. In *Collaborative Learning: A sourcebook for higher education.* Ed. S. Kadel, & J. Keehner. Vol. 2. State College, PA: National Center for Teaching, Learning, and Assessment.

Michaelsen, L. K., Black, R. H., & Fink, L. D. (1996). What every faculty developer needs to know about learning groups. In *To improve the academy: Resources for faculty, instructional and organizational development.* Ed. L. Richlin. Vol. 15. Stillwater, OK: New Forums Press.

Michaelsen, L. K., Cragin, J. P., & Watson, W. E. (1981). Grading and anxiety: A strategy for coping. *Exchange: The Organizational Behavior Teaching Journal 6*(1): 8–14.

Michaelsen, L. K., Jones, C. F., & Watson, W. E. (1993). Beyond groups and cooperation: Building high performance learning teams. In *To improve the academy: Resources for faculty, instructional and organizational development.* Ed. D. L. Wright, & J. P. Lunde. Stillwater, OK: New Forums Press.

Michaelsen, L. K., & McCord, M. H. (2000). Cases and groups: A winning combination? *MBAR Journal 1*(1): 5–16.

Michaelsen, L. K., Watson, W. E., & Black, R. H. (1989). A realistic test of individual versus group consensus decision making. *Journal of Applied Psychology 74*(5): 834–839.

Michaelsen, L. K., Watson, W. E., Cragin, J. P., & Fink, L. D. (1982). Team learning: A potential solution to the problems of large classes. *Exchange: The Organizational Behavior Teaching Journal 7*(1): 13–22.

Michaelsen, L. K., Watson, W. E., & Schraeder, C. B. (1985). Informative testing: A practical approach for tutoring with groups. *Exchange: The Organizational Behavior Teaching Journal 9*(4): 18–33.

Millis, B. J., & Cottell, P. G. (1998). *Cooperative learning for higher education faculty.* Phoenix: Oryx Press.

Moreland, R. L., & Levine, J. M. (1988). Group dynamics over time: Development and socialization in small groups. In *The social psychology of time: New perspectives.* Ed. J. E. McGrath. Newbury Park, CA: Sage, 151–181.

Nungester, R. J., & Duchastel, P. C. (1982). Testing versus review: Effects on retention. *Journal of Applied Psychology 74*(1): 18–22.

O'Connor, K., Gruenfeld, D., & McGrath, J. E. (1993). The experience and effects of conflict in continuing workgroups. *Small Group Research 24:* 362–382.

PBL Websites—University of Delaware: www.udel.edu/pbl; Samford University: www. samford.edu/pbl/pbl_main. html; San Diego State University: edweb.sdsu.edu/clrit/ PBL_WebQuest.html.

Priem, R. L., & Price, K. H. (1991). Process and outcome expectations for the dialectical inquiry, devil's advocacy, and consensus techniques of strategic decision making. *Group and Organization Studies 16:* 206–225.

Ross, W., & LaCroix, J. (1996). Multiple meanings of trust in negotiation theory and research. *International Journal of Conflict Management 7*(4): 314–360.

Saunders, C. S. (2000). Virtual teams: Piecing together the puzzle. *Framing the domains of IT management: Projecting the future through the past.* Ed. R. W. Zmud. Cincinnati, OH: Pinnaflex Educational Resources, 29–50.

Scheidel, T. M., & Crowell, L. (1979). *Discussing and decoding: A deskbook for group leaders and members.* New York: Macmillan.

Schnake, M. (1991). Equity in effort: The sucker effect in co-acting groups. *Journal of Management 71:* 41–55.

Seashore, S. E. (1954). *Group cohesiveness in the industrial work group.* Ann Arbor: University of Michigan Press.

Shaw, M. E. (1981). *Group dynamics: The psychology of small group behavior.* 3d ed. New York: McGraw-Hill.

Simmons, T. L., & Peterson, R. (2000). Task conflict and relationship conflict in top management teams: The pivotal role of intragroup trust. *Journal of Applied Psychology 85:* 102–111.

Slavin, R. E. (1983). *Cooperative learning.* New York: Longman.

———. (1995). *Cooperative learning.* 2d ed. Boston: Allyn & Bacon.

Slavin, R. E., & Karweit, N. L. (1981). Cognitive and affective outcomes of an intensive student team-based learning experience. *Journal of Experimental Education 50*(1): 29–35.

Smith, K., Johnson, D. W., & Johnson R. T. (1981). Can conflict be constructive? Controversy versus concurrence seeking in learning groups. *Journal of Educational Psychology 73*(5): 651–663.

Solomons, T. W., & Fryhle, C. B. (1998). *Organic chemistry.* 7th ed. New York: John Wiley & Sons.

Spence, L. (2001). The case against teaching. *Change Magazine 23*(6): 10–19.

Tetlock, P. E. (1985). Accountability: The neglected social context of judgment and choice. *Research in Organizational Behavior.* Ed. B. M. Staw & L. L. Cummings. Vol. 7:297–332.

———. (1992). The impact of accountability on judgment and choice: Toward a social contingency model. *Advances in Experimental Social Psychology 25:* 331–376.

Tobias, S. (1990). They're not dumb. They're different: A new "tier of talent" for science. *Change 22*(4): 11–30.

Tubbs, M. E. (1986). Goal setting: A meta-analytic examination of the empirical evidence. *Journal of Applied Psychology 73*(3): 474–483.

University of Delaware. (1995–96). Problem-based learning in undergraduate education. *About Teaching,* No. 47. Center for Teaching Effectiveness, University of Delaware, Newark, DE.

Vygotsky, L. S. (1978). *Mind in society: The development of higher psychological processes.* Boston: Harvard University Press.

Watson, W. E., Kumar, K., & Michaelsen, L. K. (1993). Cultural diversity's impact on group process and performance: Comparing culturally homogeneous and culturally diverse task groups. *Academy of Management Journal 36*(3): 590–602.

Watson, W. E., Michaelsen, L. K., & Sharp, W. (1991). Member competence, group interac-
    tion, and group decision-making: A longitudinal study. *Journal of Applied Psychology*
    76: 801–809.

Wilkerson, L., & Gijselaers, W. H., eds. (1996). Bringing problem-based learning to higher ed-
    ucation. *New Directions for Teaching and Learning Series,* Vol. 68. San Francisco: Jossey-
    Bass.

Williams, K., Harkins, S, & Latane, B. (1981). Identifiability as a deterrent to social loafing:
    Two cheering experiments. *Journal of Personality and Social Psychology 40:* 303–311.

Williams, K. Y., & O'Reilly, C. A. (1998). Forty years of diversity research: A review. *Research*
    in Organizational Behavior. Ed. B. M. Staw & L. L. Cummings. Vol. 20:33–140.
    Greenwich, CT: JAI Press.

Wilson, W. R. (1982). The use of permanent learning groups in teaching introductory
    accounting. Unpublished doctoral dissertation, University of Oklahoma.

Zalkind, S. S., & Costello, T. W. (1962). Perceptions: Some recent research and implications
    for administration. *Administrative Science Quarterly 9:* 218–235.

Zander, A. (1971). *Motives and goals in groups.* New York: Academic Press.

Ziller, R. C. (1957). Group size: A determinant of the quality and stability of group decisions.
    Sociometry 20: 165–173.

Index

Phrases in **Bold** indicate that video material about this topic can be seen on the team-based learning website: <www.teambasedlearning.org>.

About the Editors
and
Contributors

THE EDITORS

Larry K. Michaelsen received his doctorate in organizational psychology from the University of Michigan. He is a David Ross Boyd Distinguished Professor of Management at the University of Oklahoma and former editor of the *Journal of Management Education*. His primary research interests are the dynamics of group problem solving and the use of small groups for teaching higher-level thinking and group problem-solving skills. He is a Carnegie Scholar and has received numerous awards for his outstanding teaching and for his pioneering work in two areas: developing team-based learning, and designing an integrated core business curriculum based on having students create and operate an actual start-up business and use their profits to complete a hands-on community service project.

Arletta Bauman Knight received her doctorate in instructional communication from the University of Oklahoma in 1993. She has served as associate director of the Instructional Development Program at that institution since 1992. Her work in that program has involved extensive observation of, and consulting with, college teachers, coordination of training programs for teaching assistants, and editing of published documents. She has taught courses on communication, orientation to college, and a course on college teaching for graduate students in mathematics. Her research interests have been focused on teacher–student interactions in the classroom, and teacher credibility.

L. Dee Fink received his doctorate from the University of Chicago in 1976 and joined the faculty at the University of Oklahoma that same year with an appointment in geography and higher education. In 1979 he established the Instructional Development Program at Oklahoma and has served as director of that program ever since. He has published a number of books and articles on the general topics of college teaching, evaluating college teaching, new faculty members, and instructional development programs. He is currently writing a book, *Creating Significant Learning Experiences*. For more information, see his website: www.ou.edu/idp/dfink.html.

THE CONTRIBUTORS

Carolyn Birmingham is a Ph.D. candidate at the University of Oklahoma.

Jon Cragin is professor of management at Oklahoma Baptist University.

Frank J.Dinan is professor of chemistry at Canisius College.

Mark Freeman is associate professor of business, University of Technology Sydney.

Patricia Goodson is currently assistant professor of health and kinesiology at Texas A&M University.

Clyde Freeman Herreid is a Distinguished Teaching Professor of Biological Science at State University of New York–Buffalo.

Laurie A. Lucas is currently assistant professor of legal studies at Arkansas Technical University.

Mary McCord is assistant professor of business at Central Missouri State University.

Melanie C. Nakaji is a graduate intern at San Diego Mesa College in the Department of Disabled Student Programs and Services working as a deaf peer counselor.

Jiři Popovský is a professor of natural science at Charles University in Prague, Czech Republic.

G. Fred Streuling is Deloitte & Touche Professor of Accounting at Brigham Young University.